Every Day Of My Life

Published by Brolga Publishing Pty Ltd
ABN 46 063 962 443
PO Box 12544
A'Beckett St
Melbourne, VIC, 8006
Australia

email: markzocchi@brolgapublishing.com.au

All rights reserved. No part of this publication may be reproduced, stored in a retrieval system or transmitted in any form or by any means electronic, mechanical, photocopying, recording or otherwise without prior permission from the publisher.

Copyright © 2017 Gerard Bertelkamp

National Library of Australia
Cataloguing-in-Publication data
    Beeb Birtles, author.
    ISBN 9781925367973 (paperback)
    Subjects: Birtles, Beeb.
        Zoot (Musical group)
        Mississippi (Musical group)
        Little River Band (Musical group)
        Rock musicians--Australia--Biography.
        Composers--Australia--Biography.
        Lyricists--Australia--Biography.
        Musicians--Australia--Biography.
        Dutch--Australia--Biography.
        Popular music--Australia.
        Popular culture--Australia--History--20th century.

Printed in China
Cover design by Emmie Birtles
Typesetting by Elly Cridland

BE PUBLISHED

Publish through a successful publisher. National Distribution, Dennis Jones & Associates International Distribution to the United Kingdom, North America.
Sales Representation to South East Asia
Email: markzocchi@brolgapublishing.com.au

Every Day Of My Life

Beeb Birtles

A Memoir

Edited by Jeff Jenkins

In memory of John D'Arcy and Darryl Cotton

For Donna, Hannah and Emilia

CONTENTS

Foreword		.....	I
Beeb Birtles		.....	VII
Prologue		.....	XI
Preface		.....	XIII
1	Amsterdam, Holland	.....	1
2	Adelaide, South Australia	.....	11
3	Times Unlimited	.....	27
4	Zoot	.....	37
5	Frieze	.....	63
6	Mississippi — Phase One	.....	71
7	Mississippi — Phase Two	.....	79
8	Mississippi — Phase Three	.....	87
9	Mississippi — Phase Four	.....	95
10	Little River Band — Phase One	.....	101
11	Little River Band — Phase Two	.....	121
12	Donna Marie Brucks	.....	137
13	Little River Band — Phase Three	.....	147
14	Hannah Michelle Bertelkamp	.....	163
15	Little River Band — Phase Four	.....	169
16	Little River Band — Phase Five	.....	183
17	Little River Band — Phase Six	.....	187
18	Emilia Brook Bertelkamp	.....	191
19	Little River Band — Phase Seven	.....	197
20	For the Record	.....	205
21	River of No Return	.....	209
22	Midlife	.....	215
23	The Move to America	.....	221
24	Sonic Sorbet Records	.....	225

25	BIRTLES SHORROCK GOBLE	.....	231
26	ZOOT REUNION	.....	241
27	IN MEMORIAM JOHN D'ARCY & DARRYL COTTON	.....	247
28	WATCHING THE SUNSET	.....	255
ACKNOWLEDGEMENTS		.....	261
AWARDS AND ACCOLADES		.....	263

FOREWORD

The phone rang.

"Hi Baz, have you heard from the stubborn Dutch prick lately?"

"Hi Skinny," I replied. "In fact, I did receive an email from him a few days ago."

"Obviously, he's got the shits with ME this time then!" she said.

The 'stubborn Dutch prick' nomenclature has been around from 1968 when I shared a flat with Beeb Birtles. I had moved from Adelaide to Melbourne to join a band called The Town Criers as lead singer. In October '68 Beeb and his fellow Zoot band members accommodated me in their rented flat in Beaconsfield Parade, St Kilda for about a month. Then, in early '69, my cousin Lynny (aka Skinny), my sister Wendy, Beeb and I moved into a flat in Tiuna Grove, Elwood. Beeb and I then shared flats for the life span of Zoot and the Criers.

Skinny and Wendy returned to Adelaide and two friends, Dianne and Pam, also from our hometown, moved in with us for the following two years. During this period, it was only natural that we all got to know each other's idiosyncrasies. Beeb was renowned for his stubbornness as much as I was for my laziness. Beeb was always only into the music and never really comfortable wearing the pink outfits that Zoot chose to wear whilst performing, and he made a point of steering clear of the make-up rooms at various TV studios.

I remember him digging in his heels and refusing to appear on the national TV show **Happening 70**. He walked into our flat looking decidedly pissed off.

"What's up?" I asked.

"They tried to make me wear make-up," he retorted. "It's one thing to wear fuckin' pink, but make-up as well?" He didn't appear with Zoot that day. Fortunately, those shows were mimed and lead singer Darryl Cotton strapped on Beeb's bass and bluffed his way through their song. That particular clip, to the best of my knowledge, is still around.

Beeb and I were pretty green and naïve in those days and we were happy to accommodate fans who requested our address with the intention of writing to us.

It was fairly common knowledge that generally the lead singer got the chicks, a theory I was looking forward to verifying after being thrust into that position after spending a couple of years as a bass player. Ironically, that was how I met Beeb in '67. He answered the ad I placed in the newspaper to purchase my Hofner Beatle bass. Small world. We also discovered his father, Gerry, a carpenter, knew my father after working for him when my father was a builder. Beeb, inadvertently, proved that lead singers didn't always have a mortgage on the ladies. I first became aware of this after going to the letterbox to collect our 'fan mail'. There were days when there'd be more mail with his name on it than mine, which, to my mind, wasn't the way it was supposed to be … after all, I was the lead singer! If I got to the mailbox first and Beeb had more mail than me, I'd collect it and put it on his bed. If I had more than him, I'd leave it all in the box for him to collect.

We soon became aware of the repercussions of recklessly handing out our address to anyone who asked for it. In no time at all there were young girls constantly knocking on the front door, climbing through the bathroom window, waking neighbours demanding to know which flat Beeb and Barry lived in and graffiting the walls. It became a sizeable problem just walking out the front door to visit the local milk bar. It came as no real surprise to finally receive an eviction notice, mainly due to the unimpressed tenants in the block.

This time we made a pact that we'd only give out our address to the 'more mature' girls – on the condition it was viewed as privileged information and not to be shared.

Our next address, in Alexandra Street, East St Kilda, was a different dynamic. After sleeping in single beds and sharing the same bedroom in Tiuna Grove – which we both agreed seemed highly incompatible to our idea of a proper 'Rock Star' lifestyle – we decided in our wisdom that this next abode would see us in our very own separate bedrooms. Every weekend, and sometimes during the week, the parties would start and we'd arrive home after playing our gigs to find things already in full swing. Musicians, entertainers, roadies and others would get word that there was always a party at Beeb and Barry's. It was a wonderful time to be a red-blooded young man in the entertainment industry.

Leading Australian music magazine Go-Set ran an annual Pop Poll and bands such as Zoot, The Town Criers, The Masters Apprentices, Doug Parkinson in Focus and The Valentines, featuring Bon Scott on lead vocals, shared similar popularity. In '69, '70 and '71, Zoot and The Town Criers polled in the top

10 most popular acts. The competition between bands was friendly but strong and it wasn't a pleasant pill to swallow whilst flatting with Beeb to discover Zoot polled No. 1 in the '69 poll, with The Town Criers coming in at No. 6. You can't imagine my relief the following year when Zoot polled No. 5, with the Criers at No. 4! Pride, ego and dignity simply won't allow me to print the top 10 positions for '71!

Vince Lovegrove, who shared the singing duties with Bon Scott in The Valentines, became a part-time journalist with Go-Set and it wasn't long before the opinionated singer ruffled the feathers of many a fellow musician/entertainer. Zoot found themselves on the end of some of his barbed comments, as did the Criers, and I remember walking into the kitchen and finding a Go-Set mag featuring a photo of Vince – complete with daggers, sketched in ballpoint pen, protruding from all parts of his body. Signed, Beeb!

A number of years later, after hearing Vince was struggling financially when his wife, Suzi, and their young son, Troy, were diagnosed with AIDS, Beeb and his wife, Donna, sent him $1000.

Even though Beeb was prone to the occasional mood swing – and you were never quite sure if you were directly responsible for it or not – living with him was generally a delight. Anyone who's spent a reasonable amount of time with Beeb will most likely have had the pleasure of him entertaining them with his extraordinary, uncanny and hilarious chimpanzee impersonations. One could be excused for thinking they gave credence to Charles Darwin's book On the Origin of Species.

When not rehearsing, touring or playing gigs around the country, Beeb and I spent many days and nights sharing a brandy and dry, smoking cigarettes and listening intensely to records. We had very similar music tastes, often exclaiming to each other, 'Listen to this!', as we mimicked on 'air instrument' a beautiful Herbie Flowers bass line or a Roger Pope drum fill from the Tumbleweed Connection album, or a harmony at the end of a Crosby, Stills & Nash vocal line that seemed to linger forever.

We were listening to music by: Three Dog Night, Humble Pie, Jack Bruce, The Beach Boys, Spooky Tooth, Neil Young, Poco, The Rascals, Small Faces, The Who, Free, Chicago, Traffic, Nina Simone, Sam Cooke and many, many other artists.

Beeb would sit there listening intensely and absorbing the music like a sponge, frequently alerting me to a subtle vocal or musical lick in a song that impressed him and that I might not have noticed. I have no doubt that what he listened to and soaked up musically during these days became a major influence on his songwriting development in the years to come, particularly with the Little River Band (LRB).

Beeb was developing musically with Zoot as well, and, ironically, the gimmick of wearing pink, which helped launch Zoot so effectively, came back to bite them firmly on the arse. Music was getting heavier, more serious and, for better or worse, more self-indulgent. Beeb and Zoot wanted desperately to be taken more seriously and wearing pink was not conducive to that, especially amongst the male members of their audience.

I recall arriving home late one night, shortly after Beeb. We'd both been gigging and he was in a foul mood. Dianne, Pam and I asked him what was wrong and he explained how he and Zoot had been pelted with tomatoes and other assorted extremely ripe fruit, and he was 'over it!' I tried my best to lend him a sympathetic ear, before turning on my heels, scuttling to my room, closing the door behind me and almost vomiting with laughter.

Our last year or so of living together was in a house in Westbury Street, Balaclava, and while I was still partying and contemplating my future, Beeb tended to opt for more 'alone' time in his new, larger room. This became the embryonic stage of his songwriting career and a time where he practised and developed his guitar skills as he was rapidly tiring of playing bass. He would play us pieces of songs he'd been working on, during and after completion. There weren't many, but he was only just starting.

After submitting a few of these songs to Zoot in the hope of them playing and/or recording them, he came home dejected and extremely pissed off.

"What's up, lad?" I asked.

"Rick Springfield rejected my songs!"

I believe this only served to make him more determined and fuelled his desire to work harder. I can only imagine the enormous sense of satisfaction he must have felt when he provided LRB with their first single, 'Curiosity (Killed The Cat)'. To quote one of Australia's finest ever rock journalists, the late Ed Nimmervoll:

"LRB were the first Oz act to achieve gold status [in the US]. Beeb was the heartbeat, integrity and intangible glue to LRB, more interested in making an essential contribution than dominating the spotlight..."

He adds:

"Beeb's songs had, and have, heart. If you knew Beeb, you knew how true his songs were to his own life experience."

I couldn't have expressed it better. Beeb does have more integrity than most people I've met, which is not extremely common in the entertainment industry, and he's also one of the most decent human beings I've ever had the pleasure of knowing.

Last year whilst holidaying in Thailand, I was conned and ripped off badly by someone who I was lending support to, who I thought was a dying friend. Beeb recorded several CDs of artists we listened to during our years of living together. He sent them to me with a card attached: 'Hi Baz, I'm sending you these CDs to cheer you up.'

This display of thoughtfulness, compassion and kindness from Beeb was not uncommon.

Apart from the fact that from all our years flatting together, sadly, neither of us has a single photograph taken together, I probably have two other regrets: One is we never sat down with a guitar and said: "Hey, let's see if we can put some ideas together and come up with something." The second regret is that in all the years we've known each other we've never performed together. But I'm pleased to say that this might soon change. At the time of writing this foreword, Beeb and I have been informed that we are about to be inducted into the South Australian Music Hall of Fame. I'm sure there'd be those who might question my induction, but nobody on this planet would question Beeb's. His words to me were: "Hey, I'd love us to perform together on the night ... wouldn't that be fun?"

I feel thrilled, flattered and honored by this induction, particularly as it's from our hometown, but no more thrilled, flattered and honored as I am to have been asked to write this foreword and finally get to perform with my dearest friend, Beeb Birtles.

Barry Smith
2017

BEEB BIRTLES BIOGRAPHY

The world knows Beeb Birtles through his association with Little River Band – the Australian-based group that conquered the international music scene on stage and on record for a decade from 1975 – the first Australian act to achieve gold record status in the USA.

In Australian terms Little River Band was a "supergroup", made up of band members who came into the group with established reputations. Australia knew Beeb Birtles well before the Little River Band days. You might say he was the supergroup's first "super" member. You might also say he was the group's heartbeat, its integrity, the intangible glue that helped LRB's famously disparate membership manage to operate together. He was also an integral part of the group's vocal armory, and part of its songwriting strength.

But let's go back to the start. The Beeb Birtles (Gerard Bertelkamp) who arrived in Australia with his family from Holland in 1959 initially played another part in Australian history. The vast underpopulated Southern Hemisphere island colony opened its arms to post-war Europe, offering new beginnings. A generation of post-war children were set to make a significant mark on world culture. The thirst to make a difference, the quest to belong was all the more intense because of the migrant factor.

The young Bertelkamp happened to find himself growing into his teenage years in Adelaide, which more than any other Australian city had evolved into a British enclave. As the cultural and musical revolution that was about to sweep the world evolved in England it was Adelaide's heartbeat that was racing fastest, Adelaide that heard and saw the latest as migrants stepped off the ships, Adelaide that most eagerly embraced and emulated this Great Adventure. The revolution was already well underway in 1966 when Beeb joined his first group.

Times Unlimited became Zoot. Beeb was the bass playing, harmonising anchor behind the group's charismatic chick-magnet lead singer Darryl Cotton.

Beeb proved then, as he would continue to prove, that he was more interested in making an essential contribution than dominating the spotlight. He was happy to stand alongside Darryl, enough of a chick magnet in his own right to be satisfied on that level, as well as the musical one.

After Zoot moved to Melbourne and enjoyed significant success as a pop group, they – and this might have been at Beeb's instigation – were keen to improve themselves musically and brought in the multi-talented songwriting (equally handsome) Rick Springfield, pushing Beeb another step back into the shadows. He didn't mind. The group was obviously much better for Rick's entry.

Beeb next made his mark with Mississippi, Graeham Goble's group. They'd had one major debut hit, and now needed to become a working band in order to survive. Attracted by the quality of the songs, by Graeham's vision, the already famous, already legendary Beeb Birtles allowed himself to be diverted, agreed to pick up his bass again and give Mississippi the benefit of his experience and talent. Beeb and Graeham formed a unique bond. Mississippi eventually became Little River Band.

Commercially, in Australia, LRB's strength was its "Supergroup" status – lead singer Glenn Shorrock had seen success previously with The Twilights and Axiom. Artistically their strength was the combined vocal front line, Glenn, Graeham and Beeb, and their individual songwriting. Graeham was (and is) one of the most melodic songwriters of our time. Glenn's songs gave LRB its pop sense. Beeb's songs had (and have) heart. It was Beeb who provided LRB with the song they needed as their first single, 'Curiosity (Killed The Cat)'. As LRB's career and music evolved, it was always Beeb's songs that were the most honest, most real, the meat in the sandwich. If you knew Beeb, you knew how true his songs were to his own life experience.

Those LRB years are long behind Beeb Birtles, as is Australia. Life goes on. Music goes on. Whatever else has happened, whatever else will be, the essentials of Beeb Birtles' character outlined above remain. He never was and never will be a scene-stealer. The song is what's important, the task at hand, that's the ultimate objective. And inside that song, inside whatever Beeb Birtles has put his mind to, you'll sense a spirit of someone who has worked hard, thought hard, dug deep, at whatever the personal cost, in order to arrive at the result we're privileged to share.

Ed Nimmervoll
Australian Music Journalist, Author and Editor

PROLOGUE

Sometime in late 2001 I received a phone call from Graeham Goble. He asked me if I was open to a Little River Band (LRB) reunion of what fans were calling the classic lineup: David Briggs, George McArdle, Derek Pellicci, Glenn Shorrock, Graeham Goble and myself. We were going to call ourselves the Original Little River Band.

By then, it had been eighteen years since I quit the band. I told him that I would be interested because, in my mind, time had healed many things. I was also keen to hear Glenn and Graeham's voices with mine after all these years.

The reunion idea had actually come from Paul Rodger.

In Paul's own words:

In 2001, Stream AV started providing DVD authoring services to Warner Vision, which was, at the time, the largest producer and distributor of concert DVDs in the world. I was travelling to Sydney every other week to see them and on one of those visits I was talking with Warner Vision's production team about how successful the Eagles' Hell Freezes Over *DVD was. I said that we should do a similar thing in Australia.*

Darryl O'Connor, the managing director of Warner Vision, laughed and asked me who would be big enough and have the appeal to that market to make it worthwhile. I said I thought LRB would be a great choice and the room fell silent. Darryl said that LRB would be the right fit for them but how could we get it to happen? Warner Vision said if we could pull it together they would fund the production.

LRB had carved out a place in world music history and were the first Australian band to have a gold album in the USA, paving the way for other Australian artists. We informed Stephen Housden (LRB member from 1982) that we intended to perform under the name 'The Original Little

River Band'. Stephen's lawyer, Thomas Stevens, claimed we didn't have any rights to the Little River Band trademark anymore and he sent us a 'cease and desist' order. He claimed Stephen Housden now legally owned the LRB name and trademark. What was about to unravel would cost us — Graeham Goble, Glenn Shorrock and I — more than $300,000 in legal expenses.

As reported by Nui Te Koha in the *Herald Sun* on December 14, 2001:

A musician trading as the Little River Band has vowed to block plans by the group's original members to tour the US under the name.

Stephen Housden, a member of the Little River Band since 1982 and who bought the worldwide rights to the famous band name four years ago, says he will not allow a re-formed version of the group to use the LRB name in any shape or form.

"I can tell you now, there's no hope of them coming to America because I own the trademark in America and I own it for the world," Housden told the Herald Sun *from his home in Ireland yesterday. "I've been working in America for the last 20 years in the Little River Band and this new group just cannot happen."*

This 'new group' consisted of original members of LRB, first formed in 1975. I had not been paid for the loss of the name or any goodwill associated with the name of the band we had created.

On October 17, 2004, 'The Classic Lineup' was inducted into the ARIA Hall of Fame. Stephen Housden almost prevented this from happening but eventually agreed to issue a 24-hour licence to the original members, allowing us to perform one song at the awards and use the name Little River Band.

In 2005, the historical story of the Little River Band, a DVD titled *It's A Long Way There*, was manufactured, pressed and scheduled for release by EMI/Capitol, but Stephen Housden and Wayne Nelson threatened to sue EMI Records and the product was withdrawn. It was never released.

We had lost all rights to the LRB trademark that we had thought would be ours forever…

PREFACE

SEVEN SEAS

Tonight the waves are sending their spray across my bow
I ride the ocean's turbulence with a heavy brow
I keep straining as if my back is breaking
Like men who man the oars
Pressing on until I reach distant shores

Today the mist hangs low like a blanket on my deck
I sail through unknown waters never to go back
At the Captain's command I follow orders
Like soldiers on a drill
Steady course my journey left to full-

Fill my sails with Your full strength
Let Your wind blow across my breadth and length
Guide my hull through seven seas
Bring me home and bless my life with peace

Tomorrow as the dawn breaks I'll catch the sun's first light
With seagulls circling my mast the coast appears in sight
At the turn of the wheel the Helmsman guides me
Safely to the shore
Lower down my anchor to the floor

Fill my sails with Your full strength
Let Your wind blow across my breadth and length
Guide my hull through seven seas
Bring me home and bless my life with peace

I have this fascination with the number seven. It seems to pop up in front of me at the most unlikely times, like when I'm driving and for no reason whatsoever I happen to glance down at the odometer and there will be three sevens in a row. It's the strangest thing but it happens to me often. Graeham Goble, one of the other founding members of Little River Band, once told me that all of the letters in my name add up to seven, the spiritual number for perfection. I don't believe in numerology but at the same time I think it's very interesting.

I was extremely satisfied with the way the words turned out for 'Seven Seas'. The song hasn't been recorded as yet. For the longest time it remained untitled until one day when I was looking up the meaning of a certain phrase to do with the ocean, I stumbled onto the fact there are seven main seas in the world. The song has many double meanings.

This is how I see it: the song is about me. I am the ship. Here I am, at the age of sixty-eight, looking back across my life. It's been a music-filled one for the last fifty years and this song is about my journey through life. The seven seas represent the seven decades of a man's life. Riding the ocean's turbulence with a heavy brow are the trials and tribulations we go through in life. Life is not always easy but we press on, we go forward and don't look back. And as we keep moving forward we sail through unknown waters, not really knowing where we're heading.

In the chorus, the song turns more spiritual. I'm asking God to fill me with His full strength, in other words, give me all you've got to make me the best I can be for my time on earth. The image of the wind blowing across my breadth and length is the sign of the cross, a reminder of what the Christian faith is based on. I think John 3:16 pretty much sums it up for me: 'For God so loved the world that He gave His one and only Son that whoever believes in Him shall not perish but have eternal life.' The rest of the chorus is pretty self-explanatory: guide me through my life, bring me home and bless me with peace.

I invite you to embark on this journey with me. In order to do so we have to set sail north over the Tropic of Capricorn in the Southern Hemisphere, across the equator into the Northern Hemisphere and crossing over the Tropic of Cancer all the way up into the North Sea that divides the United Kingdom and the Netherlands.

Beeb Birtles
2017

One
AMSTERDAM, HOLLAND

BEEB IN SLOTERDIJK, AMSTERDAM

1945, the end of World War 2 and the citizens of Amsterdam were dancing in the streets celebrating their freedom from Nazi German occupation. It was there that my parents met. I don't know how long they dated or what set off the spark between them but I do know they were married on January 7, 1948. I was born later that same year on November 28.

My parents gave me exactly the same name as my father: Gerard Bertelkamp. No middle name, just my first name and surname. During my younger years they called me Gerardje, the *je* tagged on the end of one's name in Holland meaning 'little' or 'small', similar to the English meaning of junior.

Dad was a man of few words but I remember him telling me that the Nazis had singled him out on the streets of Amsterdam, as they did with many young Dutch men, and put him on a train to Germany to work as forced labour. However, somewhere between Amsterdam and the German border he jumped off the train at night, so he wouldn't be seen, and walked back to Amsterdam.

For a short time, my parents lived on a small boat on one of Amsterdam's canals. I remember being on it maybe once or twice and going through the canal lock system. More than likely, my parents decided that a boat was not the ideal place to live when starting their family. I have a photo of me in a rowing boat on a farm somewhere when I couldn't have been more than four or five years old. From that moment on I felt an instant love for being on the water because it gave me a great feeling of peace.

The sound of Sunday mornings in Amsterdam were of church bells ringing, tram wheels screeching and the ring-a-ling of bicycle bells from people coming up behind you, warning of their approach. I had a wonderful extended family and it was not unusual for us to go for Sunday walks and visit *Tante* (Aunt) Riek and *Oom* (Uncle) Jan. After a few hours visiting them I would be treated to a snack from the street vendors. Carts were set up with big pump jars of mayonnaise and mustard and I was allowed to buy hot and crispy *patate frite* (French fries) to eat on the way home. They were served in paper bags, open and round at the top, tapering down to a point at the bottom. It made them easy to hold for small hands. The fries at the top of the bag were smothered in either mayonnaise or mustard, whatever your choice.

For New Year's Eve celebrations family and friends gathered at someone's house, usually drinking more than they should, until midnight struck. With church bells ringing, fireworks going off and horns and whistles blowing, everyone stopped what they were doing and hugged, kissed and wished each other a *Gelukkig Nieuwjaar*! Happy New Year. When the festivities were over, we went home by taxi. More than a few times I can remember being carried, half asleep and half awake, by my father into a Mercedes taxi. Mercedes taxis were always my favourite.

We were closer to my grandparents on my mother's side. We didn't have a lot to do with Dad's parents as my grandfather was an alcoholic. When my dad was a young man my grandmother made him go get my grandfather from the local cafés and bring him home for dinner, sometimes having to support him along the way because he was so inebriated. Of course, I never saw any of this but I imagine it was humiliating for my father.

Dad was fourteen when he left school to help support his family and he worked as an apprentice carpenter. He was taught his trade by the older Master carpenters and he turned out to be an excellent wood craftsman; he could build anything with his hands.

No matter where we lived in Amsterdam Dad always made improvements to our dwellings. He provided well for us, and his work became his life. He never owned a car in Holland but drove to work on his BMW motorbike.

My parents loved to sing and were involved in performing in amateur operettas. When I was still very young, *Oma Deubel* (my grandma on my mother's side) took me to see an operetta in which my parents were performing. On recognising my mother up on stage I yelled out,

"Mama!" Oma's hand over my mouth quickly shut me up. This is my earliest recollection of seeing a live performance of any description.

Our first home was on the Wittenkade 93, overlooking one of Amsterdam's canals. Looking out the window one winter morning, I watched a daredevil kid trying to be the first one to cross the frozen canal. It was rare to see someone fall in, but it did happen. Once the canals froze over, scarf-wrapped skaters took to the ice and skated for hours on end. Some people even used the canals to skate to work in the mornings and back home again at night.

It was here on the Wittenkade that my sister was born on September 17, 1952. My parents named her after my mother, Elisabeth Hendrika Bertelkamp. Why on earth did they repeat their names with their offspring? I don't get it! My sister's name was quickly shortened to Elly.

My mother's parents also lived on the Wittenkade a little further down from where we lived but because of their age, they lived on street level. We visited them regularly, and sometimes Elly and I would stay overnight if my parents went out for a late night.

I really loved my *Opa* (grandpa) Strunk. He was Oma's second husband as her first husband had deserted her and left her with five children, starting a new life for himself in Belgium. It was a very admirable thing that Opa Strunk did to take up with a woman who already had five children.

From the Wittenkade we moved to Balistraat, into an apartment on the ground floor that was very cold and damp. It was close to a railway line that ran along the top of a dike. When it snowed in winter, kids in the neighbourhood pulled their sleds up to the top and slid back down.

We were living in that damp ground floor apartment when Dad took me shopping one Christmas to buy my first real watch. In Holland they call it a *horloge* which is a French word that means 'timepiece'. It was a particularly cold winter that year and I almost couldn't feel my toes in my rubber boots but the excitement of looking at all the different watches in the shop windows made me forget about my frozen toes. We didn't live in that damp and cold apartment very long before moving to Amsterdam East. My fondest memories of growing up in Amsterdam remain at Eikenweg, probably because I was a bit older and remember more about it. Once again we lived on the third floor with an attic on the floor above.

Dad had a workbench set up in the attic. More than likely it was here that he measured and cut all the timber for a modular beach house he assembled every summer on a rented plot at Bloemendaal aan Zee near Zandvoort. When summer was over, beach houses had to be disassembled and stored for the winter. The fierce North Sea beat against the sand dunes, or dikes as they call them, throughout the winter, and made it impossible to leave beach houses up all year 'round.

We spent quite a few summers at Bloemendaal, living at the beach for our entire summer holiday. Dad drove me down first on the back of his BMW motorbike and instructed me to sit tight and wait while he rode back to Amsterdam to get my mother and sister. Elly was still small enough to fit between Mum and Dad on his motorbike.

They were great summers: swimming in the North Sea, playing in the sand, building sandcastles and making kites with long trailing tails. There was always a strong sea breeze so I could fly my kite along the beach. Elly and I were very fortunate to have these experiences.

Living on Eikenweg was where I first became aware of listening to the radio. Two songs stand out from that time. In 1954, when I was five, I heard 'Mr Sandman' by girl group The Chordettes. It was the number one song in America and it became one of my favourites. Hearing the blend of their voices, their close harmonies, stirred something inside me.

The other song was an instrumental on a 78 vinyl record that my grandparents owned. They had one of those old-fashioned record players that you had to wind up before every song. The record was called 'La Mer', meaning the sea. It is by French composer Charles Trenet, and American composer Jack Lawrence wrote lyrics to the melody. It became known as 'Beyond The Sea' and was the title of a movie about the life of Bobby Darin, starring Kevin Spacey. I played that record over and over. To my ears it was, and still is, an incredibly beautiful melody.

When I was eight we received the news that Opa Bertelkamp had died of a heart attack. He fell down the stairs where my grandparents lived. I went to the funeral with my dad and will never forget the sight of that closed coffin slowly being lowered into the ground on a cold winter day. I didn't really understand what was happening and as I stood there holding Dad's hand I became overwhelmed with emotion and burst into tears.

When I looked up at Dad's face it was expressionless, no emotion, not one ounce of sadness. Perhaps the thoughts of those humiliating days when he had to bring his father home drunk were running through his mind. We never talked about his father's funeral and it was to be the only family burial I would ever attend in Holland.

So what do you give a typical Dutch kid for his eighth birthday? Why, that favourite instrument of all Europeans of course, the piano accordion! My parents arranged lessons for me and I can vaguely picture my teacher in my mind. The piano accordion was not my choice of instrument, even though I became somewhat of an average player and learned to read music.

One day when I was bored and playing by myself in my room, I lit some matches and started burning some crumpled pieces of paper in a small rubbish bin. I wasn't careful enough though because the curtains caught on fire and smoke started billowing out from under my bedroom door.

My parents were entertaining some friends in the living room at the time. One of them noticed the smoke and they all came running into my bedroom and quickly extinguished the fire. Oh boy, I knew I was in deep shit and when my punishment was dealt out to me it was something that I detested doing. I was ordered to practise my piano accordion for two hours straight every day for two weeks!

VOYAGE TO AUSTRALIA

BERTELKAMP FAMILY ON THE WILLEM RUYS

My father became disgruntled with the way everything was so controlled by the government in the Netherlands. He began thinking about a new life for his family in a country that offered more opportunities. He didn't agree with the socialistic form of government taking care of its citizens from the day they were born to the day they died, all for a percentage of their wages of course. He wanted to have control of his own money. I think he felt he wasn't getting ahead fast enough and those bitterly cold winters wouldn't have helped. I admire his pioneering spirit.

The Dutch government encouraged emigration because of over-population. In the late '50s Holland's population was already around twelve million, which was a lot of people for such a small country. The government sponsored special film nights where citizens could get an idea of what it was like to live in other countries around the world.

My parents attended a few of these nights and saw films on what life was like in the Belgian Congo, Rhodesia, South Africa, Canada, the United States, Australia and New Zealand. I think they quickly ruled out the African countries because of racial concerns. Over the course of a few months they became more impressed with what Australia had to offer and it wasn't long before they made their decision that this was where they wanted to immigrate. They prepared to sell some of their belongings because there was limited space on the ship.

My parents had befriended two brothers, Jan and Ary van Tielen, on one of the orientation nights and they also signed up for Australia. We departed from Rotterdam on August 7, 1959; the trip would take about four weeks. I remember the excitement surrounding our departure. Some of our extended family made the trip from Amsterdam to see us off. I had only attended school for three years before we migrated to Australia. By then, I had friends and a wonderful Indonesian teacher who was kind enough to take slides of my classmates for me to take to Australia, so I wouldn't forget them. We sailed on a ship called the *Willem Ruys* that was named after the founder of Rotterdamsche Lloyd, a Dutch shipping company. The four of us stood clinging to the guardrails waving goodbye to our family standing on the docks, as the boarding ramps were pulled away from the ship. People on the docks threw multi-coloured streamers up at us, as the ship slowly pulled away.

I was ten years old and Elly was five when we migrated to Australia. I don't remember much about the trip because most of the time Elly and I were in a crèche. We sailed to Southampton, England, catching sight of the White Cliffs of Dover, before heading down to the Mediterranean Sea. When we reached Port Said at the mouth of the Suez Canal, passengers were allowed to go ashore and sightsee. Our mother was a bit paranoid about kids being kidnapped so we weren't allowed to leave the ship.

The ship sailed at a very slow speed through the Suez Canal. It wasn't very wide and only so many ships could sail through, convoy style, until we reached the middle lakes where we parked for a few hours to allow ships travelling north to pass by. The most exciting thing I remember is when Elly and I were allowed to drink a Coke — something that didn't happen every day!

From the Suez Canal we sailed to Colombo, the capital of Ceylon, now known as Sri Lanka, where we spent a day. Once again, Elly and I weren't allowed off the ship. Singapore was the only place where we went sightseeing as a family. It was world renowned for great deals on jewellery, cameras such as Leica and Nikon, and various brands of transistor radios.

We departed Singapore for our final destination of Melbourne, Australia. The route took us through the Strait of Singapore, the Java Sea, Strait Sunda and finally into the Indian Ocean. In the Java Sea we crossed the equator. The following night we sailed through Strait Sunda and reached the Great Australian Bight. After a couple of days of closely following the south coast of Australia we sailed into Port Phillip Bay. It was early in the morning when we arrived in Melbourne on September 4, 1959.

The Port of Melbourne lies directly behind Spencer Street Station. My parents had already made up their minds to settle in Adelaide, the capital of South Australia so after disembarking from the ship we caught the train to Adelaide. We had to sit the whole way on hard, uncomfortable wooden benches.

My new life had begun.

Two
ADELAIDE, SOUTH AUSTRALIA

While still in Holland, Dad had learnt to speak a few words of English, which got him by. My mother, sister and I were thrown in the deep end when it came to learning the new language. We had to start from scratch, as did just about every family that emigrated from Europe to Australia, except for the English of course.

At the Adelaide train station we were met by a man in a Holden utility, who drove us up into the Adelaide Hills to a small country town called Woodside. This was to be our temporary accommodation, a kind of holding camp for migrants until space became available in one of a handful of migrant hostels spread around Adelaide.

As you do when you're young, I made friends with some other kids and we started exploring the area. It was spring and walking along the hot, rugged outback roads we quickly learned about magpies. They swooped and pecked the top of our heads as a warning to stay away from their nests.

Living at Woodside was communal. Laundries and toilet blocks were shared between families but they were separate from the long blocks of huts where we lived. When the women did laundry at night you could hear their screams because the possums got inside the roof and ran rampant over the rafters or on top of the corrugated iron rooftop and stared at the women with their intense beady eyes.

My father didn't waste any time finding work. Mr Smits, another Dutchman, hired him as a carpenter. We were invited to dinner at their place once. They were a religious family and gave thanks before eating their meals. I became friends with one of their sons, John, who was around my age. They also had an older son named Tony, who later became a minister in Adelaide.

John taught me to collect empty soft drink bottles because you got five pence when you took them back to the deli. We kept collecting them until we saved enough money to buy a couple of very cool plastic water pistols. We had been eyeing them in the window of the local chemist in the Smits' neighbourhood.

Building houses in Australia was something totally new to my father. He had to learn new ways of construction but because he was such a skilled carpenter, he got the hang of it very quickly.

During the first few years in Adelaide, my mother suffered greatly from home sickness. She made a couple of trips back to Holland to visit her family whereas my dad showed no interest in going back; he lived for his work.

FINSBURY MIGRANT HOSTEL

Our stay at Woodside was brief, a couple of weeks at most, before space became available at the Finsbury Migrant Hostel on Grand Junction Road, not far from Port Adelaide. All the migrant hostels in Adelaide were built like army Nissen huts, made out of curved corrugated iron with each side almost touching the ground. There were blocks and blocks of them, all numbered. They didn't have air conditioning, so they became unbearably hot in summer.

At night, families ate in shifts in the community cafeteria. During the week you could place orders for lunch to take to work or school. Your surname was written at the top of a brown paper bag and the meal usually consisted of some kind of sandwich, a piece of fruit, a piece of cake and a drink.

The Europeans complained bitterly about the bland Australian food compared to what they were used to from their countries. Most families couldn't wait to move out of these hostels. The laundries and bathroom facilities were communal and lacked proper hand-washing facilities. There was never any soap around when you needed it.

For the remaining couple of months of the 1959 school year I was enrolled at Pennington Primary School and walked there from the hostel. Being a new kid and not able to speak the language, other kids goaded me into going up to the teachers and saying swear words. I didn't have a clue what I was saying of course. As you can imagine, they were not the kind of words kids my age should be saying and I got into trouble.

Kids can be so cruel at times! But, you know, it didn't faze us not being able to communicate, we just joined in with the kids who spoke English fluently and before too long we were mimicking and forming the words they were speaking. After a while, we could put a whole sentence together and eventually join in complete conversations. Within a year of living in Adelaide I was speaking English fairly well.

At Pennington Primary I got my first taste of cricket and football. I loved playing sports and joined as many different teams as I could. On the weekends I went to the pictures, either with friends from school or the hostel. Sometimes we walked all the way to Port Adelaide and hung out on the jetty. I joined in and did the normal kid thing for a ten-year-old, until one day I got sick.

Because there was never any soap at the hostel, I neglected washing my hands after going to the toilet. I contracted an infectious liver disease called yellow fever and was immediately admitted to Northfield Infectious Diseases Hospital.

Back in those days, if you had an infectious disease they isolated you. Your family couldn't even visit until you were well again. My mother was worried sick because I was still so young and couldn't speak English and now I was being taken away from the family for at least three weeks. However, it didn't freak me out, I just took it in my stride. I was confined to bed and wasn't allowed to get up, not even to go to the toilet.

The funniest thing about my time in hospital was when the nurses tried to explain about having to urinate into a stainless steel flask. I didn't have a clue what they were trying to tell me. One night, I woke to the sound of trickling water. I sat up to see where it was coming from and, in the dark, I could barely make out the person in the bed next to me, sitting up and using the shiny weird-shaped stainless steel flask. Immediately it dawned on me. *So that's what they've been trying to tell me!* It was a major breakthrough.

My mother must have put her foot down and told my dad we wouldn't be staying at the hostel once I was released from hospital. Dad applied for a bank loan and put a deposit on a block of land in the undeveloped suburb of Netley.

43 HARVEY AVENUE, NETLEY

CARAVAN AND SHED

Netley is about halfway between the city of Adelaide and West Beach. Harvey Avenue runs between Marion Road and the edge of the Adelaide Airport. The land in that area belonged to a man named Collett.

When I was discharged from hospital, my parents took me to see the block of land. I saw nothing but sand. Recalling my wonderful summers at the beach in Holland, I took off my shoes and started running wildly across the 'sand'. Ouch, big mistake! No one had told us that South Australia had these thorns called three-corner jacks and I had about a dozen of them stuck to my feet.

Life lesson number one — don't assume that sand is the same everywhere in the world!

Behind our block of land stood a house owned by Jean and Dick Collett. Dick, Jean and their children, Merryl and Richard, were our nearest neighbours. Merryl had a horse, and a portion of their land was leased to Russell Thomas, who operated a riding school. The Collett family were instrumental in helping us get our start in Adelaide. They were extremely kind. Jean invited my mother on trips to the Barossa Valley with her friends and she would invite Mum over for afternoon tea.

My parents were the first people to buy a block of land in the area.

Dad bought a small corrugated iron garden shed that he erected and this served as my parents' bedroom, our dining area, and washing and laundry area. A deep, double concrete laundry trough was where my mother did our washing and washed the dishes after meals.

We had no running water or electricity. Our fresh water came from Dick and Jean's house. Just about every day we filled a couple of buckets of fresh water and carried them back to the shed.

My parents rented a caravan, which became the bedroom Elly and I shared. That's how we lived for a year until my parents had saved enough money to start building our house.

My father negotiated with a builder: Dad would do all of the woodwork and the builder would take care of the rest. It was very exciting seeing our house being built from the ground up. Every day when Elly and I came home from school, either something was still in progress or something had been completed. When the foundation was set, we walked across the top of it with my parents pointing out where the various rooms were going to be.

The first night we slept there was on Christmas Eve 1960. There was no carpet, just bare floors but we didn't care. It was the best Christmas present ever to be living in a real house again.

At night, we always ate together as a family. When Mum was close to serving dinner, Elly and I were ordered to turn off the television and take our place at the table. We had family conversations around the dinner table and Elly and I took turns with helping do the dishes after dinner. Mum always washed while we dried. Sometimes Mum sang popular songs of the day and I would add a harmony part. The first time I ever sang harmonies was with my mother, standing at the kitchen sink.

Elly and I earned ten shillings pocket money a week that we could either spend or save in our school bank accounts on Wednesdays. To earn this, we had to make the beds, do the breakfast dishes and sweep the kitchen floor before heading out the door for school. We alternated these duties every day of the week as my parents left the house before us to go to work.

NETLEY PRIMARY SCHOOL

Elly and I started school at the newly built Netley Primary School in

February 1960. I was held back a year because of the language barrier and my lack of knowledge of Australian subjects. In Holland, I had been taught European and world geography but I knew nothing about Australia, aside from the fact that Dutch explorers discovered it.

I was in grade five and Mrs Brown was my teacher. I will never forget Mrs Brown as long as I live because one day she called me up to her desk and took a twelve-inch ruler to the back of my lower leg, smacking me until my leg was red raw. I was flabbergasted and didn't have a clue as to what I had done wrong. She pointed out that I had misspelled 'Sydney', using an 'i' instead of a 'y'. Mrs Brown must have had a lot on her plate because her son, Kelvin, a student in our class, was the most unruly of all the kids. She smacked him more than anyone else! Looking back, I'm convinced that the Sydney incident made me determined to become a really good English student. Ever since, I have been a stickler for spelling and grammar.

I made many friends at Netley and got involved in playing all kinds of sports. I took up baseball and cricket. I hung out with friends like Bruce and Kelvin Minerds, who were Australians, and Ilgvar Daga, a Latvian immigrant. Ilgvar loved basketball and sometimes I accompanied him to games.

My memories of the three years I spent at Netley Primary are sketchy at best. By the end of my first year I could speak English fluently. Elly and I spoke Dutch at home, and outside the home we spoke English. To this day I can still carry on a conversation in Dutch. I was young enough, however, that I completely lost my Dutch accent.

I completed grades five, six and seven with flying colours. Even though I was held back to start with, I had an advantage with a couple of subjects like mathematics and geography. I was taught these in earlier grades in Holland and that came in very useful by the time I entered grades six and seven.

Girls flirted with boys and led them around like sheep. Blair was a really good-looking girl but she lost interest very quickly and went from one boy to the next. It was all so innocent back then: getting friends to pass notes to girls you liked. Giggling girls flirting with boys behind the shelter sheds, and boys following girls home to see where they lived.

I liked a pretty girl called Linda, who was so sweet and innocent in primary school. A few years later, she became a rocker and a biker chick, complete with black eyeliner, mascara and black leather clothes. She grew up way quicker than I did! I was innocent and naïve to the extent that I didn't experience sex for the first time until I was twenty and living in Melbourne.

Another girl I really liked was Wendy Newman, who had a brother, Robert. I was friends with him and I used to go over to their house after school. Wendy and I loosely became boyfriend and girlfriend and I made the mistake of bringing her home to meet my mother.

Life lesson number two — don't bring someone from the opposite sex home to meet your mother, no matter what age you are!

The minute Wendy was out the door, my mother picked her to pieces, pointing out she had a crooked nose and was poorly dressed.

I learned that lesson very quickly. I think I brought maybe two other girls home after that. It didn't matter who the girl was, my mother was always extremely critical. No one was ever good enough for me, or for Elly, for that matter.

If my mother only knew that what she was doing at the time was pushing me away from home. After the incident with Wendy I decided that everything I did would take place outside of our family home. Don't get me wrong, when it came to Elly and me, my mother was very loving and generous. I've lost count of the times that we went to the pictures together. We would catch the bus to the city and walk to The Majestic Theatre in King William Street. We saw every Jerry Lewis and Dean Martin comedy and every Elvis Presley movie together. When the new technology of curved Panavision movie screens was introduced in Adelaide we went to see *South Pacific*. I loved doing that with Mum. While Mum did lots of things with me, Dad never did. I've heard other baby boomers say the same thing about their parents, that they weren't involved in their lives and not very demonstrative with their emotions.

I hugged my father one time and told him that I loved him and I felt him straighten up like a piece of wood. I could tell it made him feel very uncomfortable, so I never did it again. Maybe because his own father had never shown him any love he didn't know how to handle it. He hardly ever talked to me about his childhood.

My mother was more demonstrative with her love. She would run her fingers through my hair and talk to me about what was going on in my life. After all, I was her firstborn and we had that mother-and-son bond, but that was only when I was young.

The last time my mother came to visit my wife Donna and me in Nashville she showed us some photos of my dad. They were from shortly before he died. She admitted that my father's only downfall was that he never did anything with me when I was growing up.

Dad died on May 4, 2000 from Alzheimer's disease. I chose not to go back to Australia to see him because I didn't want to remember him that way. At that time, Donna and I and our two daughters had been living in the US for ten years and I hadn't been back to Australia during that time. It greatly disappointed my mother and sister that I didn't fly back for his funeral. For some reason I had developed an attitude about Dad never doing anything with me and it made me angry. I thought: *Why should I fly back for his funeral when he never did anything with me?* Now that I'm older I understand that my parents were a product of their generation. Even though Dad may not have remembered who I was, I should have flown back not only for his sake, but mine as well. I now know from having attended my mother's funeral that it brings closure.

Along with the British music invasion came the fashions of the day. The Beatles had long hair and wore Cuban-heeled boots. We all wanted to look and dress like The Beatles or The Rolling Stones. I wasn't allowed to grow my hair long or own a pair of Beatle boots. And I was especially not allowed to wear skintight jeans!

I defied my parents about this. Sitting in my bedroom, with the door closed, I spent hours hand-stitching the legs of my jeans tight. When they were done I could barely pull them over my ankles. I mean, they were skintight!

I also saved my money and bought my own pair of Beatle boots that I kept at my friend's place.

Richard Trout and his sister, Charmaine, lived on the corner of Harvey Avenue and Beare Avenue. Whenever I went out, I swung by their house and swapped my shoes for my Beatle boots. I grew my hair as long as I could get away with at the front but the back remained short. It was my feeble attempt at looking cool. It was a ridiculous look when I see old photos of myself now!

Most of my friends were mods, not rockers, and we used to go to a shop in Rundle Street called Scott's Menswear, where we could get tartan pants and bright-coloured silk shirts made – it was the happening look at the time. Scott's was downstairs from a long narrow snack bar called J. Sigalas & Co., where we used to buy pop dogs. The owner took long bread rolls and slid them onto metal rods that heated the inside of the bread. When he removed the warm bread roll, he'd squirt tomato sauce or mustard into the bottom of the roll, followed by the hot dog. Those pop dogs were outrageously delicious!

My old friend and fellow music lover, Valda Rubio (née Valtenbergs), remembers this:

The cultural phenomenon of the mods (and later the sharpies) came straight out of the UK. Every weekend scores of young men would assemble outside The Scene in Pirie Street, until a suitably attired mod damsel would choose one, on the basis of his haircut, cravat and scooter (the Vespa was far more superior to the Lambretta), then to be whisked off to adventures unknown.

At the end of the night the summary of events could include driving twenty-abreast on Anzac Highway and gate-crashing parties. It was seen as an honour if a scooter gang discovered your 21st and demolished the food and drink. I was over the moon when they turned up at my party and parked their scooters all over my parents' lawn in middle-class Beaumont.

For my fifteenth birthday, my parents bought me a Maton Alver acoustic guitar that was right-handed. It was cherry red, the kind that had F holes in it. Being left-handed I immediately turned the guitar over and tried to play it upside down. It was hopeless trying to form chords with my left hand so I flipped the strings over and tried to form chords with my right hand. That still didn't work because the bridge was set at a slight angle to compensate for the thickness of each string. No matter how I tried I couldn't get the guitar in tune so I gave up.

My parents' friends Ary and Jan van Tielen had also chosen to live in Adelaide. However, Ary had returned to Holland after two years, which was the minimum period immigrants were required to live in their country of choice. Jan stayed for five years before moving to California in June 1964.

Because of the difference in voltage between Australia and the US, electrical appliances had to be left behind. When Jan left he sold his combination radio and record player to my parents who bought it for my sixteenth birthday in 1964. The bonus was that I also inherited Jan's small record collection. I didn't care that it was second-hand, I was thrilled to have my own record player and my ears became glued to the radio. This was by far the best birthday present my parents had ever given me!

Jan left behind 45s as well as long-playing records. A couple of albums I inherited were *Rock Around The Clock* by Bill Haley and His Comets and *One Dozen Berrys* by Chuck Berry. I also had an extended long play album by a singer called Dick Haymes, who was popular in the '40s and '50s in the US.

Some of the singles were 'Shop Around', with 'Who's Lovin' You' on the B-side, by Smokey Robinson and the Miracles, 'Mule Skinner Blues' by Rusty Draper, and 'Do Not Forsake Me: (The Ballad of High Noon)' by Frankie Laine. I had a Teresa Brewer single, the name of which escapes me now, plus quite a few other records by popular artists of the day. The Kriesler record player awakened my passion for music.

I was already interested in the hit parade of the day. The most popular radio station in Adelaide was 5DN and every week in *The News* they printed the 5DN Big Sixty, the top sixty records of the week. This was before the term Top Forty was coined.

Printed in a little separate section underneath the chart they listed the five predictions of songs waiting to get in as the older songs slipped out. Every week I cut the charts out and kept them on a clipboard. And every week I would accurately predict which songs dropped out and which ones made it into the charts.

Once the British invasion was under way I bought the English music magazine *Fab*. Each issue was jammed with great photos of the latest English rock bands. Bands whose records we heard on the radio. My bedroom walls were covered with photos of them, from the floor to the ceiling.

We watched national television shows like *Rock Around The Clock* and *Bandstand*, which featured all the current pop stars and bands. The Easybeats were the most popular Australian band. They were made up of Dutch, English and Scottish migrants. I bought their very first album.

I could name dozens of artists who appeared on television around that time. The Bee Gees were regulars on *Bandstand* as were the duo of Olivia Newton-John and Pat Carroll. Little Pattie and The Delltones were also regular guests. Then there were The Atlantics with their instrumental surf music, and Rob E.G. playing his Hawaiian steel guitar.

Rob would later form Sparmac, the label that recorded that first incredible Daddy Cool album, *Daddy Who? Daddy Cool!* He also produced Rick Springfield's first solo single, 'Speak To The Sky', and 'Feelings', the first single for Darryl Cotton and me when we were in a duo known as Frieze. But all that was a long way ahead of me — in Adelaide in the mid '60s, I had just started becoming a huge music fan, I was obsessed.

PLYMPTON HIGH SCHOOL

All through Primary School I was known by my given name of Gerard but, as I entered into Plympton High School in 1963, that was about to change.

The Dick Tracy Show was a popular cartoon series on television during those days. Some of the characters had names like Mumbles, Pruneface, Flattop, Itchy, Joe Jitsu and B.B. Eyes. I have no explanation for why but my school friends – it may have been Bruce Minerds, he was always the class comedian – started calling me B.B. Eyes and that's how my nickname started. The name stuck and was soon shortened to B.B. and for the rest of my high school years that's what I was called.

In my first year at Plympton High I met Peter Grigorenko who turned me onto new music. I distinctly remember him playing me Van Morrison's second solo album, which was jazz-influenced, and Bob Dylan's very first album. Out of my group of school friends Peter was ahead of his time when it came to music.

In my second year at high school I became very good friends with John

D'Arcy. John's family came from Manchester and they lived at Glenelg Migrant Hostel. John was a huge fan of The Hollies, a vocal harmony group from his hometown. The Hollies were also becoming extremely popular in England following the success of The Beatles and The Rolling Stones. Their first chart single was a cover of the Coasters' 1961 single '(Ain't That) Just Like Me' from their début album *Stay With The Hollies*.

John and I were also fans of the English group The Zombies, who had a gigantic hit with 'She's Not There'. I can't tell you how many shillings I spent selecting that song in jukeboxes all over Adelaide. It was so electrifying to hear the intro.

After dinner, I rode my bike to either Tony de Vries' house or John's place, where we learned some of the popular songs of the day. John played guitar and was great at working out the chords and then teaching us our respective harmonies.

Tony was another friend from Plympton High whose family had migrated from Holland. I went to his house every chance I got because he had a really good-looking sister. She was typically Dutch-looking with beautiful fair skin, a round open face and white blonde hair.

Alas, Tony didn't last long with us. I don't know if it was because he didn't have the same passion for music or the fact that John's family moved from the Glenelg Migrant Hostel to Christies Beach.

Gordon Rawson, another good friend from high school, sent me this memory:

John D'Arcy introduced us to the Liverpool sound and guitars. We all went to the Sheff's College of Music and paid for ten music lessons. It was in Glenelg. I used to ride my bike after school, with a guitar that I bought for five guineas in a cardboard box under my arm.

Beeb, John and Tony de Vries started learning a few songs together and then invited me to join the group. The first song I remember doing with the guys was 'Under The Boardwalk' by The Drifters. It was also my first attempt at singing background vocals. Not long after that, Tony decided he wasn't interested anymore and the three of us continued on.

I remember playing The Shadows' 'Apache' in front of Beeb's mum and her friends in their kitchen at Harvey Avenue. We were rewarded with Dutch salted licorice and pancakes.

English migrants gravitated towards living in one of two outer areas in Adelaide. One was the Salisbury and Elizabeth area and the other was Christies Beach. When John's family moved to Christies Beach around Christmas of 1964 it became my hangout on weekends.

I completed only three years of high school. As I was getting older and the teachers were getting younger it became hard for them to maintain control in the classroom. Some classes were complete chaos with kids mucking around all the time. That made it impossible to pay attention to what was being taught. Consequently, my grades started to suffer and I lost interest in subjects like Chemistry and Physics. They bored me to tears. French and Mathematics were my strongest subjects.

I completed third year of high school but failed the final examinations. I had the choice of repeating that year or going out into the workforce. The thought of having to repeat without my friends didn't enthral me, so I dropped out of school. A choice I have regretted ever since!

I guess I must have been about sixteen when I started going out at night on the weekends. I still didn't drive so I either walked everywhere or caught the bus. I heard about a dance called Sixth Avenue that was held in a hall on Marion Road towards South Road. Gordon Rawson and I walked there a couple of times. I can't remember whether we had to pay to get in but it was a dance that was chaperoned by adults. A small sound system amplified records that were played from a record player set up in one corner.

At Sixth Avenue most of the kids just came to dance and pash on with each other during the slow songs when they dimmed the lights. They had some kind of mirror ball set up that rotated coloured lights around the hall during these slow numbers. Working up the courage to ask a girl to dance was always a pretty uncomfortable thing for me to do. I was very shy but eventually I did ask a girl to dance during one of the slow songs. As we were dancing I could feel that she was wearing a corset made of very stiff material. It was a total turn off and, to top it off, all she wanted to do was pash on for the duration of the song. I couldn't wait to get the hell out of there!

My friend Barry Smith (lead singer of The Town Criers) knew Darryl Cotton at Marion High School, where they were both on the cricket team – Barry was captain. He also remembers this:

There were two dances and the one I played at was in Fifth Avenue. It was called The Pad. My first band, The Acorns, played there a few times. I don't recall going to Sixth Avenue but I do remember the venue and it would have been a bigger dance than The Pad. It was just a coincidence that the two dances were only a street away from each other.

I think the first time I met Beeb was when he and his dad came around to my folks' place in Glandore and he bought my Hofner Beatle bass that I played. Beeb took the scratch plate off and played it upside down with the control knobs at the top. It was the first of its type in Adelaide.

When I first saw it in the window of Allans Music it was like the Holy Grail. I had to have it and I stood guard over it for several Saturday mornings trying to hide it so no one else would buy it. I finally snared it on hire purchase. It was like my first girlfriend, car and cigarette all wrapped up in one.

Sixth Avenue didn't last long for me and I moved on to clubs in the city. One of the first clubs I went to on a regular basis was Beat Basement at the top end of Rundle Street. Man, did I see some great bands performing there. Bands like Hard Time Killing Floor, The Others, Blues, Rags and Hollers, Dust and Ashes, The Bentbeaks, and The Mustangs, who would soon become The Masters Apprentices. Harmonicas were very in at the time and many bands had lead singers who played them. I went to The Cellar in Twin Street a couple of times but the scene there was more folk music and jazz. I was more into pop and rock and roll music.

One of the biggest thrills was when I bought tickets to see The Rolling Stones. Bev Harrell, The Newbeats and Roy Orbison were the opening acts. Seeing the Stones in action gave me chills up my spine and made me want that kind of life.

Some of the best bands in Australia came out of Adelaide. The melting pot of Australian, English and European kids produced fantastic groups. At that time The Twilights were by far the best band in Adelaide. They were the resident band at The Oxford Club in King William Street.

Darryl Cotton and I went to see them there one Sunday night when The Bentbeaks supported them. The club was jammed shoulder to shoulder with pop music fans. No other band in Australia could duplicate the popular songs of the day like The Twilights could. Between the six guys in the band they had such a cool image and a fantastic sound. Glenn Shorrock was one of the two lead singers and Darryl and I loved his voice.

There was a group of us who hung out at Big Daddy's in the city. Jim Popoff was the man who ran the club. I'm pretty sure this is where I met Skinny (Barry Smith's cousin whose real name is Lynette) and Dianne and Pam. Big Daddy's is where we saw Five Sided Circle, The Y?4, The James Taylor Move and visiting Melbourne bands like The Loved Ones.

In those days, alcohol wasn't served in clubs and we knew no different. When the clubs closed we usually ended up going to someone's place and having a few drinks there. Skinny's parents were very relaxed about kids coming over late at night and drinking and having fun at their house.

Valda Rubio remembers this about living in Adelaide during those days:

I was fortunate enough to be born in Adelaide. I am of that opinion more now than when I was growing up there. Melbourne was where it was all happening but Adelaide is where much of it began. For some reason, whether it was the huge influx of British immigrants or just some collective unconscious, Adelaide was the breeding ground for progressive ideas and excellent bands.

The Scene, Scots Church, The Cellar, Big Daddy's, Opus, Twenty Plus Club, The Oxford Club, Beat Basement, Snoopy's Hollow and my favourite, Sergeant Peppers, were just some of the popular venues in which local and interstate acts played. Many musicians got their start in Adelaide before moving interstate or overseas.

All I thought about was which band, which venue and what to wear. I remember even going to Big Daddy's during my lunch hour to get in a quick dance, only to find myself explaining to a slightly bemused supervisor, how I had managed to sprain my ankle during my lunch break.

Those years were some of the most exciting times in my life. We all made so many friends at these clubs and dances, some of them would follow us to Melbourne when our bands moved there to try to make it in the big smoke. Some of us are still friends after all these years, and when we get together we reminisce about those great old days in Adelaide.

Three
TIMES UNLIMITED

Beeb (playing his homemade bass guitar), Darryl and Ted
Photo courtesy of Terry Higgins

On weekends I started to hang out and make friends in the Christies Beach and Port Noarlunga areas, about twenty miles from Adelaide. Every weekend I hitchhiked there and crashed the night at someone's place. If for some reason I couldn't find somewhere to sleep, I slept on the beach under the Port Noarlunga jetty or in bus shelters. On winter nights I froze my arse off trying to keep warm in my black duffle coat and sleeping on hard bus shelter benches. I didn't care though, it beat hitchhiking all the way back home to Netley.

I got to know so many people through hanging out in Port Noarlunga during the day and going to dances at the Masonic Hall in Christies Beach at night. Popular up and coming bands like The Masters Apprentices, The Others, Blues, Rags and Hollers played at the Masonic Hall on Saturday nights.

Sometimes a local band like The Mermen would play. The Mermen had an unusual lineup because they had two lead singers, one of whom was Darryl Cotton. Malcolm 'Rick' Brewer was their drummer and he lived in McLaren Vale, a suburb near Christies Beach and Port Noarlunga.

John D'Arcy, Gordon Rawson and I kept rehearsing and we added Ted Higgins (who later became Zoot's first drummer) on drums. Ted lived in Port Noarlunga with his mum and sisters and had his own bedroom out the back, separate from the house. This is where we rehearsed. His bedroom was big enough that we could fit his drums as well as a couple of amplifiers. I wasn't playing an instrument at that time so by default I became the lead singer. We found a bass player in David Murdoch, a little guy who wore glasses. We practised and practised, learning our favourite songs until we had a set list long enough to go out and perform for the very first time.

We named our band Times Unlimited. Our first performance was at a dance that was held in the Plympton Scout Hall on Marion Road. The gig was an embarrassing night to say the least because we made lots of mistakes, with the guys playing wrong chords and me forgetting the words. It was awful! David Murdoch, our bass player, was so disgusted with the way we played that he promptly quit. When the band was discussing this later, I asked, "Well, what are we going to do now?"

John looked at me and said, "You'll have to learn to play bass guitar and sing at the same time, lad." He made it sound so simple! I didn't own a bass guitar, let alone an amplifier, but we just bulldozed ahead.

We asked my dad to help shape the body of a bass guitar from plywood. John knew how to measure exactly where to lay the frets on the neck and we slapped a few coats of shellac on it for the finish. We bought a cheap pickup (a pickup is a transducer that captures or senses mechanical vibrations produced by musical instruments, particularly stringed instruments such as the electric and bass guitar) and we positioned it where we would get the optimum sound out of the bass.

When we finished building the bass, I had my work cut out for me. I sat down in front of my Kriesler record player and started picking off the bass lines to every song we had been rehearsing. When I had a few songs under my belt we rehearsed them that weekend, and so it continued until I had learned every one of the songs in our set. This may sound like a difficult task – but I was at that age where nothing seemed impossible. The thought, *Gee, I don't think I can do this*, never occurred to me. I did it because I loved it.

I still didn't know if I could play bass and sing at the same time but it became easier with every rehearsal. Much more importantly, through learning to pick what were sometimes difficult bass lines off records, my ear training had begun and that would serve me greatly in the years to come.

I needed a bass amplifier but I didn't have the money to buy one. As I was still under twenty-one, I asked my parents if they would sign a hire purchase agreement on a Goldentone bass amplifier from one of Adelaide's music shops. They agreed.

Now I was really cruising. I had my homemade bass guitar and a

Goldentone bass amp. It was with this combination that I played all of our earliest live shows in the Christies Beach and Port Noarlunga areas.

Ted Higgins remembers:

When Times Unlimited was formed and we started playing shows, we'd go to the local Masonic Hall on a Saturday night where a guy called Paddy and an English bloke used to hold dances and bring good bands in.

We went to see The Mermen and that's where we saw Darryl Cotton. We discussed afterwards that for the band to become popular we had to have a good-looking lead singer, a front man who the chicks would like. After we spoke to him, he said he would consider it.

However, we still advertised for a lead singer. Jim Keays applied but John D'Arcy didn't like him because he was from Elizabeth. I remember John saying he wouldn't drive all that way for practices and that he thought Jim's voice sounded like shit. I liked him because he was a good-looking guy.

At Willunga High, every girl at school wanted to go out with Darryl Cotton and, after continually talking to him, he decided to join our band.

I wasn't very keen on lead singers because they didn't have to buy any gear. To my mind, they just stood there and sang. It took some time for John D'Arcy to convince me that Darryl would be an asset to the band, that with him as our lead singer we could move up to the next level.

Eventually, I came around because we were limited in what we could achieve with just the four of us. Gordon, John and I all sang but it took the focus off playing our instruments. Plus none of us felt really comfortable talking to an audience and that's where I realised lead singers earn their weight in gold. Darryl was a good-looking guy and he was a chick magnet. When he joined as our lead singer we decided to change the band's name.

DOWN THE LINE

Darryl Cotton was born at Henley Beach Private Hospital in Adelaide on September 4, 1949. In his early years he sang in the school choir and one year they were chosen to participate in John Martin's Christmas Pageant. John Martin's was a well known department store in Adelaide. Darryl's ambition was to become a school teacher and, like me, he also went to see Elvis Presley movies, not with his mother but with his aunts; his mother had a couple of much younger sisters who were around the same age as he was.

Rick Brewer happened to overhear him singing 'Ferry Cross The Mersey' to himself in a coffee shop in Port Noarlunga one day. Rick thought Darryl had a really good voice and invited him to join his group, The Mermen.

Darryl was the first person to call me 'Beeb'. He shortened B.B. to Beeb. From the time we met that has remained my nickname. I also took the first part of my surname and shortened it from Bertelkamp to Birtles, anglicising the spelling. From that time on, Beeb Birtles was my professional name.

All of us, including Darryl, were still mad Hollies fans and on their latest album they had a song called 'Down The Line'. We changed our name from Times Unlimited to Down The Line, though the new name didn't last long.

Being the kind of inquisitive musician who always wants to know who wrote the song, I have since found out that 'Down The Line' was actually called 'Go Go Go (Down The Line)' and it was the very first song Roy Orbison ever wrote.

Gordon Rawson left the band. At one particular rehearsal we could tell he was in a really bad mood and he threw his guitar down. We had seen these moods before but somehow it came to a head that day. Not that I'm being critical because I can be the moodiest prick of all at times! I think I inherited that from my dad because his moods could swing one way or the other at the drop of a hat. Anyway, on this particular day we either asked Gordon to leave the band or he quit.

Gordon remembers that day:

I had had a fight with Bev, my girlfriend. I had a bit of a rejection problem in those days. In more recent times while suffering some depression it was traced back to 1965, probably to do with my father's death. The music used to help get me through.

Our band started gaining a following in the Christies Beach and Port Noarlunga areas. Word was getting around. One weekend, two guys from Elizabeth approached us about management. They were checking out new bands to play at some dances they were promoting in the Elizabeth area.

One of the guys was Doc Neeson and the other was a friend of his, Alan Hale. They said they thought we had a lot of potential but they didn't like our name.

Doc said, "Why don't you call yourselves something like Zoot, a short punchy name that doesn't mean anything?"

I've since read that Doc's inspiration came from his admiration for the English singer Zoot Money's Big Roll Band. We looked at each other questioningly and thought, *What kind of a name is that?* The guys left and we never heard from them again. We kept throwing the Zoot idea around and at some point decided that, yes, it was kind of a cool name. From then on we became known as Zoot.

John Rose, the drummer for Five Sided Circle, remembers this:

I was already playing in Five Sided Circle during the early days of Zoot. One Saturday morning our bass player rang excitedly to tell me of a fabulous new band he'd seen at the Port Noarlunga Institute and how he couldn't get over the great harmony vocals, in particular the way that John D'Arcy could sing 'I'm Only Sleeping' by The Beatles. The following night I confirmed this while watching Zoot's first night at a real local breeding ground for bands called Beat Basement.

Five Sided Circle had lots of gigs lined up and people were always asking us to recommend new bands. Naturally, we recommended Zoot and not long after we were playing shows together. Within a short time, Zoot had surpassed our ambitions and moved to Melbourne. The bastards!

Lots of my music friends in Adelaide would say: "Hey, wouldn't it be fantastic if we became popular all over Australia and got on the telly and everything?" And I would think: *Popular all over Australia? Forget that, I want to be playing music all over the world.* I always had big dreams.

THE APPRENTICE

Through my dad's contacts in the building trade, he arranged for me to get a job as an apprentice with a ceramic tiling company. He knew a German man by the name of Gunther who owned The North Adelaide Tiling Company. Right from the start, I think Gunther was reluctant to give me a try, but for my dad's sake he did.

For the next two years I worked for the various ceramic tile layers who worked for Gunther. I learned how to mix cement and cut ceramic tiles to size. I soaked the ceramic tiles in buckets of water and got everything ready for them to tile shower stalls, bathroom walls and floors as well as kitchens. Occasionally we worked on the street, tiling the front of shops.

I've never been a lazy guy so I didn't mind the hard work. At that time I still didn't own a car so Dad would drop me off on a particular street corner and whoever I was working with that week would pick me up and give me a ride to the job site. I worked during the day and at night played with Zoot. I was making more money playing in the band than I was as an apprentice. When I think back to those days I don't know how I kept it up.

I regret the way I treated my mother during these years. I was very disrespectful and I'm ashamed of the way I yelled at her at times. She would come in to wake me in the mornings and I would scream at her to get out of my room, shut the door and leave me alone.

Thinking back on all that now, the only possible excuse I have is that I must have been so tired from working all day and playing music late into the night that I was totally exhausted. I was truly beat when I climbed into bed at night. But still, I can't believe what a prick I was to her during those years.

It wasn't unusual for me to come home from work, jump straight into the shower and immediately head out the door again for a gig. There wasn't enough time to sit down and eat dinner. I'm sure my mother was worried about me, though she never really said anything.

Towards the end of my time as an apprentice I was given small jobs to do by myself. Most of them were tiling windowsills and kitchens. I was never very fast because I cared more about doing an excellent job. But all Gunther cared about was getting the job done so he could invoice the builder. The fact that I was slow must have really frustrated him. He complained about me taking too long. One day when he confronted me about this, I'd had enough and I quit.

After quitting the tile business, I got a job at the Chrysler car factory in Christies Beach, drilling holes in parts for car doors. During the week I stayed at Christies Beach, sleeping on the floor of Darryl Cotton's bedroom at his parents' place so I wouldn't have far to go to work. I can't say I exactly leapt out of bed every morning, eager to go to the factory. By this time, Zoot had become the number one band in Adelaide and we were thinking about going professional. Drilling holes in car doors was not part of the dream!

Four
ZOOT

Zoot at the 5KA Big Beat Spectacular

Zoot's success didn't happen overnight. There was a span of about three years from the time we started rehearsing in Ted's bedroom to when we had become Adelaide's most popular band. We played all over Adelaide wherever we could get the bookings. Zoot's lineup consisted of Darryl Cotton, John D'Arcy, Ted Higgins and me. We realised we had to move on to bigger and better things or else forever play around the traps in Adelaide.

Ted Higgins remembers these times:

It wasn't long after Darryl joined that we started getting more gigs but it was our ambition to play at the better venues in Adelaide. Dances like Kommotion Klub, Shindig, and the ultimate club, The Scene, in Pirie Street, where only the best bands in Adelaide could play.

Our first notable show was when we supported The Harts at the Port Noarlunga Institute during the summer shows they used to run. I remember using their equipment and it was the first time I had played on a good name kit, Slingerland. Shortly after that show I bought a Drouyn kit.

We started playing some really big shows at the Railway Institute. 'Big Beat Spectacular' was a dance run by Jim Slade, a popular DJ at 5KA. This was the first time we played a big show with screaming teenagers and from then on things really started moving.

We were becoming the most sought after band in Adelaide and went into Gamba Studios and recorded 'I Can Hear The Grass Grow' by The Move. We performed it on In Time *on Channel Ten.*

I was in the dressing room talking to this weedy looking guy with a strong English accent. He was dressed in a red frilly shirt. I told him we were going to be on television for the very first time. Then I asked him, "So what do you do?"

He said, "I'm a drummer as well."

I found out later that it was Keith Moon from The Who! How stupid did I feel?

Zoot was booked exclusively through Central Booking Agency (CBA), run by Joyce Washington. Bob Lott was a booking agent there and he was a great guy. One weekend Zoot decided to drive to Melbourne to check out that scene. Before we left for Melbourne, Bob gave us a bit of a lecture, warning us to stay away from drugs and alcohol and to try to live decent lives. I think he was genuinely concerned about us because we were still so young.

When we got to Melbourne we were very bold in asking Jeff St John and Yama at Sebastians (a club) if we could get up and play a few songs. We already had friends who had moved there and they told us about The Catcher in Flinders Lane. It was a very cool club set in a warehouse. The Chelsea Set, with Ray Arnold on drums, was playing there that night. We also checked out The Thumpin' Tum in Little Latrobe Street. For years, David Flint was the promoter who ran The Thumpin' Tum. All of these clubs were located in the city.

When we got back to Adelaide Joyce Washington from Central Booking Agency had entered us into the Hoadley's Battle of the Sounds at the Thebarton Town Hall.

Ted remembers this well:

The Masters Apprentices, who were already a professional band and had moved to Melbourne, came back to Adelaide specifically to enter the competition.

Everybody was pissed off about this! When we went on, the place erupted and we killed them. When the Masters went on, everyone booed. Everybody was saying afterwards that we should have won but after a very lengthy delay it was announced that the Masters had won.

The hall erupted in booing and it was later revealed that the Masters' manager had forced that decision because it would have looked really bad for a professional band to lose to a local Adelaide band. There was a write-up about it in the next week's Go-Set *magazine.*

The event caused quite a stir because The Masters Apprentices really weren't an Adelaide band anymore and it was a pretty underhanded thing to do to the Adelaide music scene.

Peter Tilbrook, the Masters' rhythm guitarist, spoke about this in the book *It's Our Music, 1956 – 1986* by David Day and Tim Parker:

To get into the national heat we had to win a state competition or otherwise compete against all of the Melbourne bands. There were so many of them that the chances of winning were a lot less. So quite legally we were entitled to enter in South Australia because we were a South Australian band. We won but it was disappointing for Zoot because they'd put on a marvellous show themselves.

It seemed to me and the rest of my band that the front twenty rows were packed with Zoot fans and they certainly let us know. There were a few missiles thrown on that occasion. But our fan club was in the next twenty rows so it started to make up for it.

From the same book, Bob Lott, who was one of the judges that day, adds:

There was a twenty-minute time delay. The judges wanted time to get out of the hall before the announcement. They knew there would be a riot when the decision (against which I voted) was announced. So they made their getaway down a fire escape at the side of the building. The judges thought The Masters would represent Australia better as an original band if they won the national contest. But it wasn't rigged.

As it turned out, The Masters Apprentices lost the national Hoadley's Battle of the Sounds to The Groove in 1968. One night there was a big concert at Glenelg Town Hall and Zoot was on the bill. The headliners were The Twilights, who had come back from Melbourne. Paddy McCartney, the other lead singer in The Twilights, must have thought we had potential because when The Twilights returned to Melbourne he told David Mackay, their record producer, about us. David, in turn, sent manager Wayne de Gruchy to Adelaide to check us out. He came to see us at Sergeant Peppers and, in between sets, talked about his ideas. He was looking for a young band he could turn into Australia's next big teenybopper sensation.

John D'Arcy told us in no uncertain terms he would quit the band if we were going professional and moving to Melbourne. He planned to go to Flinders University and finish his degree. We were adamant about turning professional, so we parted ways.

Up until that time, John had been a big part of my life and I had learnt a lot from him. However, as you do when you're young, friendships come and go, though I missed our friendship because I could always make John laugh. He stayed in Adelaide, earned his degree and joined Five Sided Circle. A year or two later he ended up joining Graeham Goble's band, Allison Gros.

Zoot went on the hunt for a new lead guitarist. We were all impressed with Steve Stone, who was playing with The Silhouettes at The Scene in Pirie Street, and we asked him to join.

Ted Higgins remembers it this way:

Tim Ferrier approached us about management. He ran a dance in Kent Town where we first saw Procession. He offered us a contract for $30 a week each — provided we got rid of John D'Arcy. We agreed, and then approached Steve Stone, who jumped in.

We also met Darryl Sambell, who was promoting a young lad called Johnny Farnham. We became his backing band at St Clair. We recorded 'In My Room' at what is now Carclew.

I remember recording at Carclew because I had traded my Hofner Beatle bass for a deep red Guild semi-acoustic bass that had F holes in it. I think we also recorded backing tracks for April Byron, who was a popular female singer then. April was Johnny Farnham's girlfriend at the time.

The two songs we recorded at Carclew were 'Half Heaven, Half Heartache', a hit song by Gene Pitney, and 'In My Room', an original composition by Johnny Farnham. Whoever was recording us that day was not impressed with me. I felt way out of my depth because I wasn't a good enough studio bass player. They brought someone else in to play bass on 'Half Heaven, Half Heartache', though I did play bass on 'In My Room'.

David Mackay, who produced The Twilights, secured a recording contract for us with EMI Records.

David says:

I had told Bill Robertson at EMI about this new young band and they had a guy I knew who had a lot of promotional ideas (Wayne de Gruchy), so I thought we should take them on. I scoured for songs, ever hopeful that I was encouraging Aussie writers to come up with fresh songs. But in the end, it was a cover ('You'd Better Get Goin'' by Jackie Lomax) that seemed to work well. I doubt there was a greener band that I had signed, but at the same time I doubt there was one fresher and more committed with raw talent. They were fun times and ones I cherish.

As we were all under twenty-one, Darryl Cotton's dad, Brian, signed the contract on our behalf. On June 9, 1968 we drove to Melbourne specifically to record the song. 'Three Jolly Little Dwarfs', another song David Mackay had found, was on the B-side. We weren't very keen on that particular song. Both songs were recorded at Bill Armstrong Studios on Albert Road in South Melbourne, one of the best recording studios in Australia at that time.

'You'd Better Get Goin'' made a reasonable showing on the Australian pop charts but really served more as an introduction for Zoot to Melbourne, Hobart, Sydney, Brisbane and Perth audiences. Being an Adelaide band, it did very well on our hometown charts.

THE MOVE TO MELBOURNE

ZOOT LINEUP: TED HIGGINS, STEVE STONE, DARRYL COTTON AND BEEB BIRTLES

Tim Ferrier didn't last long as our manager. I can't remember whether it was the $30 a week wage he had us on or that we weren't impressed with what he was doing for us. I do remember that we had to *pay him* to get rid of him. The last gigs we played in Adelaide were mainly at Sergeant Peppers.

We supported many interstate bands there like Perth's Johnny Young and Kompany; Brisbane's Thursday's Children, with the rhythm section of Barry Sullivan (Big Goose) on bass and Barry Harvey (Little Goose) on drums; Melbourne's Party Machine, with Ross Wilson and Ross Hannaford; and Max Merritt and the Meteors, who were originally from New Zealand. We also played with a local soul band, Impact, and Geoff Kluke, their bass player, played a Rickenbacker bass just like Paul McCartney. I was green with envy.

Jeff Joseph, a manager from Melbourne, had also seen us play. Jeff had come because of Joyce Washington's recommendation.

Jeff says:

Joyce wanted me to see the band when I was in Adelaide, as she always did when she wanted an act to move to Melbourne. I had seen several acts for her and none of them really interested me or showed much potential. I told her that Zoot would be the last act I would see. She took me to this downstairs club where Zoot was on stage. When I went through the front door I could tell straight away that the band had something — that little extra.

Jeff was impressed. We had long discussions about our desires etcetera, and agreed that we should come to Melbourne to further our career. It was organised that we would go over on the train and Jeff would pick us up at Spencer Street Station.

Unfortunately, Jeff had an attack of bronchitis and was unable to make it to the station. This was before the days of mobile phones, and Wayne de Gruchy knew of the plans for the train trip and he met us instead. Wayne and Tony Knight undertook the band's management.

To promote the release of 'You'd Better Get Goin'' the four of us piled into Wayne's car and drove up to Queensland to personally deliver our single to DJs at radio stations. Somewhere just outside of Melbourne we stopped to pick up some speed to keep Wayne awake and he drove all the way without sleeping. We were terrified, thinking: *This guy's on drugs and driving a hundred miles an hour!*

Wayne was living with his girlfriend in Darling Street, South Yarra, and we would meet at his place for talks to plan the band's career. Back in those days, groups played all night long at the same venue. Wayne had brilliant ideas. First of all he wanted to dress us in outrageous bright pink clothes. Matching outfits for each one of us. I wasn't exactly thrilled with having to wear pink, but I went along with it.

His other strategy was to create a demand for the band. He would only allow us to be booked for sets of forty minutes each. That was it. Before we knew it, we were on and off the stage.

Picture this: four pretty good-looking guys, dressed head to toe in matching pink outfits, hit the stage, play their forty minutes and are whisked off to the next venue. It created an unbelievable demand with the teenybopper girls who just couldn't get enough of us. Screaming young girls! On the other hand, guys hated us because they thought we were 'poofters' for wearing pink clothes.

Within weeks we were being booked all over Melbourne at three, sometimes four different dances a night. It was like we were the evening's 'guest spot'.

Wayne worked for Tony Knight, who ran a very successful club called Berties. Berties was on the corner of Flinders and Spring Streets in the city. At the other end of Spring Street, his brother, Phil, ran Sebastians.

We left Adelaide for good in August 1968. Wayne de Gruchy had arranged for us to rent a two-bedroom flat on Beaconsfield Parade in St Kilda. Ted and Steve shared one bedroom, and Darryl and I shared the other. We slept on mattresses thrown on the floor.

Living in that flat were some of the poorest days I remember. We'd get to Berties and hang out until it closed before we started rehearsals for our big début. It had been pre-arranged that we could order food from Berties' kitchen at night free of charge, but during the day we had no money to buy anything.

Between the four of us we used to scrape enough coins together to buy a box of Kellogg's Corn Flakes and on our way home after rehearsing from midnight till dawn, we stole bottles of milk from the porches of houses near our flat. These were tough times.

Barry Smith stayed with us and he recalls:

There were only two mattresses on the floor in the bedroom so whoever got home last generally wound up sleeping on the floor. Occasionally, if one was lucky enough to score a spot on the mattress it wasn't uncommon to wake up with maybe a couple of extra female bodies squeezed in with us!

There was no power at one stage, possibly due to insufficient funds, and sometimes we'd go to bed in the dark or by the light of a match, not knowing who the hell we were jumping into bed with. I remember thinking: I'm really gonna enjoy this pop star life, even if we don't make any money.

Wayne de Gruchy and Tony Knight started planning the 'Think Pink – Think Zoot' campaign that introduced Zoot to Melbourne audiences. Advertising banners and flyers went up all over Melbourne making the announcement. The date of the launch was set for September 3, 1968.

The band wanted to live up to all the publicity, so we started learning all these new songs instead of just sticking to our known repertoire. The Twilights used to store their big Marshall amplifiers in a room behind the stage at Berties and they allowed us to use them for the launch. So not only were we performing new songs but playing through equipment that wasn't ours!

Life lesson number three – stick to what you know when playing your first all-important gig!

Wayne and Tony had also invited well-known musicians from bands like The Wild Cherries and other music industry people, so the pressure was on to put on a great show. Unfortunately, it didn't turn out that way. I think our nerves and expectations got the better of us, and we all walked off the stage embarrassed and disappointed.

Not long after Zoot's début at Berties, Ted Higgins and Steve Stone quit the band. They were in Melbourne for maybe three to four weeks at the most before they headed back to Adelaide. Darryl and I were adamant that we would re-form Zoot no matter what. We were in Melbourne to stay. After all, what more could we achieve back in Adelaide?

Rick Brewer, the drummer in The Mermen, had come to Melbourne shortly after us and we asked him to join Zoot. He also moved into the flat on Beaconsfield Parade. Then we went on the hunt for a guitar player. We really didn't know of anyone in Melbourne, so we had to rely on Wayne and Tony to help us out.

Going to Berties every night of the week, we got to know a lot of people. The Coffen sisters, Jill and Nanette, were sharing a flat in Gourlay Street, Balaclava and I would often give them a lift home. All my life I've been a neat freak and I quickly grew tired of our living arrangement in the flat. I couldn't stand living with three other guys who were not as neat and tidy as I was; in fact, they were slobs!

When things became unbearable between the guys and me, I asked if I could move in with the girls. They were sharing a three-bedroom flat with other friends but said I could put a mattress down in the living room and sleep there. They knew that Zoot wasn't making any money.

As soon as I moved out of Beaconsfield Parade, everything changed. Living with the girls was perfect. I was much happier and the band became a much happier unit.

The sisters were seamstresses and both of them sewed Zoot's very first pink outfits. While living in Gourlay Street, Nanette sewed me numerous pairs of pants. We'd drive to one of the fabric shops in Chapel Street and choose the material and then she would cut the pants from a pattern. She was very gifted. She had an artistic flair and was completely self-taught.

Jill Coffen (Braithwaite) remembers:

I clearly remember Beeb asking whether he could stay at our place because he said, "Every time I come home there are girls in my bed."

Nanette and I loved having him flat with us because he was like a brother. When he went on tour he would send postcards signed, 'Your brother, Beeb'. Beeb wasn't noisy, or regularly drunk or drugged, he was reasonably tidy and conscientious about paying his share of the bills and ... he had a car!

The only time he ever got mad at us was when he found that someone had broken his Beatles double White Album. He went nuts and gave us a lecture on respecting other people's things. I think some large friend had accidentally sat on it.

NATIONAL SUCCESS

DARRYL COTTON, ROGER HICKS, BEEB BIRTLES, RICK BREWER

I thought we found out about Roger Hicks through Wayne but Roger remembers differently:

I used to go to Berties a lot and I was there the night Zoot did the opening pink extravaganza. It was just a matter of days afterwards that I heard Ted and Steve had left the group and Zoot were looking for a guitar player, so I popped in to say hello. I remember that meeting quite clearly, and something about me must have taken their fancy … it sure wasn't my legs!

Roger Glanville-Hicks lived most of his life in Bay Street, Brighton. When we met him, his parents temporarily lived in a maisonette in Toorak before moving to Mt Eliza. His father was a doctor and his aunt was the famous Australian composer Peggy Glanville-Hicks.

Roger had attended Wesley College in Prahran with David Briggs and Paul Grabowsky who was a few years younger. He took the bus in St Kilda Street, Brighton every morning, which passed through Elwood, right in front of Molly Meldrum and Ronnie Burns' place. He remembers Molly getting on the bus a few times when he was still at school.

In 1969, Cream and The Jimi Hendrix Experience were the latest and greatest groups to emerge from England. Roger had worked out all of

Jimi's intricate guitar parts and could play them perfectly, note-for-note. He could also play 'Hideaway', the instrumental on John Mayall and the Bluesbreakers' 1966 album, which featured Eric Clapton on guitar.

He had worked out José Feliciano's version of 'Light My Fire', originally recorded by The Doors. He was fantastic on his nylon string classical guitar and this talent later found its mark on the intro to Russell Morris' classic single, 'The Real Thing'.

Roger adds:

I also played on 'Part Three Into Paper Walls'. I consider this track to be musically and sonically far superior to 'The Real Thing'. But I always thought of it as part of 'The Real Thing', it's like a big coda. There is a lot of acoustic guitar in it. The opening of 'The Real Thing' reappears at the end of 'Part Three Into Paper Walls' and is more clearly audible and complete than in 'The Real Thing'.

Roger greatly impressed us with his guitar-playing ability. So with Roger and Rick Brewer, Zoot was complete.

At twenty, I still had not experienced sex, but Berties was a great club for picking up girls. We met so many people by going there every night. One night I was introduced to a girl from Sydney who was a couple of years older than me. You'd think that I would remember the name of the first girl I had a sexual relationship with but I don't. She took me home to her flat on St Kilda Road and showed me what it was all about. *So this is what I had been missing out on for all those years living in Adelaide?* I'm telling you, I was very innocent and naïve when I was young.

We went out for a while, usually hooking up at Berties but the relationship didn't last for long. It probably hadn't occurred to her but she had opened up the wonderful world of sex for me and I was ready to go and sow some wild oats!

I wasn't interested in having a steady relationship with anybody because this was all so new to me. I was young and played in a band that was becoming idolized all over Australia. I turned into a bit of a loose goose after that.

In doing so, I also became the unluckiest guy in Melbourne when it came to sexually transmitted diseases. I visited the free government venereal diseases clinic in Gertrude Street, Fitzroy so often that the guys and I joked about me having a key to my own room there!

Valda remembers these times of Zoot establishing themselves as a band in Melbourne:

Zoot had been living in Melbourne for some time and were really getting popular with the teens. Darryl was the pretty front man and Beeb was the hilariously, cheeky side-kick with the great voice. They were tight right from the get-go. Roger and Rick were sympatico and while Zoot were a band, this pairing was the most comfortable for all the four members but it was, for the most part, a case of 'us and them'.

Darryl and I were very straight whereas Rick and Roger were much more open to experimenting with drugs. They would pop pills and were probably introduced to marijuana long before I decided to try it; Darryl was a teetotaller. Rick and Roger moved in together in a half-house in Douglas Street, East Malvern where some of our rehearsals used to take place.

David Mackay had left for England and the next producer to take over was Howard Gable, a New Zealander who was brought to Australia by EMI to become the in-house producer for the Columbia label. He was married to a New Zealand singer named Allison Durbin.

As none of us wrote our own music, we were always looking for great songs to record. Once again, we crossed paths with The Twilights. Terry Britten, The Twilights' lead guitarist, was writing his own songs as well as producing records for other artists.

He played us a song called, 'One Times, Two Times, Three Times, Four'. It was very catchy and commercial and we all agreed it should be our next single. Howard Gable produced the single and it reached number thirty-two on the Melbourne charts and fared decently all over Australia.

To promote the single, we appeared on national television shows like *Uptight* on Channel Ten and *Dick Williams' Hit Scene* on the ABC. We were also being interviewed for magazines such as *Go-Set* and *Gas*. In short, a buzz was starting to get around about us.

I don't remember all of the circumstances surrounding our change in management. All I know is that Wayne de Gruchy and Tony Knight didn't manage us for very long.

The Australian Management and Booking Organisation (AMBO) was our booking agency and it was here we got to know people like Mike Barnett, Bill Joseph, and Darryl Sambell, who managed Johnny Farnham. Johnny was already off and running with his first huge hit, 'Sadie, (The Cleaning Lady)'.

Darryl Sambell rented the penthouse at the top of the same block of flats where Zoot was living on Beaconsfield Parade. When Wayne and Tony were no longer on the scene, Jeff Joseph and Darryl Sambell jointly managed us.

It turned out to be the screwiest arrangement because Sambell basically kept Jeff in the dark by not telling him anything he was doing for the band. In the meantime, we were busy travelling all over the country and building our fan base. As well as managing Johnny Farnham and us, Sambell also managed The Masters Apprentices. At some point in time it all came to a head and we split from Sambell, feeling he had his hands full. Zoot continued on with Jeff Joseph as our sole manager.

During the pink phase, all we had was a handful of singles produced by different people. David Mackay produced 'You'd Better Get Goin'', released in August 1968. Howard Gable produced 'One Times, Two Times, Three Times, Four', released in December 1968. Ian 'Molly' Meldrum produced 'Monty and Me', written by Hans Poulsen and Bruce Woodley from The Seekers. On the record there's a whistle that Darryl couldn't do. Johnny Farnham happened to be outside at Armstrong's so he did the whistle and sang the harmonies with Darryl and me. It was released in June 1969 and reached number one in Brisbane but only number thirty-three in Melbourne.

Roger Hicks' time with Zoot didn't last long. Conflicting musical aspirations and disillusionment with the image of the band were getting to him. He became friends with The Brisbane Avengers, who introduced him to marijuana, and he began hanging out with them. Eventually, they asked him to join their band, quitting Zoot.

Rick Springfield was a very good-looking guy who had toured Vietnam with a re-formation of MPD Ltd. Pete Watson, the bass guitarist from MPD Ltd., formed a band called Wickedy Wak in which Rick was the guitar player. They recorded a song by Johnny Young called 'Billie's Bikey Boys' on which I was one of the background singers. Molly Meldrum produced the single.

RICK SPRINGFIELD, RICK BREWER, DARRYL COTTON AND BEEB BIRTLES

In Rick Springfield's memoir, *Late, Late At Night*, he says:

I will never be more excited about a recording session than I am for this very first one. Everything is happening so fast. Johnny Young and Molly both want me to sing lead vocal on the song, and I'm euphoric. Paul, the bass player — and the other singer in Wickedy Wak — is not nearly as euphoric as I am about this decision. In fact, he's so pissed off that he won't even play on the session, so we bring in a bass-playing ringer named Beeb Birtles. Beeb is in a popular teen band called Zoot, a poofy-looking bunch of pretty-boys who dress in pink and are adored by the girls.

The Brisbane Avengers and The Valentines were looking for guitar players at the same time and they were courting Rick heavily. Rick saw more potential in joining Zoot. He was there for part of the Think Pink phase but as we progressed we played less of the hit songs we were known for and started performing more original material.

Rick Springfield:

I thought the unattractively named Wickedy Wak had a pretty good handle

on the girl market, but joining Zoot takes it to a whole new level. They are cute and famous ... how can you beat this?

In 1969 bands like Black Sabbath, Led Zeppelin and Deep Purple were emerging with their harder-edged sound of rock music. Zoot took songs like 'Summer In The City' by The Lovin' Spoonful, 'I'm Only Sleeping' and 'Hello Goodbye' by The Beatles, 'Shilo' by Neil Diamond, and 'Hurdy Gurdy Man' by Donovan and gave them much heavier arrangements.

When Rick Springfield joined, we used to rehearse in an old church in South Melbourne. We'd get the key from one of the old ladies who attended the church and load our gear into the main hall. It was in that church that we came up with many of the arrangements to other artists' songs, including The Beatles' 'Eleanor Rigby'.

Darryl and I were instrumental in encouraging Rick to write his own music. I remember a number of times when we sat around at his parents' house in Parkdale and listened to the latest bits and pieces of songs Rick had written. And this was where Rick taught us his new songs acoustically.

For a number of years, 3AK was the most popular radio station in Melbourne. They had a slogan, 'Where No Wrinklys Fly', meaning it was a station for young listeners only. During the summers they promoted concerts on the beaches along the Mornington Peninsula as well as on the other side of Port Phillip Bay, from Geelong all the way down to Apollo Bay. We were booked to play at these concerts and travelled there in the band's cream Volkswagen Kombi Van.

We had some fantastic times playing those shows. We always finished the set with 'Eleanor Rigby' and right before the ending, when Rick Brewer went into his drum solo bit, Rick Springfield would throw his white Gibson SG high into the air and catch it just before strumming the sustaining end chord.

During one of these shows it was rather windy and when Rick threw his guitar into the air the wind caught it. His Gibson SG flew a few yards along the beach. Rick was left standing on the stage with egg on his face.

It wasn't long after Rick joined Zoot that we decided to do away with the 'Think Pink – Think Zoot' gimmick. A big publicity campaign was organised around the burning of our pink clothes on *Happening '70*, with Ross D. Wyllie as the host.

A drum barrel was placed on the set and we dropped our pink outfits into it. Dry ice in the bottom of the drum created the fake smoke. We did interviews with all the pop magazines to let people know. From that time on we weren't known as Pink Zoot anymore, it was just Zoot.

Zoot's early recording career was pretty spotty as we were told what to record and with which producer. We were constantly at the mercy of EMI and we were getting tired of being told what to record. My pet peeve all along had been that people were mistakenly calling us 'The Zoot'. So when it came time to find a title for our first album I suggested *Just Zoot*. The guys liked the idea and that's what our first long play album was called.

Just Zoot ended up being a mixture of singles, some Terry Britten songs and a few of Rick Springfield's first original songs. It was released in early 1970 and to this day I don't have a clue how well it sold. We were young, naïve and under age. All we cared about was playing our music. Our recording contract with EMI only ran for one year and a new contract was never signed when we would all have been over twenty-one. Over these last fifty years EMI have continued to repackage *Zoot Locker*, a compilation album of our most popular songs. Our biggest hit single, 'Eleanor Rigby', continues to pop up on CDs like Australia's Biggest Hits From the '70s without any compensation to the band. In fact, Zoot have never received any royalties from sales of records and the band is currently disputing that with Universal Music Group which is now the parent company of EMI Australia.

With Howard Gable we went into Bill Armstrong's to record four new songs from which we'd choose one as our next single. One of the songs was a Brian Cadd and Don Mudie composition called 'About Time'.

Without our knowledge or consent, EMI released it as our next single and it made us furious. We didn't know we had a new single out until we saw the advertisements for it in the music magazines. What could we do about it then? We had to go along with it and promote the single by appearing on all of the Australian pop music television shows.

Howard Gable adds:

I had the same shock as the band as I thought they were demos. I was amazed when I got the call to urgently return from New Zealand to record more tracks, as EMI Australia needed 'follow-up hits'! I couldn't believe our demos had been released, let alone charted.

In June of 1970 we left the world of pink behind with a stinging Rick Springfield song called 'Hey Pinky', also produced by Howard Gable. The lyrics knocked the guys who knocked us for wearing pink outfits. And we decided to do something totally outrageous to advertise the release.

Jeff Joseph had an office in a building on the corner of Alma Road and St Kilda Road in St Kilda. A photographer had his studio set up in the same building. Jeff spoke to him about us wanting to take some rather unconventional photos. Because so many guys thought we were gay and hated us for wearing pink on stage, we decided to bare our bums for the camera, as if to say, 'Kiss My Arse'.

The four of us took all our clothes off and stood side by side with our bare bums to the camera. When the advertisements for the release of 'Hey Pinky' appeared in all the music magazines it created an unbelievable stir.

Despite the fact that the single didn't do that well on the Australian charts (the Australian record ban was in force at the time), a couple of very funny incidences resulted from us appearing *au natural*, and both of them occurred in Sydney.

The Australian record ban was a 'pay for play' dispute in the local music industry that lasted from May until October 1970. During this period, a simmering disagreement between commercial radio stations — represented by the Federation of Australian Radio Broadcasters (FARB) — and the six major record labels — represented by the Australian Performing Right Association (APRA) — resulted in major UK and Australian pop songs being refused airplay.

Directly due to the naked bums shot, our bookings at the Sydney gay clubs skyrocketed. In particular, I remember playing at one place in St Peters where the backdrop behind us was an oversized, blown up photo of us standing with our naked bums to the audience.

When we hit the stage, the gay boys screamed. We thought: *What's this? We thought we were done with the Think Pink – Think Zoot thing?* They screamed and squealed through our whole set. After the show, one guy kept hanging around and made it obvious he had eyes for me. He wanted my body bad enough to offer me $500 — a lot of money to me in those days — to walk to the nearby racetrack with him. I politely declined at least three or four times, and for the rest of the night I didn't let my band mates out of sight!

The other funny incident occurred at Chequers nightclub where we played every time we went to Sydney. It was an all-night affair. We played until two or three in the morning. When we took a break, we went out into the crowd and had drinks with the people we knew.

One particular night an attractive woman kept hanging close to where I was seated. She made it very obvious that she was waiting around specifically for me. When we finished playing, she took me home with her.

She didn't waste any time undressing me and positioning me with my bum facing her dressing table mirror. Then she said, "Do you know how many weeks I've been waiting to see this in the flesh?"

All this attention due to the naked bum shot – yeah, baby!

This was the time of conscription in Australia and it was in Jeff Joseph's office that I sweated bullets about being called up for National Service. I was one of the unlucky ones whose marble with the number twenty-eight was chosen for all those young men whose birthdays fell on the twenty-eighth day of the month.

I was able to defer my National Service for a year because at that time I still had my Dutch nationality. The music industry saw what National Service had done to Normie Rowe's career. It was never the same after he came back from Vietnam. Normie had been a gigantic Australian pop star, having had many big hit records until he was conscripted for National Service.

On June 6, 2015, Paul Cashmere posted this on the Noise11.com web site:

Australian '60s pop legend Normie Rowe has confirmed his conscription into the Australian army to serve in Vietnam was a set-up by Liberal Prime Minister Harold Holt to generate publicity by sending 'Australia's Elvis' to war.

In recent years Rowe was contacted by the son of a Holt advisor who said his father confessed to the conspiracy before he died and wanted Normie to know the truth … He said his dad was in Harold Holt's office and Holt was struggling with popularity and the anti-war movement.

The officer said to Holt, "What you need is an Elvis Presley. Get Normie Rowe called up."

If the Prime Minister says something is going to happen then there is a pretty good chance it is going to happen.

Rowe has long suspected something was not quite right with his conscription. "I guess it was about '78. I was driving round the Eastern Freeway and came off at Hoddle Street still doing 120 kilometres per hour. I was pulled over and the cop said, 'You were born on the same day as me. How come you went into the army and I didn't?'" Normie thought that was interesting.

By the time he had returned from the war, the music world had changed and the fans had moved on, leaving him without a career.

"I did a show on February 1, 1970. Zoot were on it and all the kids clamoured for Zoot," he said. "They walked away from me completely."

Normie successfully reclaimed his position in the music industry but never returned to the heady days of being Australia's biggest pop star. After his return from the war, along with Zoot featuring Rick Springfield, the new kid in town for pop fans was a guy called Johnny Farnham.

The dreaded letter arrived in the mail, telling me that I was required to show up for a medical examination somewhere in the city. I had to read and mark off a very long column of ailments and diseases listed on the questionnaire. There were all kinds of stories going around about ways to help guys get out of having to serve in the army and one of them was to drink glucose and it would make your blood sugar go up. The doctors would then think you were a diabetic.

I formulated a plan. I wasn't going the route of overdosing on sugar or anything like that. One of the conditions listed on the questionnaire was 'bed-wetting'. When I got to that question I marked it as positive.

Barry Smith was there:

On the morning of Beeb's medical appointment, I remember being woken to the sounds of trickle, trickle and giggle, giggle coming from his bedroom. Not thinking too much of it and still being half groggy, I went back to sleep.

Upon getting up that morning and checking out Beeb's bedroom, I was confronted by his bed which had the biggest pool of urine on it. That's when I put the puzzle together and realised he had gone for his medical and decided that just in case anyone doubted his bed-wetting story and came to check his bed for evidence, he had backed up his claim and would be ready for them.

Of course the possibility of having too much evidence crossed my mind — I couldn't understand the necessity of having the entire lineup of Zoot emptying their bladders onto his bed! It certainly explained all the giggling.

What was I thinking? Of course, they wanted to know why and how often I wet the bed. I said it was something that was out of my control. When they dismissed me at the end of the physical examination they said I would be required to go for a psychiatric evaluation for my bed-wetting condition.

After a few weeks of not hearing anything, another letter arrived in the mail with a phone number to make the appointment with a psychiatrist. I showed up and the psychiatrist told me to take a seat while he proceeded to question me.

"What has your doctor told you about your perpetual bed-wetting problem?"

I said, "Nothing much, other than he's convinced it's a psychological condition."

"Do you know there are pills you can take now to control bed-wetting?"

"If there are, my family doctor hasn't informed me about them because he says it's all in my mind."

The whole time he was questioning me I was sizing him up, thinking: *Is he the type of guy I can come clean with? Will I risk opening up to him or not?* I decided I was going to appeal to his sympathetic side.

I took a deep breath and said, "Look, it's not that I don't want to serve my country, I'm willing to fight for Australia because I love living here.

It's just that my band is starting to do really well and for me to get called up right now will take everything I've worked for over the last two years away. The army will literally pull the rug out from under my music career."

He listened intently to what I said but I couldn't tell from his facial expression what he was thinking. All he said was, "Okay, that will be all for now. You will be notified by mail what I recommend to the army officials." And with that, he got up and walked me to the door. I heard the door close behind me as I made my way down the hallway.

I had almost reached the elevator when I heard a voice calling out to me,

"Oh, by the way, Gerard," he said, "more than likely you will be discharged from National Service for medical reasons."

And with that, the psychiatrist disappeared back into his office. I received the official letter from the army confirming my discharge about a week later.

Ian "Molly" Meldrum presents Zoot silver discs for sales of 25,000 singles of 'Eleanor Rigby'
left to right: Beeb Birtles, Rick Brewer, Darryl Cotton, Rick Springfield and "Molly" Meldrum

In 1970 Zoot won the Victorian heat of Hoadley's Battle of the Sounds. The finals were held in Sydney where we came second to The Flying Circus. The whole show was recorded. We performed our version of 'Eleanor Rigby' and 2SM started playing the live recording on air, receiving incredible response. As a result it was Howard Gable who insisted on us recording 'Eleanor Rigby' as a single. We received incredible crowd reaction wherever we played it. It was released in December 1970 and within weeks, radio stations all over Australia were playing it.

John Rose, the drummer with Five Sided Circle, remembers this:

One day whilst walking on Moana Beach in South Australia, I heard 'Eleanor Rigby'. You can drive and park your car on Moana Beach. Car radios were tuned to the one and only station that played anything resembling modern music.

All together the car radios made it sound like the band was there too. The arrangement was out there, in your face and I loved it. I was walking along saying to people, "I know those buggers!"

Zoot's last recording together was a Rick Springfield song called 'The Freak'. It was the most adventurous original recording we had made. It entered the Melbourne charts and peaked at number twenty-seven. It was our final disappointment.

'The Freak' was a hard-rocking song with a melodic finger-picking extended middle eight that featured some great harmonies. It was released sometime in early 1971 but the band had peaked musically and it was obvious to all of us that we were at the end of the road.

Zoot travelled all over Australia, but we were extremely popular in Brisbane where we played to some really big crowds. At one show at Brisbane's Festival Hall the girls climbed up on stage and tore Darryl's pants off. The bouncers had to escort him off the stage because of indecency. I think he put something else on and came back to finish our set. Most of the time we flew to Brisbane but drove to Sydney and Adelaide in our Kombi van. My recollection of why Zoot broke up is a little sketchy.

Jeff Joseph, Zoot's manager, remembers it this way:

We had received an offer from RCA in the States to go over as part of a package with Healing Force. RCA wanted to record and tour Zoot and Healing Force. The original EMI recording contract had been signed by Brian Cotton, Darryl's father, on behalf of the band because all the guys were under twenty-one at the time. The contract covered all territories of the world.

I went to Sydney and met with Ken East, the managing director of EMI, who had recently returned from working with EMI UK after a number of years. I felt he would understand our position, having just returned from working in the international market. I put our case forward and his reaction was one of flat refusal. As far as he was concerned, EMI had Zoot worldwide and that was the way it was going to remain.

At the conclusion of the meeting I told him that if EMI wasn't prepared to release Zoot from the American and northern hemisphere territories, giving EMI the band for Australia and New Zealand, the group would split up within a month as it had achieved everything possible within Australia. He told me at that point not to threaten him and I replied, "I'm not threatening you, Ken, I'm promising you." One month later, Zoot split up.

Rick Springfield launched his solo career and signed with the Sparmac label. They released his first single, 'Speak To The Sky', which became a huge success in Australia. It wasn't long after that he took off for the United States and since 1972, Rick has made Los Angeles his home.

Two very significant things happened in my life after the break up of Zoot. The first was this: it dawned on me that I was not progressing any further on my instrument, the bass guitar. I stopped playing bass and switched to acoustic guitar. At the time I had been given, or maybe I bought, a pretty bad acoustic guitar. I can't even remember what brand it was and I'm sure it wasn't left-handed. I sat around for hours and hours teaching myself how to play chords.

The second significant thing was that as I was learning these chords, I began forming melodies in my mind and words to accompany these melodies. I started recording bits and pieces of these early songs on a cheap tape recorder that Maria, an avid Zoot fan, had given me. A whole new world opened up and I was totally absorbed. I considered myself to be a late starter as a songwriter, at twenty-three, but it quickly became my all-consuming passion.

Sometimes, Darryl would come over to my flat and we would write songs together. Even though Zoot had broken up, I did the same with Rick Brewer. Rick didn't play guitar and didn't consider himself a singer at all but, man, he could come up with some bizarre lyric ideas. We had a lot of fun and I've still got some of those early song ideas on reels of tape.

With the impact Zoot had, most people assume the band was around for quite a few years. In actual fact, from the time we moved to Melbourne to when we broke up amicably in April 1971, it was only about two-and-a-half years. During that time we became the biggest teenybopper band in Australia.

However, those fun days were over and it was time to get more serious about music if it was to be my chosen career. When I switched to playing a six-string acoustic guitar I became very focused. Some of my song ideas were acceptable while others were not very good, but I began to learn what not to do instead of just accepting that everything was good. It was this period in my life that would set me up for what was to come, and it started with my year in the duo known as *Frieze* with Darryl Cotton.

Five
FRIEZE

Frieze: Beeb and Darryl

At the AMBO offices in Latrobe Street, Melbourne, Jeff Joseph, Darryl Cotton and I had a meeting with a couple of guys from the Noel Paton Advertising Agency. One of their national accounts was a Melbourne company called Frieze Brothers who manufactured men's suits. The company wanted to target a younger age group with a new range of suits. The guys proposed that Darryl and I form a new band called 'Deep Frieze'.

In true advertising form, they came up with the bright idea to name each member of the band after a particular cloth, material or fabric. So Darryl, with his surname being Cotton, was fine. However, their suggestions for the other members' names were quite hysterical. They wanted me to be called Terry Lene, after the synthetic fabric Terylene, and I was to have a brother named 'Crimp', as in Crimplene... Darryl and I looked at each other as if to say: *You've got to be kidding, right?* Oh no, these guys were dead serious!

It hadn't been that long since we put the 'Think Pink - Think Zoot' gimmick behind us and here were these guys proposing we do something very similar. We didn't go for it. We told them that if we were to pursue their idea we would get laughed out of the music business. Instead, we proposed the idea of a duo and simply calling ourselves 'Frieze'.

All through the Zoot years, Darryl and I barely scraped by on whatever money we made. The duo idea appealed to us because it meant some steady money plus free clothes and a new car. The ad men liked the idea and took it back to the owners of Frieze Brothers. They also went for it.

With the money we were given, we bought a Holden station wagon, a sound system and a stereo Teac tape recorder to use for our pre-recorded backing music. Plus we were both fitted for a wardrobe full of brand new Frieze suits!

As Rick Springfield had done before us, we also signed with the Sparmac label. Label boss, Robie Porter, found a song written by Barry Mann and Cynthia Weil that he wanted us to record. It was called 'Feelings' and on the B-side we recorded one of Darryl's first original songs, 'Young Man's Lament'.

I knew Robie Porter better as Rob E.G., who I had watched countless times on *Bandstand* playing his Hawaiian steel guitar in the early '60s. Robie had since moved to the States and was in partnership with a successful businessman and television producer named Steve Binder. Unfortunately, our single stiffed, getting virtually no airplay and that marked the end of our association with Robie Porter and his Sparmac label.

Darryl and I set up a meeting with Bill May at Maton Guitars, on Canterbury Road in Surrey Hills, to have a couple of custom-designed acoustic guitars made. Bill was always very sympathetic towards Australian performing artists and gave them great deals on custom-made guitars.

I remember my first Maton was a left-handed Country and Western model. It would be the start of a longstanding relationship and I still play Maton acoustic guitars exclusively today. I love their guitars because you can be gentle playing them or you can really lay into them without getting any fret rattle, but it's the tone of the Australian timbers they use that make them so unique. I am also currently the representative for Maton Guitars in the US. I'm their man on the ground in Nashville.

One of the earliest gigs we played as Frieze was at The Tottenham Hotel in Sunshine. The Cycle was the resident band, featuring David Briggs on guitar, Geoff Cox on drums, Keith McKay on keyboards and Rick Berger on bass.

We approached The Cycle to record the backing tracks to the songs we wanted to perform as Frieze. We booked TCS Studios at Channel Nine in Richmond. For live purposes, each song had a count in so Darryl and I would know exactly when to strum along and start singing.

Some of the songs we recorded were 'Teach Your Children' by Crosby, Stills, Nash & Young, 'At The Zoo' by Simon and Garfunkel, 'Cinnamon Girl' by Neil Young, and we also put together a fabulous Everly Brothers medley.

Basically our job was to appear at department stores like Myer, David Jones and Grace Brothers whenever a fashion show was organised. Male models walked up and down the catwalk modelling the latest Frieze Brothers suits and we were the draw to get people there to stop and have a look. Jeff Joseph operated the tape recorder and the sound system while we performed. He was still our manager and took care of all our bookings.

Meanwhile, Darryl and I continued writing original songs and we were both growing in that area. Jeff managed to get us a recording contract with Paul Turner, the managing director of WEA (Warner Elektra Atlantic), and we set out to record our first album of all original songs.

Brian Cadd, who had been the keyboard player in The Groop and with whom we crossed paths in Zoot, was recruited as our producer. He was back in Australia after the demise of Axiom in England.

We used Phil Manning on electric guitar and Barry Sullivan on bass (both from the band Chain), and Ray Arnott on drums. Charlie Gould was on acoustic guitar, Graeme Lyall played saxophone and flute, Peter Jones scored the string arrangements, while John French was the recording engineer.

The album featured the first original songs I had written. Songs like 'Friend', 'Love Is A Feeling', 'You And I' and 'Jackie Girl'. Darryl and I co-wrote the country-flavoured 'All Because Of You'.

Once again I came up with the idea for the album title, *1972 B.C.* I wanted it made clear that it was Birtles and Cotton over and above the name Frieze. It was really a bit cheesy to be associated with the conservative suit manufacturer. They weren't exactly the hippest-looking suits around.

Overall, the album wasn't a bad effort and I was very proud hearing the final mixes of the songs we had written. This was so much better than the lame version of 'Feelings' we had recorded for the Sparmac label. That wasn't really who we were.

As well as performing at department stores all around Australia, we started playing live gigs with the backing of a Queensland trio called Burke & Wills. Peter Moscos was the lead guitarist, Jamie Dunn was the drummer (Jamie would later find fame as the voice of the puppet Agro), and the bass player was Warren Adams. We played at the Mulwala Easter '72 festival that was held on April 1, 2 and 3, 1972.

Stephen Stills' Manassas and Canned Heat headlined the festival. Manassas featured some great musicians like Chris Hillman, Dallas Taylor, Joe Lala, Fuzzy Samuels, Paul Harris and Al Perkins. I had their first album in my record collection. After moving to Nashville I met Al Perkins when he played steel guitar on one of my demos.

The year as Frieze was a year of growth for both Darryl and me. It served as a bridge from Zoot to whatever was to come next for both of us. For me, it became the springboard to the three years I consider to be my true musical apprenticeship – my time with the band Mississippi.

I grew unhappy performing as Frieze and missed the interaction of playing with other musicians and the camaraderie of being in a band. Only problem was I didn't know how to tell Darryl.

I've always had an immense problem confronting awkward situations such as these. Instead of just coming out with it and saying what is on my mind I tend to bottle things up and withdraw, becoming extremely unhappy in the process.

I've noticed throughout my life that when I find it difficult to make an important decision I leave it in the hands of those around me. I know this is not a good attribute, and in this particular instance, it was Darryl who drew it out of me.

He said something along the lines of, "Look, I get the feeling you don't want to do the Frieze thing, do you?"

And, of course, the minute I had that opening I found the courage to say, "No, I'm not happy doing this anymore." We wrapped it up very quickly and went our separate ways. Darryl started planning his solo career and stayed with Jeff Joseph as his manager.

It was now July 1972 and I didn't have a clue what I was going to do next. Jean Gair, who was the office manager at AMBO for many years, came to my rescue. We knew her well from visiting the office for band meetings as well as getting our wages and seeing what bookings were coming up. It was obvious she was very fond of both of us.

When she heard that Darryl and I had parted ways she offered me the job of answering the phones at AMBO for $50 a week. She was a lifesaver because I still had to live and pay rent.

Through working at AMBO I met Megan Tudor who also worked there. Megan was the daughter of Jean and Ron Tudor. Ron was well known in the music business, having started the Fable label and later forming the Bootleg label with Brian Cadd. Megan and I started having counter lunches together at the pub on the corner of Exhibition and Latrobe Streets. At the time she still lived at home with her parents.

I was really enjoying this time in my life and then one day, about three months into my stint at AMBO, I answered the phone and heard the voice at the other end ask, "Oh hi, I was wondering if you could help me, I'm trying to get in touch with Beeb Birtles."

It was a phone call that would change my life.

Six
MISSISSIPPI — PHASE ONE

Left to right: Russ Johnson, Graeham Goble, Derek Pellicci,
Beeb Birtles, John Mower and Colin DeLuca

The voice on the phone belonged to Graeham Goble. Graeham, Russ Johnson and John Mower were three Adelaide guys in a group called Allison Gros. They came to the attention of Ron Tudor, owner of the Fable label in Melbourne, and recorded a chipmunk version of the song 'Daddy Cool'. It was a national number one hit under the name of Drummond.

Due to the success of 'Daddy Cool', Ron offered the guys a deal to record an album of original songs. When the album was completed they needed a new name and it was Ron who came up with the name Mississippi. The self-titled *Mississippi* album was released on the newly formed Bootleg label in 1971. Brian Cadd and Ron Tudor formed the boutique label as an offshoot to Fable. It was the hipper label of the two, recording Brian Cadd as a solo artist as well as with The Bootleg Family Band. I think Brian got the idea when Leon Russell and Denny Cordell started Shelter Records in the US.

Both labels had a family feel. The Bootleg Family Band had a top ten hit with a cover of Loggins and Messina's 'Your Mama Don't Dance' in 1973. In 1972 Mississippi scored a national top ten hit with 'Kings Of The World', written and sung by Graeham Goble. All three Mississippi guys sang.

Russ Johnson was an extremely inventive guitar player and wrote some excellent original songs. He was a young musician but very mature. He struck me as an old man trapped inside a young body. I can still picture him smoking his pipe when I first went to the house they all shared on Auburn Road in Hawthorn.

Graeham played acoustic and electric guitar but was more a parts player and a rhythm guitarist. He was the genius who worked out their fantastic harmonies. He sang all the high harmonies in a very strong falsetto voice.

Out of the three, John Mower possessed the sweetest voice. He was yet another English migrant who had settled in Adelaide. Graeham was Australian-born, as was Russ, though Russ had spent some time growing up in California.

With the runaway success of 'Kings Of The World', the guys wanted to form a band to promote the album. That's what prompted Graeham's call to AMBO. I'm sure he was taken by surprise when I answered the phone. He invited me to the Fable label's office at 180 Bank Street in South Melbourne to listen to their brand new album.

Ron Tudor rented office space in the same building that now housed Bill Armstrong Studios (soon to be renamed AAV for Armstrong Audio Visual). The building used to be an old butter factory. The recording studios were located a few steps down to a basement. Everything above the studios was turned into offices.

I showed up at the appointed time and Ron introduced me to the three members of Mississippi. Then we all crammed into a tiny little office that served as a listening room. The guys hung back while I sat and listened.

From the time the needle hit the vinyl I was floored by what my ears were hearing. The blend of their harmonies was so sweet. They were as good as, if not better, than the greatest harmony bands that had influenced me over the years. Not only did their harmonies sound amazing but their original songs were fantastic as well. As I sat listening all I could think was, *'Somehow, I have to be a part of this band!'*

I guess because of my reputation with Zoot, they assumed I was still playing bass guitar. In fact, that was the main reason for contacting me. They were looking for a bass player and a drummer to complete their lineup. I told the guys I was very interested in joining the band but I'd have to buy a bass as I was now playing acoustic and electric guitar and writing songs of my own. They still wanted me to try out. I phoned Merv Cargill down in Frankston and asked if he knew of someone who was selling a left-handed bass guitar. Merv was very well known and respected amongst musicians, with a reputation for being the best guy in the business for repairing musical instruments. He also acted as a middleman for selling musicians' instruments and amplifiers.

I was determined to join this band and even if it meant putting myself in debt I was going to do it. It was a miracle that Merv knew of a left-handed Fender Precision bass for sale. I drove to Frankston and bought it.

Before deciding, the Mississippi guys wanted to rehearse a few songs with me to see how I would fit in. The rehearsal took place at their house. I knew I wasn't cutting it on bass anymore because I had come to that conclusion shortly after Zoot broke up.

After hearing me play, I got the feeling that John and Russ were not impressed and didn't want me to join the band. But Graeham said, "Well, let's hear how your voice sounds with our voices."

He taught me some specific harmony parts and I added my voice to theirs. I was just being myself and, as I would do in any instance such as this, I gave it my all. But I still got the feeling that John and Russ were not all that keen. I guess they didn't see the need for another voice in their band. On the other hand, Graeham loved the sound and strength of my voice. He heard something in the blend of our voices that John and Russ were not hearing.

As they discussed whether I was in or out, I was totally taken by surprise when Graeham suddenly told them, "Well, if you guys don't accept Beeb in the band, I'm leaving and going with him."

What the hell? Now what would make him say that without even knowing me? Perhaps we all make choices at times when our gut feelings tell us that this is the absolutely right thing to do. On that day, I joined the band known as Mississippi.

As the guys in Mississippi didn't know any Melbourne musicians, they turned to me to throw some names in the ring. We contacted Derek Pellicci, who I knew had been in a couple of bands called Plum and Ash, and asked if he was interested in coming to the guys' house for a rehearsal. Derek auditioned and we all liked the way he played drums on our songs.

Derek had a girlfriend, Anne, and a part-time job as a window dresser at Myer in the city. I remember we went through a hell of a time convincing him to quit his day job and commit to the band full-time. He was being pulled in two directions because Anne was pushing for him to have some security in his life. You know, save up a deposit and buy a house and all that jazz. So there were a few months of not really knowing whether he was willing or not. Eventually, we convinced him to quit his job and join the band.

It was through Derek's Plum connection that Paul Beschi auditioned for Mississippi as the bass guitarist. Paul was the younger brother of Terry and Phil Beschi, the lead guitarist and bass player in Plum, but we didn't think he had the right feel for our music. Then we heard about Colin Deluca.

Colin was a funny character who loved W.C. Fields' humour and he even looked a little like him. Colin is one of those guys whose life is the water. When we met him, I'm pretty sure he owned a boat. He spent his time living on the boat or in a small recreation vehicle wherever he parked it. He lived a real vagabond kind of life. His mother lived in Essendon and he had a brother but it was very obvious that Colin was the black sheep of the family.

One thing that was undeniable about Colin: he was an excellent bass player. His feel for our songs was fantastic. Colin and I always got along very well, but he could be a rascal. He and I did some pretty outrageous things together.

The band stayed in some very cheap motels on our travels and a complimentary breakfast was included at most of them. You filled out the menu the night before and either dropped it at the office or hung it outside your room.

We were somewhere in the Victorian countryside on a string of dates. Colin and I shared a motel room. We filled out our breakfast menus the night before but when we lifted the metal lids off the plates in the morning, what we'd ordered was not what we received.

Our eggs were very undercooked and looked disgusting. This really pissed Colin off, so, in retaliation, he went to the toilet and dropped a turd on the plate and put the metal lid back on. The plate was put back on the tray with all the other dirty dishes.

We didn't think any more about it until we got a call from Michael Chugg the next day. Chuggi was our booking agent who worked at the Let It Be Agency. He was yelling down the phone line, "Okay, who did it? Who dropped the turd on the plate?" Colin and I couldn't keep a straight face.

We burst out laughing and were rolling on the floor, absolutely cracking up.

The very first song I ever recorded with Graeham Goble was his entry in The Yamaha Music Festival. It was an international song contest and Graeham had written a beautiful acoustic guitar-picking style of song called 'Time'. We recorded it in Studio B at Armstrong Audio Visual.

He double-tracked his acoustic guitar with his Gibson Dove. Peter Jones played a piccolo flute for the solo section and it sounded very haunting. It was a fantastic song and it's a shame it wasn't recognised in the contest. In recent years, I have urged Graeham to resurrect the song and re-record it.

Around that same time, Brian Cadd was writing and recording jingles for advertising agencies and he used me to sing jingles for Onkaparinga blankets and Suzuki Motor Bikes. Graeham and I also wrote a commercial for Kentucky Fried Chicken that Mississippi recorded. I wrote a couple of jingles for Motor City Preston as well.

Things like that were typical if you were hanging out at AAV. The studio complex had a real family feel about it and the same people came and went on a daily and weekly basis. I spent a lot of time there because Megan, who was now my girlfriend, was working upstairs for her dad at the Fable label.

Over the three years of Mississippi's existence, the band went through a number of lineup changes but always retained the core of Graeham Goble, Derek Pellicci and me. The first lineup included Derek on drums, Colin Deluca on bass and John Mower as lead singer. Russ Johnson, Graeham and I all played guitar.

The band's début performance was at Corbould Hall in Ballarat on October 20, 1972 followed by a show in Adelaide at the Thebarton Town Hall on November 3. Mississippi was an extremely hard-working band, performing all over Australia. As I mentioned, I regard my time with Mississippi as my true musical apprenticeship. Having come through Zoot and Frieze, I sought the approval of my peers in the Australian music industry who may have viewed me as an average musician. I wanted to be accepted and recognised for my talent.

I made the decision to stop playing bass and played six-string guitar and continued writing my own compositions. Mississippi made me a better singer, a much improved guitar player and a pretty good songwriter. The three-year apprenticeship would serve me well for my time to come in Little River Band.

In July 1973, Bootleg released a new Mississippi single called 'Early Morning', written by Graeham, Russ and myself. The B-side was a song called 'Sweet World' that had been recorded on the first *Mississippi* album. The single did very little on the charts. Not long after the release, Russ Johnson quit the band to join Greg Quill and Country Radio.

I don't recall the specific reason for him leaving but he could be a little unstable at times. Graeham thought it might have been because Russ had experimented with LSD during his time in California.

I remember one particularly disturbing night at Auburn Road when Russ and his wife Clemene had an argument. She bolted out of the house and ran down the street with him chasing after her and yelling that he was going to kill her. Clemene was very frightened of him and he was a bit of a control freak. I didn't respect him for the way he treated Clemene and was glad he decided to leave the band.

Kerryn Tolhurst, the guitar player in Country Radio, quit that band and stepped in temporarily to play lead guitar for Mississippi until we found another guitarist. Kerryn later formed The Dingoes with Broderick Smith. Mississippi went on the search for another guitar player.

Seven
MISSISSIPPI — PHASE TWO

Colin DeLuca, Harvey James, Beeb Birtles,
Derek Pellicci, John Mower and Graeham Goble

Graeham Goble wasn't happy living in the house on Auburn Road so we decided to find a place together. We rented a flat above a bank on the corner of Maud Street and Burke Road in North Balwyn. Megan and I were now going out exclusively and it was just down the road from where she lived with her parents.

To give you a glimpse into how the odd couple lived: Graeham wanted all the comforts of home and immediately carpeted his bedroom. He had curtains made for the window overlooking Burke Road. He had a proper single bed with a box springs base and a mattress on top. He also owned a long cabinet, on which sat his record player.

I, on the other hand, bought seagrass matting to cover the bare floor in my bedroom and threw a double mattress on top of it. I bought a big round white Chinese rice paper lamp and stuck a coloured light bulb in it. I suspended it slightly off-centre so that it hung low over the bottom half of my mattress. Strategically positioned for those romantic moments in my bedroom, of course. Back then I was very much living the hippie lifestyle.

Our co-living arrangement suited me because during the first six months or so, Graeham was so homesick for Adelaide that whenever the band had a few days off he would get in his car and drive back home.

Kerryn Tolhurst played only a handful of shows with us before we found Harvey James. Harvey was an English migrant who had the looks of a rock guitar hero and he could also really play. We got along extremely well. I remember the day he came over to our flat in North Balwyn and we ran him through the songs in our set.

Graeham and I were always the ones to work someone new into the band. We would sit with a new member for as long as it took to get it right before we rehearsed as a full band. Harvey was the perfect addition to our lineup as he fitted in very well. His first gig with Mississippi was on November 3, 1973.

Live, the band was improving all the time because we were always on the road. Through the constant touring it got to the stage where Colin Deluca couldn't take Graeham's pedantic ways anymore and he also quit. We found André Santos to take Colin's place. I can't remember where we first saw him. I didn't get that guy at all! He had Graeham convinced that he could expel drugs from his body on demand. He would sit there and make himself perspire as if he had total control over his bodily functions. To me he was a strange guy and too different from the rest of us. Consequently, he didn't last long.

Mississippi pushed on, however, performing around Australia, honing our craft as musicians and songwriters.

INITIATION

Sometime during 1972, shortly after I joined Mississippi, I started searching for some kind of deeper meaning in my life. I had never been heavily into drugs, though I did experiment with smoking pot and I took LSD a couple of times. When I experimented with LSD I never swallowed a whole tab but would cut it in half.

The first time I took it was when a friend of a friend came down from Sydney to stay with me. She was going to the Sunbury Music Festival but had nowhere to stay. Even though I shared my bed with her, we had no romantic involvement whatsoever. For me to even hang out with another woman must have meant that it was during the time when Megan had broken off our relationship. My new friend from Sydney stayed with me at the flat and I distinctly remember she had the tab of LSD taped to the underside of her watch.

The Sunbury Festival ran from January 25 to 28 in 1974. Queen had been booked for the festival. I chatted with their bass player, John Deacon, on the back of a semi-trailer where the musicians tuned their instruments before going on stage. John was telling me how rooted he was from the flight from England to Australia, and we both commented on how stinking hot it was that day.

My guest was roaming around the grounds doing her own thing. We decided that we wouldn't indulge in dropping the acid until after dark. I remember bumping into Valda that day as well. At the time she had a thing for Ross Wilson from Daddy Cool. Anyway, as nighttime approached, the Sydney gal found me and we split the tab of LSD and swallowed half each.

I felt sorry for Queen because the crowd was not very accepting. I had never heard of Queen until Mississippi drove to Perth for the first time for a couple of weeks of engagements. It was the Perth nightclub scene that introduced me to their music.

The Sunbury audience booed Queen and yelled for them to get off the stage and go home, and that they were just a bunch of 'English poofters'. I didn't think they were given a fair shot. How could you not like Brian May's unique guitar sound coming from that wall of Vox AC30s? Their harmonies were also amazing and Freddie Mercury was a charismatic lead singer.

Madder Lake, the Sunbury headliners, was one of Australia's most popular rock 'n' roll bands at the time. I had never seen them before, so I wanted to check them out. I was totally blown away by their music. I was impressed by the way their lead singer, Mick Fettes, moved and by his gravelly voice. He was a very charismatic front man and the band sounded great. But, of course, I was under the influence of the LSD.

That was it, my introduction to LSD. The next day, when my female guest flew back to Sydney, my skin broke out in ugly pimples. I'd never had a problem with bad skin so I figured it was because of the drug.

The thing that ultimately stopped me taking drugs was that I disliked the feeling of not being in control of my mind and body. And whatever you took, you never knew how long it was going to last.

The only other time I was on LSD I didn't know about it. Unbeknownst to me, Allan Burke, a roadie friend of mine, decided to surprise me one night by stirring LSD into a beer. Allan was one of those friends you have for a time and a season. Over a period of months we hung out and drank a few beers together while we listened to music.

When I was well and truly under the influence of the LSD, Allan placed the *Jeff Beck Group* album on his turntable and I heard electric guitar being played like never before. My ears were opened to the most amazing feel for guitar playing I had ever heard. Each note, every run of notes, gave me chills up and down my spine. And the sound Jeff Beck got out of his guitar and amplifier was so unique!

Once again, for the next couple of days I paid the price by seeing my skin break out. It was enough to put me off forever. I never dropped acid again. But hey, it was the thing to do in those days. We were all caught up in the '70s hippie movement. I even became a vegetarian for a while.

All through the Mississippi years and the first year of Little River Band I smoked some marijuana, but even that affected my body in an adverse way. Whenever I smoked, it left me feeling vague the next day. I preferred having a few drinks instead because I was more in control of how far to take it.

When I reached the age where I started thinking there had to be more than this in my life I began searching for something that would really fulfill me. It was through Megan that I got to know about the Theosophical Society Bookshop in Russell Street in Melbourne. The songwriter Hans Poulsen was a good friend of Megan's and he was into pure living and the whole spiritual thing. It was probably through them that I first heard about The Findhorn Foundation, a spiritual community, eco-village and an international centre for holistic learning, helping to unfold a new human consciousness and create a positive and sustainable future.

I went to the T.S. Bookshop and allowed myself to be drawn to certain books. *Initiation* was the title of one of the books I came across. The book, by Elisabeth Haich, was about reincarnation, which I was totally open to at the time because spiritually I was searching for something.

In one of the first chapters, Elisabeth described our human life here on earth as having 'fallen from paradise'. I liked the phrase and used it for the title of a song Graeham Goble and I would later write. 'Fall From Paradise' was the first track on side two of *Sleeper Catcher*, Little River Band's fourth studio album.

I also read *Autobiography Of A Yogi* by Paramhansa Yogananda, though it didn't really grab me. One book I did connect with was called *The Practice Of The Presence Of God* by Brother Lawrence.

I read some fascinating books during that time but none of them really convinced me to the extent where I could say, "Yes, this is it, I've found what I've been looking for and this is what I believe in one hundred per cent."

Eight
MISSISSIPPI — PHASE THREE

Derek Pellicci, Beeb Birtles, Graeham Goble,
Charlie Tumahai and Harvey James
Photo courtesy of Philip Morris

Mississippi was booked through the Let It Be Agency, but we really needed the guidance of a good manager. It was through Let It Be that we found Barry Earl and appointed him as our manager. Barry really believed in the band's music and had grandiose plans for us.

Barry grew up in Garden City, a municipality behind Port Melbourne. He was bitten by the music bug after he met George Harrison and Ringo Starr in Tahiti and went fishing with them. After he returned to Australia he became a manager with the reputation for spotting new talent. Whilst in New Zealand he saw The La De Das and brought them to Australia. He also managed Leo de Castro before Leo joined the Melbourne band King Harvest.

Barry and his wife, Mal, were living in a ground floor flat on Alma Road in East St Kilda where we would go for band meetings. It was across the road from Alma Park East. I remember that's where Barry turned us on to Paul Butterfield's *Better Days* album that totally floored us.

Barry knew Charlie Tumahai and asked if he would be interested in joining Mississippi on bass guitar. Charlie agreed, and his very first gig with us was actually on my twenty-fifth birthday, November 28, 1973.

Charlie was a very cool cat who possessed a beautiful Maori voice plus great feel for playing the bass. Once Charlie joined we went back into AAV studio B and recorded a song that Darryl Cotton and I had written three years earlier.

Over a three-year period, Mississippi was a very hard-working band, playing in pubs and clubs all over Australia. Some of the venues where we performed were the Largs Pier Hotel, Pooraka Hotel and The Lion in Adelaide; The Broadbeach Hotel in Queensland; the Savoy Club in Newcastle; The Manly Vale Hotel in Sydney; Southside Six, the Village

Green, Croxton Park Hotel, the Station Hotel, the Matthew Flinders and Q Club in Melbourne; Beethoven's, the Orient Hotel, the Whitesands Hotel and the Sandgroper Hotel in Perth.

We also supported international artists like Gary Glitter, The Jackson 5, Chuck Berry, Leon Russell, Little Richard and The Faces.

When we played at Chequers, I bumped into my old friend Valda, who was now living in Sydney, sharing a house with Zac Zytnik from Taman Shud and Blackfeather.

Here's what Valda remembers:

I was still working at Chequers, one of Sydney's premier music venues, when Beeb returned in a brand new band called Mississippi. He asked if I could put some of the guys up at my house in Blues Point Road. It was a fantastic three-storey terrace that had backyard views of the harbour.

Most days I was working at The Old Spaghetti Factory but I made sure that the guys had plenty to eat. I was a staunch vegetarian at the time. Whether it was the vegetable casseroles or my passionate rhetoric, Beeb, Derek and Graeham were persuaded by my lifestyle. Beeb went vegetarian for three whole weeks, and when I caught up with Graeham recently, he told me he still had not eaten red meat since those days.

When it looked like I was going to be called up for National Service, I got the idea for writing a song about all the young guys having to go through that experience and asking themselves some very serious questions about life.

'Will I' had become a favourite with Mississippi audiences wherever we played. Harvey's guitar work was outstanding, especially the long sustaining guitar lines at the end. The B-side was the very first co-write by Graeham and me. It was called 'Where In The World', and Charlie and I shared the lead vocals. Harvey played some amazing sustaining guitar lines on it as well. It was definitely a specialty of his, being able to control feedback and hold long guitar notes.

'Will I' was released on the eve of the band's departure for England. As a band, we were very disappointed with the lack of support from radio as well as our label, Bootleg. It was obvious Ron Tudor wasn't going to pay for us to record another studio album so we decided to try our luck in England.

Barry Earl secured free passage to England with the Sitmar line by booking the band as the on-board entertainment for the six-week voyage. I think we had something like $10,000 saved up to sustain our new life in the UK.

So on April 21, 1974 we set sail from Sydney on the ship *Fairsky*, and took off for fame and fortune in England.

VOYAGE TO ENGLAND

MISSISSIPPI ON BOARD THE *FAIRSKY*
PHOTO COURTESY OF PHILIP MORRIS

The voyage on the *Fairsky* to England was the worst six weeks of my life. We were required to play every night in the Lido bar. It was quite pathetic because our song list wasn't that long and we had to repeat some of the same numbers. We tired of that very quickly and it became a tedious chore to perform.

Graeham had met Narelle, who was the receptionist at a hotel in

Sydney where the band stayed. They were married shortly before we left for England, so they had their own cabin. I hated being confined to the ship, so I drank too much just about every night. I remember our roadie, Trevor, being disgusted with me because I was so wasted all the time.

The only memory I treasure of that boat trip is the day I spent with Charlie Tumahai, our bass player, on Tahiti. We had two or three days there. On the first day some girls and guys, who I had become friendly with, rented a car and we drove all the way around the island along the coast road. It was a fantastic day and I remember we took a lot of photos.

On the second day, Charlie and I got up at the crack of dawn and ate a traditional Tahitian breakfast. We drank strong black coffee and ate freshly caught fish. Then we drove to watch a crowd of school children playing. One of the children was Charlie's daughter from a previous marriage, who he hadn't seen in a long time. I stayed in the car while he went over to say hello.

I don't know whether Charlie's ex-wife was Tahitian or Maori, but that's one of the things I will never forget doing with him. Sadly, Charlie is no longer with us. He died suddenly in New Zealand on December 21, 1995, at the age of 46. He collapsed and died from a massive heart attack at the Auckland district court where he was working as a member of a volunteer organisation helping the Ngati Whatua tribe.

On the ship, I started experimenting with a new guitar tuning I'd found called open G. I was messing around with that when I stumbled onto the chord progression that became the start of my song 'I'll Always Call Your Name'.

I initially wrote the song about leaving Australia behind, but many people think I wrote it as a reference to God. Believe me, I don't think there was any connection between God and me at this particular time in my life. I couldn't wait to get off that fucking ship!

From Tahiti, we sailed to the Spanish city of Port Balboa on the Pacific Ocean side of the Panama Canal. After sailing through the canal our next port of call was Willemstad in Dutch Curacao. From Dutch Curacao we sailed on to Sintra, Portugal where we made a stop. Then on to Amsterdam, Holland and Southampton, England, where we finally disembarked.

Hooray, we had made it and we were all relieved to step back on land.

We rented a van barely big enough to fit us and all our equipment, and we drove to London to look for accommodation. As most Australians do in London, we ended up in Earls Court and rented some single rooms as temporary accommodation. We then all looked for our own places to live, wherever we could find them.

Graeham, Narelle and I decided to look for a house to share. We found a very comfortable little half-house at 28 Broadmead Avenue, Worcester Park, Southwest London. It was close to Kingston on Thames. The smartest thing Graeham and I did was prepay our rent for six months. That turned out to be a lifesaver later on when it was time for us to return to Australia.

Beeb & Elly in Amsterdam

Bertelkamp family in Amsterdam

Beeb with bike
Christmas 1951

Zoot 1969. Left to right: Roger Hicks,
Darryl Cotton, Beeb, Rick Brewer

Zoot, left to right:
Darryl Cotton, Beeb, Roger Hicks & Rick Brewer

Go-Set Pop Poll Winners 1969

Beeb, Darryl Cotton, Rick Brewer and Rick Springfield

Think Pink - Think Zoot

Gas magazine poster

Beeb, Rick Brewer, Darryl Cotton
and Rick Springfield

Advertisement for new Zoot single, 'Hey, Pinkie'

Zoot - live at Chequers
Photo by Philip Morris

Beeb in Frieze
Photo by Peter Bennett

Beeb, Jamie Dunn, Warren
Adams, Peter Moscos
and Darryl Cotton
Photo by Angelique Moscos

Mississippi - acoustic set at Sunbury
Left to right: Derek Pellicci on drums, Harvey James,
Charlie Tumahai, Beeb & Graeham Goble
Photo by Philip Morris

Beeb at Sunbury

Publicity photo from the '80s

Graeham and Beeb in Mississippi.
Photo by Philip Morris

Beeb in Mississippi playing his right-handed Epiphone upside down

Little River Band - Beeb in action
Photo by Mitch Karam

Diamantina Cocktail

LRB - Diamantina Cocktail gold record

Publicity photo of Beeb in
Nashville, Tennessee

LRB - Beeb with his Gibson SG

LRB - TV Week giant pinup poster
Left to right: (back) David Briggs, Glenn Shorrock, George McArdle,
Graeham Goble, (front) Beeb Birtles & Derek Pellicci

Beeb & Donna

Birtles family photo

South Australian Premier Don Dunstan with Donna 1978

Nine
MISSISSIPPI — PHASE FOUR

Harvey James, who had sailed all the way to England with us, didn't play one show with us in London. He quit the band on arrival in Southampton. Out of desperation, Graeham phoned Russ Johnson and asked him to rejoin. I wasn't exactly thrilled, as I felt we'd gone our separate ways, but Russ agreed and flew to London. Harvey spent some time visiting his relatives in England and then flew back to Australia, where he joined Mike Rudd and Bill Putt in Ariel (and later joined Sherbet).

When I heard that Harvey was dying from cancer in 2010 I phoned him and we talked for about forty-five minutes. At one point in the conversation I asked him why he had quit Mississippi and he told me it was because of Graeham. I think it was more a personality difference than a musical one. More than a few musicians who crossed paths with Graeham couldn't handle his eccentric ways. Harvey James died on January 15, 2011, aged 58.

Mississippi's first show in London was at The Greyhound Hotel on July 5, 1974. Barry Earl booked us into a few prestige venues like The Speakeasy, Ronnie Scott's and the Greyhound, but we played some dives as well. In particular, a dreadful place called Hatchetts. It was a dance club where we were the live entertainment in between disco records being spun. We had to squeeze onto a tiny stage and play four or five sets a night. It was degrading!

As a lot of Australians in London tend to stick together, word got out that we were playing at the Greyhound. Glenn Wheatley and his wife, Allison, were in London after a year in Los Angeles. They were staying at Carol and Marty Kristian's house. Marty Kristian was a member of The New Seekers.

When Glenn was still the bass player in The Masters Apprentices, he took over the band's management. The Masters had also gone to England to try to make the big time. They came close when they recorded a couple of very progressive albums at Abbey Road Studios, *Choice Cuts* and *A Toast To Panama Red*. But the albums received little attention and they broke up.

Glenn and Allison stayed in England, where he went to work for David Joseph's Gem-Toby Organisation (GTO). David Joseph managed Procession and The New Seekers. He was married to Robyn Alvarez, a very popular Australian singer we used to watch on *Bandstand*. After opening the Los Angeles office of GTO, David sent Glenn over to run it. However, Glenn and David butted heads over an incident that took place after the Presidential Inauguration in January 1973. It was the night The New Seekers performed for President Nixon.

Glenn, in his book *Paper Paradise*, said:

David Joseph was not so pleased that night. Something had gone wrong with his travelling arrangements. He was unhappy and dressed me down in front of everybody. I was shaken and close to breaking. I knew from that night on it would only be a matter of time before our relationship disintegrated completely.

Glenn resigned over the incident. He and Allison returned to England, where Glenn found a job building roads during the day and working in a pub at night, while Allison was working as a model. They had already made their decision to go back home, hitchhiking their way back to Australia the long way through Europe, the Middle East and down through India.

In London they came to see Mississippi play at the Greyhound and after the show they came backstage to say hello. The writing was already on the wall for Mississippi as the trip to England had been a disaster. It couldn't have been more than six to eight weeks before our money ran out and we were all forced to fend for ourselves.

Russ Johnson flew back to Australia. Derek Pellicci got a job working in a shoe shop that sold the kind of high platform boots Elton John made famous. Charlie Tumahai stayed in London and joined the very progressive English rock band Be Bop Deluxe. Graeham and Narelle took off to Europe for a belated honeymoon, and I got a job packing albums in boxes at Decca Records.

Before the band all went their separate ways, Graeham, Derek and I had already made a commitment to re-form the group. We just weren't sure whether to stay in England or go back to Australia.

The three of us sat around discussing why Mississippi wasn't a bigger success than we thought it should have been. We decided what was missing was a really good front man, someone who could be the liaison between the band and the audience. We needed a lead singer with a good voice who could move on stage and be the focal point for the group.

The problem with Mississippi was we were five musicians who played instruments and sang but not one of us felt comfortable communicating with an audience. I said to the guys, "Well, the best guy I can think of is Glenn Shorrock." I knew that Glenn was still living in London after the demise of Axiom, the band he had with Brian Cadd.

We decided to contact Glenn Wheatley to get his opinion. We drove over to Marty Kristian's house where Wheatley and Allison were staying and had a brief meeting with him. We were there to more or less pick his brain. Wheatley told us that his plan was to go back to Australia and find a band to manage and break them in the United States, not England. In telling us this, he convinced us that we should go back to Australia and re-form the band there.

After Axiom broke up, Glenn Shorrock joined the multinational progressive rock band Esperanto, who released their début album, *Esperanto Rock Orchestra*, in 1973, featuring Glenn's song 'Statue of Liberty'. He left Esperanto before their third album was released in 1974.

While in that group, Glenn had a publishing deal with MAM Music to write songs. He also sang background vocals on records for Cliff Richard and Olivia Newton-John. When I phoned Glenn, he said he'd been knocking his head against a brick wall for the last five years. He'd had enough and wanted to go back to Australia.

In Glenn Shorrock's own words from the unreleased Little River Band retrospective DVD, *It's A Long Way There*:

Having tried to break the English market with The Twilights and then with Axiom, both of which failed, I found myself in London for about five years and I did whatever I could to earn a living and that included serious songwriting.

I invited Glenn to our house in Worcester Park, and, with Graeham, we sat around and played each other songs we had written. We could tell Glenn liked some of our songs and we liked some of his as well. Then we decided to hear what our voices sounded like together.

One of the first songs we rehearsed was Graeham's 'It's A Long Way There'. We taught Glenn his part and when we hit that first 'and it's a long way there, it's a long way to where I'm going', the three of us heard something magic. The blend of our voices was amazing. Right then and there we knew we had a unique vocal sound.

Glenn Wheatley:

The three vocalists were Beeb, Graeham and Glenn and they absolutely just blended so fantastically right from the word go. It was a natural and everybody got terribly excited. Glenn Shorrock even said he would consider relocating back to Australia as well. We started to put the formulation together of what would be a band with the criteria of basing ourselves in Australia but trying to take on the world from there.

It was now September 1974 and we made a loose arrangement to meet back in Australia sometime during January 1975. We already had half the band, with Graeham Goble, Derek Pellicci, Glenn Shorrock and me, plus we had Glenn Wheatley lined up as our manager.

Megan flew over to be with me and was working temp jobs in London. I was broke and had no way of getting back to Australia. I wasn't going to ask my parents or anyone else to lend me money to get back home. I took as much overtime at Decca's packing plant as they would give me.

I walked the mile-and-a-half to work every day and walked back home at night, rain or shine. My job was packing Engelbert Humperdinck, Tom Jones and a variety of classical albums in boxes, ready to be shipped off.

That's what I did for three months straight. I saved every penny I could because I needed so many pounds for my plane ticket back to Australia.

One day, one of the big wigs came to inspect the plant. It was Ken East, the head of EMI Australia when Zoot were riding high. He was the dickhead responsible for fucking up the band's chances to sign with RCA in the US. At some point I had met Ken and he would have known who I was, but when he toured the Decca plant I didn't make myself known to him. I was too proud to let him know I was working there as a mere packer.

During that time in London, Megan and I went to some great rock concerts including The Sensational Alex Harvey Band, from Scotland, and a fantastic Welsh band called Man.

When I had saved enough money to buy my plane ticket home, I gave Decca notice that I was quitting. Megan and I caught the Hovercraft over to Holland to visit my extended Dutch family who I had not seen since my family migrated to Australia in 1959.

Our trip to Amsterdam coincided with the city's 700th birthday. Can you imagine? It was 1974 and Amsterdam was celebrating 700 years of existence! We had a great time, even though it was mainly catching up with members of my family, and I remember doing a lot of walking.

We returned to London the day before our scheduled flight home. We bought the cheapest tickets we could, with Air India. The flight was a bit of a milk run. We touched down in the Middle East to refuel and of course we stopped off in India. I can't remember if it was New Delhi or Bombay. As awful and crowded as the Air India flight was, Megan and I were on a high because we were heading home.

Megan's mother, Jean, loved the quaint little town of Maldon in the Victorian countryside, which is where she was when we arrived back in Melbourne. We decided to show up unannounced. Driving through the Victorian countryside feeling the Australian sun beating down on us felt so good. We took Jean totally by surprise, she couldn't believe we were back. It was so good to be home!

Ten
LITTLE RIVER BAND — PHASE ONE

LRB 1st lineup: Glenn Shorrock, Derek Pellicci,
Graeham Goble, Beeb Birtles,
Ric Formosa, Roger McLachlan
Photo courtesy of Roger McLachlan

Glenn Shorrock and Graeham Goble were the first guys to make it back to Australia. They both returned to Adelaide to visit their families and Derek Pellicci arrived next. When Megan and I arrived we lived with her parents for a while until we found our own place.

When Glenn Shorrock came back to Melbourne he stayed with Jim Keays and his wife, Vicki, in a terrace house in Carlton. Some of our initial acoustic rehearsals took place in the park across from where they lived. We set our sights on finding a guitarist and a bass player to complete our lineup.

We heard about Roger McLachlan, a New Zealander who was playing bass in the musical *Godspell*. Roger was a tall, lean, good-looking guy. We asked if he was interested in auditioning for the band and he was keen. He passed the audition, so we asked him to join the group.

In trying to remember how we found out about Ric Formosa, Ric tells me this:

The band found out about me through Phil Manning (from Chain). I had met him a little while before I auditioned for the guys and he was really impressed with my playing and promised he'd look into finding me a gig. I took it with a pinch of salt and really had no expectations. Then Glenn Wheatley rang me one day, saying that the band had asked Phil Manning to join, but he turned it down because he was promoting his own solo album. Phil highly recommended me. So Glenn asked me to come over and audition.

We were very impressed with the fact that Ric, at the tender age of sixteen, had been asked to join Edgar Winter's White Trash when Rick Derringer quit that band. Ric's family had migrated to Canada from Italy and were living in Toronto at the time. His parents were adamant that Ric was way too young to go to live in New York, so he had to pass up the opportunity.

The Formosa family moved from Canada to Australia and had only been here a short time before we contacted Ric about auditioning for us. Ric had a unique style of guitar playing. He was incredibly fast on runs of notes and had his own distinctive sound. He agreed to join the band.

We were all so broke when we arrived back in Australia that we applied for the dole. That extra bit of money helped us get through a tough period while Glenn Wheatley was hustling up some bookings.

Megan and I rented part of a house at 3 Young Street, Kew that backed onto the Yarra River. It was close to the walking bridge across to Victoria Street, where the Skipping Girl Vinegar neon sign was. I remember living there when Glenn Wheatley phoned to say that the band could make some instant money if one of us could write a jingle for the national Witchery chain of clothing shops.

I was suffering from a really bad head cold at the time but I was intrigued by the name of the chain. I was sitting on the front porch step with Megan where I hammered out the skeleton of 'Witchery' in no more than ten minutes.

I played it for Glenn and within days we were in AAV (Armstrong Audio Visual) recording the jingle. However, there was a far more profitable payoff waiting for us a couple of years down the road. We also wrote some commercials for the ANZ bank that we recorded later in studio A at AAV. These commercials were a great way for the band to make some extra money.

The Wheatleys rented a place near the corner of Glenferrie Road and Toorak Road and this was where Wheatley's office was. I remember going around there to sift through his record collection and he let me borrow whatever I wanted. When he made his first trip back to the States to score a record deal for Little River Band he returned with albums by Al Jarreau and Hall and Oates.

All my life I've been an avid music fan and it was always a thrill to discover someone new. Al Jarreau's first album was called *We Got By* and it blew me away. The grooves on it were fantastic, in particular a song called 'Spirit'.

Glenn also had the second Hall and Oates album, *Abandoned Luncheonette*, with 'She's Gone' on it, as well as the album that was just called *Daryl Hall & John Oates*, with the silver cover of their two faces made up in drag. That album featured 'Sara Smile'. They were all very influential albums at the time.

The very first lineup of Little River Band consisted of me, Graeham Goble on guitar, Ric Formosa on lead guitar, Roger McLachlan on bass, Derek Pellicci on drums, and Glenn Shorrock was our lead vocalist. We played our first gigs under the name of Mississippi because that's what we were called before going to England. Our first show was at Martini's in Carlton on March 20, 1975.

Right from the start, we had fans coming to our shows. Fans of Glenn's from his Twilights and Axiom days, fans from my Zoot and Mississippi days, and fans of Graeham and Derek's days in Mississippi. It got back to us that our fans felt strongly we shouldn't be an Australian band with an American name. We agreed wholeheartedly and it was during those first few gigs as Mississippi that we started looking for a new name.

One day, Glenn Shorrock and I were sitting in the back seat of a car driving down Princes Highway to play a gig at The Golf View Hotel in Geelong. As we passed the Little River exit sign, Glenn said, "Little River, that'd be a good song title."

I nodded my head, but within a split second he said, "Hey, what about Little River Band?" We ran the idea past the other guys and Wheatley and we all agreed it was the perfect name for us.

Little River is a sleepy little town between Melbourne and Geelong. A few years later we shot one of our film clips at the Little River railway station. I liked the name change for the reason that Little River Band was more a universal name. There's bound to be a little river in every country around the world. Plus I liked the shift from Mississippi, one of the biggest rivers in the world, to Little River.

Wheatley didn't waste any time shopping for a record deal. Some people in the music business regarded us as Australia's first supergroup. Stephen Shrimpton, the head of EMI Australia, was very interested in signing the band and by June of 1975 we had an EMI recording contract. They gave us the very generous budget of $15,000 to record our first album.

LITTLE RIVER BAND

Glenn Shorrock had quite a few songs from his writing deal with MAM Music in England that he presented for our first album. During our three years with Mississippi, Graeham and I had also written many songs that had not been recorded. In studio B at AAV we recorded rough demos of all the songs. The long list for that first album must have been at least sixty songs, from which we had to pick ten.

Within Little River Band, song selection was always a very democratic process. All six members voted on which songs we thought were the best to record. Graeham's song 'It's A Long Way There' had already become a kind of anthem for Mississippi but it had never been recorded. The song was eight minutes and thirty-nine seconds, which greatly reduced the number of other songs we could fit on that first album. The final selection ended up being nine songs.

The album was self-titled as *Little River Band*. From start to finish it was recorded in three weeks with Ross Cockle as our recording engineer. Ross was very much into our music. He had a great personality and was very easy to get along with.

Every song was recorded live with the five instrumentalists in the studio. The music went down as a band. On 'It's A Long Way There' all of Ric's lead guitar solos were recorded at the same time as the band track. He was whingeing afterwards, saying he could do much better. We gave him some time to try to top what he had but stopped him after a few takes because it wasn't as magical as what was already on tape. The whole album was pretty much recorded live that way.

After recording Glenn's lead vocals, Glenn, Graeham and I sang all of our harmony parts around one microphone. Very few overdubs were recorded on that first album. Because the string arrangements had to be scored, they were recorded separately at a later time.

Here's what Graeham said about writing 'It's A Long Way There':

I wrote 'It's A Long Way There' on June 2, 1972. I was in my twenties and I had just left my hometown of Adelaide to pursue a music career in Melbourne. I was having a difficult time emotionally with missing home but I was very aware that the journey I was taking was my destiny. These were my first tentative steps into a new and unfamiliar world.

I didn't want to leave Adelaide but I knew it was something I had to do. I was very anxious and I missed my home enormously. For the first few months I used to travel back to Adelaide (nine hours by car) every three weeks to see my family and eat home-cooked food. It took a long time for me to let go.

The idea for 'It's A Long Way There' came from that nine-hour road trip I used to make. I realised much later though that there was something deeper within the words and, looking back on it now, it was a premonition of where life was taking me.

It's one of those recordings that still sounds great even today. I think that has a lot to do with the guys who played on it. We were playing eight gigs a week those days so when we went into the recording studio we were so well rehearsed we could just focus on the performance. We recorded it live, including the guitar solo work by Ric Formosa. We overdubbed the string section and vocals. I remember cutting the vocals at 3 a.m.

Each take we did was a little under nine minutes long and there was no Pro Tools back then so you had to get it right. Of course, with today's technology you wouldn't try for the whole band having to get everything right at the same time but there was magic in the way Little River Band used to record. It was like the collective energy in the room was the seventh player. You can definitely hear that on the record.

As well as being the band's lead guitarist, Ric was also an arranger. He scored the string arrangement for Glenn's song 'The Man In Black'. He was also very influential with turning us onto new music like the Pat Metheny Group and the Brecker Brothers. The musicianship on those albums was phenomenal and we were in awe of their playing.

In those early days, our agreement with Wheatley was that his cut was as the seventh member of the band. In other words, he didn't take a twenty per cent commission for management as most managers did. Everything was split seven ways. That's the reason why he is credited as a co-producer on our first couple of albums. Wheatley had next to nothing to do with producing us. We hardly saw him in the studio at all.

When the album was finally completed we ran into a couple of snags. The first was that EMI hit the roof because they found out we had gone over budget by $2000. Can you imagine? Our first album cost them just $17,000. How much money do you think they made from the eventual worldwide sales of that album? They would have made millions!

The next snag was this: Wheatley came to us and said that EMI didn't think there was a second single to pull off the album for radio airplay. He also talked to me privately and said the guys in the band felt that 'Love Is A Feeling' was the weakest song on the album. 'Love Is A Feeling' was one of the first songs I had ever written and it had already been recorded on the *1972 B.C.* Frieze album with Darryl Cotton. Wheatley tried to appease me by saying that the song would be used as a B-side on a future single.

I was a little disappointed, of course, as now I had only two songs on the album: 'Curiosity (Killed The Cat)' and 'I'll Always Call Your Name'. But I could see the reasoning behind us needing to release two singles.

In Australia, unlike the US, the life of an album was very short. An act might be lucky to sustain one album release for a year, at the most. This all comes down to the population difference between the two countries. In America, by the time your record saturated the country from the west coast to the east coast, an album could sustain your career for eighteen months to two years. That took the pressure off needing to come up with new material all the time. We definitely needed to have two singles on the album for radio in Australia.

Another song Glenn Shorrock had written during his time with MAM Music in England was called 'Emma'. We went back into AAV and recorded it. 'Love Is A Feeling' was taken off the album and 'Emma' was included as one of the nine songs. 'Emma' was a very catchy and commercial song.

EMI picked 'Curiosity' to be the band's first single, and it was released in September 1975. It became a top twenty hit, reaching number fifteen on the Australian charts. When 'Emma' was released as our second single it went up the charts the same way 'Curiosity' had done, reaching number twenty. 'Love Is A Feeling' was the B-side of 'Emma'.

Peter van den Elshouts, a graphic artist at EMI, came up with the artwork for our first album cover. He drew blown-up caricatures of our faces coming out of an English Zephyr driving down a country road. The cartoon-looking cover had no connection whatsoever to the music on the album inside.

It was embarrassing to say the least. Thank God Capitol Records insisted on a new cover for the US release. EMI released Little River Band's self-titled début album in November 1975. The band went on the road to promote it and it jump-started our career in Australia.

AFTER HOURS

The recording of our second album, *After Hours*, wasn't anywhere near the pleasant experience the first album had been. Once again we entered AAV and recorded a long list of demo songs from which to choose the tracks. Ross Cockle was again our recording engineer. But having three strong songwriters wanting things their own way means that it can become extremely competitive.

Unintentionally, the second album took on a country-rock flavour with songs such as Glenn's 'Seine City' and 'Sweet Old Fashioned Man' and Graeham's 'Country Girls'. My songs stayed more in the pop-rock vein. Wheatley was now in full swing managing us and wasn't around much for the recording of *After Hours*, which was also produced by the band.

There were many disagreements over song arrangements. It got so bad at one stage that Wheatley had to ask two writers not to show up to the studio whenever the third writer was working on one of his songs. Graeham and I had a major disagreement over the arrangement of 'Broke Again', a song I had started but he finished. I was ready to blow a fuse when we recorded the backing track.

Some seriously bad vibes were floating around the studio during the recording of *After Hours*. It turned out to be a very laidback, moody kind of album and not very commercial. We recorded Graeham's 'Days On The Road' which we'd already been playing live, as the opening track.

When I think back to those days now, Wheatley and I were never very close. It seemed to me he wasn't interested in listening to what I had to say. I was always pushing for the band to move ahead faster. For example,

I saw the need for some kind of backdrop on stage long before the other guys did. I could see we needed some production for our live shows. I had returned from England having seen some great bands and what they were doing with their backdrops on stage. It didn't need to be anything expensive, just something that set the scene.

I got so frustrated with mentioning this time and time again, with nothing being done about it, that I wrote the song 'Everyday Of My Life'. The lyrics speak of my frustration and came out of one of our many tedious band meetings.

I don't know whether the other guys put two and two together and realised I had written the song about our band meetings. I also don't remember there being any question that I would sing the lead vocal. I also wanted to sing the lead vocal on 'Broke Again' but the guys felt strongly that Glenn should have that song, and I agreed. The only reason I sang a couple of songs live on stage was to give Glenn a breather. Glenn and I never butted heads over who should sing the songs.

I had the body of 'Everyday Of My Life' written but I needed a middle eight. I keep every piece of music I write. I listened back through all my bits and pieces and came across a very short piece of music I had written in 1971, complete with lyrics. It was in a minor key but miraculously it slotted in perfectly as the middle eight. It's the section where the lyrics begin with, 'Don't know why life's hard for us cause we sure do try, forget your cares and worries, you know that we'll get by'. And that's all it was. I couldn't believe how perfectly it fitted. The song was complete!

I was pleased with the way the track turned out. I was especially thrilled with the synthesizer parts and the brass section. Ric Formosa arranged and conducted the brass. The bonus was the song was selected as the first single off *After Hours* and became a hit for the band. 'Broke Again' was released as the follow-up single but unfortunately it didn't even chart.

Glenn had written 'Seine City' about a romantic involvement with a woman in Paris when he was living in England. 'Take Me Home' was another song I had written in open G tuning while I was in London and it was one of our stronger live songs.

When I visited Ric Formosa and his family at their house in Caulfield

I had the idea to write a song about his family having migrated so often. I imagined his mother standing on the tarmac with her suitcase in hand, getting ready to board yet another plane. Ric showed me how to play the opening chord to 'Another Runway' and from there we wrote the song together. He was a genius with his knowledge of music. I thought it turned out to be a beautiful ballad, especially the repeat echo on the flute played by Graeme Lyall as the song fades out. It had a very haunting and lonely feel.

Ric wrote and sang his song, 'Bourbon Street'. It borrowed heavily from his favourite band at the time, Little Feat. Ric was a huge fan of Lowell George. He also arranged and conducted the strings and cor anglais on the album.

Graeham's 'Country Girls' was another song we were playing live. It's hard for me to listen to that song all the way through now because of all its different musical sections. It goes on a bit and never seems to end.

After Hours turned out to be a very unpleasant experience for all of us, and it's a miracle the band didn't splinter altogether after the recording. Somehow, we kept it together and went on the road to promote the release. Wheatley booked us to play at all the popular venues around Australia.

After three years of playing the pubs as Mississippi, the pub scene was still very much alive. In that first year as LRB we played at countless pubs, such as The Sentimental Bloke, The Matthew Flinders, The Council Club Hotel, Southside Six, The Sundowner and The Village Green, just to name a few. We also played at all the universities like Melbourne University, Monash and La Trobe, as well as appearing on the popular television shows *Countdown*, *Hey Hey It's Saturday* and *GTK*.

If you saw Little River Band live, or if you ever saw photos of the band, you would have noticed that I was always standing next to Derek. I liked to play tight with the drums and bass. I saw myself as part of the rhythm section.

Within the first year of the band being together, Wheatley flew to the US with our début album tucked under his arm. We were fortunate he still had connections in Los Angeles from his time at the Gem-Toby Organisation. He called on these people, hoping to secure a release for our first album. He told us of his disappointments with more than a few well-known music industry heavyweights in LA. He related some of those on the unreleased *It's A Long Way There* retrospective DVD.

In Glenn Wheatley's own words:

I did the rounds and got no fewer than twelve knockbacks, some very serious knockbacks. I was very disgruntled for a while because it looked like maybe I wasn't going to get the deal. Maybe it wasn't going to be that easy after all.

One in particular was United Artists Records and a president called Artie Mogull whose infamy was that he was the one who allegedly discovered Bob Dylan and Laura Nyro and all these people, so he was a bit of a legend. I had a reel-to-reel tape in those days and brought it into his office.

"Mr Mogull, pleased to meet you, my name's Glenn from over there." And he had this big highback chair and he's sitting behind his desk. He turned around away from me so I couldn't see him. All I could see was the highback chair with these two arms coming out as he threaded the tape. He hit the play button and we're listening to the first three minutes of 'It's A Long Way There', an eight-minute song.

He didn't turn around, there was no nodding of the head and no chair movement. So I'm dying, I'm starting to think, oh my goodness, he doesn't like this at all. *The finger came out again to the stop button. He stopped it halfway through the song. He still hadn't said anything and he hadn't turned around to me. He finally turned around very slowly and said, "You know, Mr Wheatley, have you ever run your fingernails down a blackboard? You know that feeling you get through your body? That's what this music does to me."*

Well, I swear to you I almost cried in front of this man. He upset me so much that I went, "I, I, can I have my tape back please, Mr Mogull?" He rewound it and gave it to me. I, fair dinkum, bolted into the car park and sat there with my heart pounding. It was the worst rejection I'd ever had. I mean, this was Artie Mogull, the man who discovered Bob Dylan, telling me that this music was like running your fingers down a blackboard. I mean, I was shattered. I had no idea what to do. I went back to the hotel, regrouped my thoughts and kept at it.

On Christmas Eve 1975 I received a phone call from Capitol Records, from Rupert Perry who was running the company at that time, and he said, "Glenn, we love it, we'd like to do a deal with you."

Wheatley had secured a recording deal for us with Capitol Records on their Harvest label. A little over a year after our self-titled album was released in Australia, it was released in the US. Wheatley also signed us to a booking agency in LA called Headquarters. The agent assigned to us was a young guy just starting out in the business, John Marx.

Glenn Wheatley:
I only had three confirmed dates. I had to sit the band down with their wives and girlfriends and say, "Look, we're going to America, we're giving this thing a shot but I don't know how long we're gonna be."

When Wheatley returned from the States with his good news he was confronted by a very unhappy band. Some major changes were around the corner. After the recording of *After Hours* it was decided that we needed to work with a producer, someone who could act as a mediator between the six of us.

Bill Halverson, who was very well respected for having worked at Wally Heider's Studio in Los Angeles and San Francisco as a recording engineer, was in Australia finishing off some recordings with Skyhooks. His reputation came from having worked with Crosby, Stills & Nash on their early albums. We may have just been testing the waters with him because we cut only three tracks at TCS Nine studios, with John French as the assistant engineer.

We recorded a song called 'Good Wine', written by Ian Mason. Ian sang the lead vocal but we also had a version with Glenn singing. We also cut 'Time To Fly', one of my songs and another that I wrote in open G tuning.

Ian Mason was a keyboard player we started using in the studio because we didn't have one in the band. He was a very good piano player and had an excellent voice as well. Graeham was convinced Ian should be a permanent member of the band and he pushed hard for him to join our lineup, but the rest of us didn't think his personality would fit. It wasn't that we didn't like Ian; I guess the majority of us didn't think we needed another member in the band. 'Emma' was the first song we hired Ian to play on and he also played keyboards on the *After Hours* and *Diamantina Cocktail* albums.

I can't remember exactly how Roger McLachlan's dismissal came about. Sometime during the tour to promote *After Hours*, Derek felt Roger's bass playing wasn't keeping up with the way he was progressing on drums. This is always a difficult issue in bands because there will be times when some musicians progress faster than others.

So what does a band do about that? What did The Beatles do? Think about how drastically their music changed over a period of just seven years. The four of them stuck together until the very end when they decided to break up. You're either great mates and overlook the fact that some guys have limitations and you carry them along, or you approach it strictly from a business point of view, forget about friendships and replace members with new ones. And, really, that's the cold, cruel reality of life, isn't it, no matter what occupation you may be in?

Derek approached the band and told us he was unhappy with Roger's bass playing. Right off the bat, Glenn Shorrock was opposed to sacking Roger. He disagreed vehemently with Derek. Glenn and Roger had become good friends early on. None of us had a personal problem with Roger because he really was a great guy. Personally, I never had a problem with Roger and would have carried on with him as our bass player. We were also friends.

Roger remembers it this way:

So what went wrong? Good question! I don't know who instigated me getting the flick from the band. I always suspected that it was Graeham, but maybe it was Derek not being happy. I guess the thing that pissed me off more than anything was the way it was handled.

Unbeknownst to me, while Glenn Shorrock and I were in Sydney doing promotion, the band was secretly checking out other bass players. If certain members of the band were not happy with my playing ability, no one ever came to me and mentioned it.

So out of the blue one day, when Glenn Shorrock and I were living in Peel Street, Prahran, I received a phone call from Glenn Wheatley telling me that my services were no longer required. Just like that, no warning, no face to face! I thought that was really weak and gutless, but hey, rock and roll is littered with stories like that. Glenn Shorrock was really pissed off and threatened to leave the band because we were really close...

I thought that some of the songs being presented at the time were just okay. So I was never inspired to whip out my bass and practise. In my mind I had it all covered. In hindsight, after hearing what George McArdle was into, I needed to re-evaluate. And that's just what I did, becoming the number one bass guitar session player in Melbourne and far surpassing the musical abilities of most of the former and later members of the band ... Given the opportunity to do it all again I would probably choose the same path because it made me the musician I am today. They were great days for me!

I spent many nights dropping around to Peel Street, Prahran where Roger and Glenn Shorrock were living. We'd all hang out and listen to the latest albums by artists and bands we loved. There was always some female company around. Peel Street may have been where I first met Jo Swan, who later married Glenn. I remember having some great times there.

Around the same time, Ric Formosa and Glenn Shorrock butted heads over issues that were more than just musical. Glenn's approach to show business comes from the very English working class form of entertaining and he treats it like a job.

Here's what Ric remembers:

I loved the band for the first year or so but it had sort of become the Glenn Shorrock cabaret show and I hated it. I was young, an idealist, in a hurry, and going places. I certainly didn't think or see myself as a little guitar player in Glenn's backing band.

Session work was starting to come in big time and I was much more interested in being in the studio, playing, writing arrangements and producing, rather than being on the road eating shit food, living out of a suitcase full of dirty clothes and playing the same solos every night, with Glenn dancing and tripping up drunk or stoned all over my pedals.

He's a sweet little old guy, and the odd time we have bumped into one another it's been all hugs and very emotional. I do like him a lot and have nice memories of our time together.

CHRISTIANITY

One evening, in May 1976, Narelle and Graeham, Megan and I were invited to attend a movie in a church on Punt Road in South Yarra not far from Toorak Road. I don't remember how the invitation was extended to us but quite a few people in the arts had been invited because I remember seeing Phil Manning, the guitar player from Chain, there as well.

The movie was called *The Road To Armageddon* and it was an adaptation of a book called *The Vision* by Reverend David Wilkerson, which was first published in 1974. David was better known for having written a book called *The Cross and the Switchblade*, a very popular book in Christian circles.

In *The Road To Armageddon*, Wilkerson said he had been subjected to three consecutive nights of visions he believed to be from God. In *The Vision*, his eyes were opened to see about 20 years into the world's future. Along with disturbing graphics, the movie talked about the coming oil crises, the shortage of food in African countries and other parts of the world, disease epidemics, gangs roaming the streets of some big cities, nudity and pornography in daily newspapers and magazines and on daytime television, plus many other dire predictions.

Forty years later, much of what Reverend Wilkerson predicted is accepted as the norm in today's society. We have slowly become conditioned to the world around us.

I sat through the whole movie and took it all in with interest but remained sceptical about all those things actually coming true. After it was over, the four of us drove back to Megan's parents' house in North Balwyn where we continued to discuss the movie. I had a wall up, not wanting to believe any of what we'd seen, and I stood my ground.

Graeham and Narelle did most of the talking that night. They could see the reality of David Wilkerson's predictions and, before the night was over, they had convinced me.

I went home to bed and slept as usual that night. When I woke the next morning, something had changed in me. I felt a peace I had never felt before and was very calm and relaxed. On that morning, I viewed the world through different eyes.

I stayed in that state of enlightenment for three days and then on the fourth day, when I woke, it was like, boom … I felt like I had been dropped back into my old shoes and was back to my old self.

In thinking this through, my reasoning told me that God had given me a taste of how great I could feel every day of my life but that it was up to me to elevate myself to that level. I thought I had to work at it to maintain that level of serenity.

On May 11, 1976, Little River Band flew to Brisbane. From there we drove to Toowoomba for the start of our national tour to promote *After Hours*. I know I wasn't imagining things because the guys in the band noticed that something had changed in me as well. They were bumping elbows as if to say, "Check Beeb out. What do you think is up with him?"

I will never forget one particular incident. When we drove to the motel in Toowoomba I got out of the rental car and started walking towards my room. Mick Lillie, our lighting guy, walked out of his room and greeted me. When he made eye contact, the words that came out of his mouth were, "Man, what have you been smoking?"

I was, in actual fact, as straight as a die. Yet he saw something in my eyes. He noticed something was different about me.

On that fourth day in Toowoomba, when I was back to my old self, I walked straight to the nearest bookshop. I said to the salesperson that I wanted to buy a Bible in today's English. I wanted to read the Bible in a language I could understand.

After three or four years of searching and reading books on Eastern religions, mysticism and reincarnation, I decided there was only one spiritual path left for me to pursue. Good, old-fashioned Christianity!

The salesperson recommended *The Living Bible*. I bought it and read it from cover to cover in a matter of days but it didn't mean all that much to me. The words didn't jump off the page to enlighten me any further; in fact, I found parts of the Bible extremely tedious and boring.

The important thing, however, was that this was the start of my life as a Christian. The three days of enlightenment were such an amazing and powerful experience that it made me a believer in the trinity.

I believe in God, Jesus Christ and the Holy Spirit. Christianity makes total sense to me. Knowing what I know now, I believe that those three days of enlightenment were what Christians call the 'born again' experience. It was my spiritual birth.

If you believe that we are created mind, body and spirit, I personally believe that your spirit can lie dormant in you until it is awakened. God won't interfere in our lives because he gives us free will to choose. This is something that people who are not 'born again' find difficult to understand and accept.

Many people also have a problem accepting Jesus' birth as the immaculate conception. Either you believe it or you think it's a load of crap. Unless you have experienced rebirth for yourself, it's extremely hard to convince people that Jesus is the way, the truth and the life.

It's the same as when people have a problem with accepting the Bible as the word of God. Please understand I am only speaking from my own experience here. For me, it was like striking gold, I had found the mother lode.

From that time on, I dived exclusively into the Bible and other books written by Christian authors. It opened up a whole new world for me. I couldn't get enough of learning more about this great new discovery of mine.

Megan and I were living in Maud Street, North Balwyn at the time and I was so excited and keen to share this incredible revelation with her but she remained aloof and didn't show any interest.

That didn't deter me however, because with every book I read I was applying those principles to my life. I didn't go to church and maybe I wasn't even a praying man yet, but it was the start of an incredible spiritual journey for me.

For the rest of my time in Little River Band I was full-on into my Christian faith. The guys in the band were clueless as to how much I learned from them over the next seven years by applying my Christian teachings. I was learning principles beyond what their understanding of Christianity was.

The problem with human beings believing in Christianity is that the mind or the intellect gets in the way. In the same way I put a wall up when confronted by David Wilkerson's predictions in *The Vision*, people put up a wall with believing in Jesus. After experiencing what I experienced, I don't question it – I just accept it.

Eleven
LITTLE RIVER BAND — PHASE TWO

LRB 2ND LINEUP: GEORGE MCARDLE, DEREK PELLICCI, DAVID BRIGGS, GLENN SHORROCK, BEEB BIRTLES, GRAEHAM GOBLE

The majority vote in the band was for Roger to go, with Ric choosing to leave at the same time, so we had to find replacements for both of them. We started holding auditions at Crystal Clear Studios in South Melbourne. Phil Manning was one of the guys we auditioned but we felt he wasn't right for us. At the time, David Briggs was playing in a funk band with some younger musicians and I think we went to see him play before asking him to audition.

In the same band, George McArdle was an inventive young bass player with a thumb-slap style of playing that he'd learned from his idol, America's Stanley Clarke. David and George auditioned for us at the same time and we were immediately impressed with both of them.

We really had our work cut out for us. We had two weeks to work the guys into the band before our first scheduled overseas tour. We rehearsed as much and as often as we could.

George McArdle:

Yeah, that was quite a change for me being in such a high profile band, playing with all these guys that were my heroes. There I was playing with them and knowing that in a couple of weeks I'd be touring Europe.

The band flew to Europe, where the tour kicked off in West Germany, supporting The Hollies. You can imagine how excited I was! Even though Graham Nash was no longer with them, they were still the band I had imitated for most of my early music years. I had every one of their albums in my record collection. Now Little River Band was sharing the stage with them.

The Hollies were still a great band playing all of their hit songs. Terry

Sylvester was singing all of Graham Nash's high harmonies. They were really nice guys as well and we'd talk with them at the various hotels we shared.

Throughout my entire career, I've always been a big fan of Graham Nash and have compared myself to him. I think we have somewhat similar voices. It's Graham's cutting voice that gave The Hollies and Crosby, Stills & Nash their distinctive harmony sound. In the same way, I think it was my voice that gave Little River Band its unique harmony sound.

After playing in Europe for a couple of weeks, we flew to the States. Our agent, John Marx, worked his butt off trying to book us as the support for some of the popular bands at the time. Our very first US show was at Madison University in Harrisonburg, Virginia, in front of about 5000 college kids. We were the opening act for the Average White Band, a fantastic Scottish band. At the time they had a huge hit with an instrumental called 'Cut The Cake'.

The tour was a mixed bag of clubs, small theatres and big concert stages, depending on where John Marx booked us. One night we'd be on stage in front of 5000 college kids, and the next night we might be in a small club that held no more than 200 people. I remember playing at The Childe Harold restaurant and saloon in Washington DC with the Sanford-Townsend Band. What a great band those guys were! They had a big hit with a song called 'Smoke From A Distant Fire'.

In those early days of touring the US, we rented hire cars and flew everywhere. We spent hours and hours in airports, either waiting to catch flights or waiting for the rental cars to pull around to pick us up. I was always one of the designated drivers.

We also spent quite a bit of time getting directions to hotels where we were staying. In the beginning, we shared rooms: two guys in one hotel room. I dreaded having to share with Shorrock because he snored so loudly. You may have the impression we were successful right from the start in the US, but in reality we all put up with a lot of shit. We were learning as we went along.

Overall, it was a pretty tough tour because we were away from home for more than three months. The band was determined to make it in America. What helped tremendously was we were all willing to do radio interviews and television appearances and as much press as we could get.

The Capitol Records reps fell in love with the band because we were so easy to work with. As opposed to some of the egocentric American acts who couldn't be bothered doing radio interviews and making television appearances, we were always ready to accommodate. So right from the beginning, the guys at Capitol Records worked harder for us. We became the darlings of the record company.

In Jacksonville, Florida there was a radio program director named Bill Bartlett. He programmed WPDQ-FM and WAIV Radio. He had a real passion for Australian rock and roll bands and played their records on his FM station. Bill played 'It's A Long Way There' in its entirety, which ignited a college following for us throughout the South East region.

In fact, Little River Band broke out of Jacksonville, Florida. The band was immensely popular there and sold out shows in a matter of hours. It was from there that the fire spread throughout the rest of America. Bill's radio station was also responsible for the introduction of AC/DC and Skyhooks to American audiences, and Jacksonville became a magnet for Australian music.

When we returned to Australia in mid December 1976, after having been gone twelve weeks, we were $70,000 in the red from that first world tour. Capitol Records picked up the tab and advanced us the money against our royalties. That's how much they believed in the band. They knew that eventually we would start making money from our tours.

DIAMANTINA COCKTAIL

Having survived the recording of *After Hours*, and with David Briggs and George McArdle now firmly entrenched in our lineup, it was decided that we needed a producer for our next album. We hired John Boylan, an American producer who had worked with Linda Ronstadt and a bluegrass band called The Dillards. John was friends with the guys in the Eagles and had attended the same college as Steely Dan's Donald Fagen and Walter Becker.

Funnily enough, I had the two Dillards albums that John produced in my record collection from when I was listening to bluegrass and country rock. Later on, he also produced the bands Boston and Quarterflash, who had a worldwide hit with 'Harden My Heart'. John flew out to Australia and we started work on *Diamantina Cocktail*, our third studio album.

Once again we took over AAV in South Melbourne with Ross Cockle as our recording engineer. We now had another songwriter in our midst with the addition of David Briggs. David contributed 'LA In The Sunshine'.

At rehearsal one day, David was playing some chords and I said to him, "I really like the sound of those chords. How do you play them?" He showed me the two chords and I took them away with me and wrote the bulk of 'Happy Anniversary'. When I needed a middle eight for the song I went back to David and we finished the song together. I love the middle eight in that song. I remember triple tracking my falsetto vocals to get that sound you hear on the record.

Glenn Shorrock had written 'Help Is On Its Way' back in his days with MAM. We were still catching up on songs that had been presented for our very first album. Glenn also wrote 'Home On Monday', for which I came up with the music for the middle eight.

We were all disappointed with the way the Witchery chain of shops hadn't used our jingle to its fullest advantage, so we resurrected it and Graeham and I wrote another verse to turn it into a three-minute song.

Graeham also contributed 'The Inner Light', 'Changed and Different' and 'The Drifter'. I wrote 'Raelene, Raelene' about Raelene Milne who I met when I shared the flat with Nanette and Jill Coffen in Balaclava … I was heavily influenced by David Crosby at the time and the song's mood reflects that in the chord changes and the melody.

I reconnected with Raelene in Sydney when the band was performing at the Bondi Lifesaver and we started the relationship I had always wanted to have with her. But it didn't go anywhere because of my guilt at the time. I didn't have the balls to end my relationship with Megan and give that up to be with Raelene full time.

Months later, Raelene and I met for dinner in Sydney and she confronted me about this. I felt really terrible that I had hurt her by not staying in contact every time the band returned to Melbourne. I don't remember Megan ever commenting on 'Raelene, Raelene', and if she suspected something had been going on, she never let me know.

Even though John Boylan was the producer, most of the song arrangements still came from within the band. John was instrumental with influencing us with the acoustic guitars on 'Help Is On Its Way', introducing us to Nashville tuning.

Nashville tuning is when you take the higher set of strings on a twelve-string guitar and string them separately on a small body acoustic but keep the high tuning the same. Musicians use this tuning as a way to split the sound of a twelve-string guitar. Both the higher tuning and the regular tuning can then be panned to the left or the right in a stereo mix. Tricks of the trade, you might say.

Graeham Goble:
'Help Is On Its Way' ended up being a very clever song because it's in so many different keys. It changes around a lot and it's a real challenge to do that. I think it's one of the best LRB songs we've ever done because of the lyric and the melody. It's a fabulous song.

From the high harmony point of view it's pretty hard to sing in concert because it's up there all the time, but it's got a great lyric and a great message.

George McArdle:
Glenn started playing a little upright piano in the corner of a room backstage at some venue in the US and I had my bass around my neck with a little practice amp and started playing that bass line. Everybody just thought, "Hey, this sounds quite good." It's amazing that someone with such a voice could also be so good at writing songs but he had so many strings to his bow.

'Help Is On Its Way' was released as the first single from *Diamantina Cocktail* and became our only number one in Australia. In all, four singles were released from the album: 'Help Is On Its Way', 'Witchery', 'Happy Anniversary' and 'Home On Monday'. The album went gold and eventually double platinum in Australia and it also went gold in New Zealand. 'Help Is On Its Way' was voted Australian Record of the Year. Glenn Shorrock was voted Best Australian Songwriter, while the band was voted Best Australian International Performers at the King of Pop Awards.

But now we ran into a problem with Capitol Records regarding the release of our second album in the US. They had been living with *After Hours* and didn't think the album was strong enough. They also felt the same way about *Diamantina Cocktail*. So they suggested taking the best songs from each album and coming up with an American version of *Diamantina Cocktail*.

The band agreed, and Capitol chose 'Days On The Road', 'Another Runway', 'Everyday Of My Life', 'Broke Again' and 'Take Me Home' from *After Hours* and 'Help Is On Its Way', 'Happy Anniversary', 'Home On Monday' and 'The Inner Light' from *Diamantina Cocktail*. We trusted Capitol with knowing the record buying market as well as radio.

When the album was released in the US, we took off on the road. We were gone from May until October 1977, promoting it all around the world. Our time away from home paid off with *Diamantina Cocktail* becoming the first album by an Australian band to go gold in the US, an achievement that made us all very proud.

People ask me all the time what life on the road was like and how I handled it. "Didn't you hate living out of a suitcase for all those years?"

No, I didn't. I didn't hate it because I kept myself occupied. I always had a pair of running shoes, running shorts and workout T-shirts with me. Whenever we arrived at the hotel or motel, I'd take off for a 45-minute run. It was my way of staying fit on the road. And if I wasn't working on a new song, I would write long handwritten letters back home to family and friends.

The majority of our tours were during the American summer and if we weren't required to do newspaper or radio interviews we'd lay out by the pool and boost our tans until it was time to head off to sound check. Most of the time we would stay at the venue after sound check and wait to go on that night.

On our rare nights off, we'd ask the concierge at the hotel where the best restaurant was and a group of us would go and have a really nice dinner together. Sometimes, Capitol Records would take us all out to dinner. I never had a problem being on the road, travelling all over the world, a different city just about every day. I took it all in my stride. I was living my dream.

SLEEPER CATCHER

In 1978 we recorded the *Sleeper Catcher* album, which I consider to be the peak of our recording career. Some of the guys in the band feel it was *First Under The Wire*, but, to me, all the songs on *Sleeper Catcher* were strong and vocally it was our best. John Boylan was again the producer and this time both Ross Cockle and Ernie Rose engineered the recordings in the AAV studios.

Ernie was someone I had known and respected for years, going back to the days of Armstrong Studios on Albert Road when Zoot recorded there. He was also the recording engineer and co-producer of the Mississippi album with Peter Jones who played piano. On the road, Ern was our out-front sound guy.

We had just finished recording the basic track for 'Fall From Paradise' when I bumped into Marc Hunter from Dragon. I was a fan of their music and had gone to one of their shows at the Dallas Brooks Hall in Melbourne. We knew each other through the music business.

I pulled him into the studio A control room and said, "You've got to hear this." We played him the bare bones track that consisted of drums, bass, electric guitar and piano, and it totally blew him away. He said he couldn't wait to hear the finished track.

The highlight of *Sleeper Catcher* for me is how Glenn, Graeham and I sang some of our best backing vocals on just about every song that was recorded. In particular, 'Fall From Paradise' and Glenn Shorrock's 'Sanity's Side' have some great backing vocals, not forgetting 'Lady' and 'Reminiscing'.

I knew Ed Nimmervoll through doing interviews with him for various music magazines he worked at. From working at *Go-Set* he knew Glenys Long, a redhead who was very well known throughout the music industry. It came as a complete shock to the industry when Glenys took her own life. Because of their close working relationship at *Go-Set*, Ed wrote a set of lyrics titled 'Red-Headed Wild Flower'. I had known Glenys for all my years living in Melbourne, going back to the Zoot days. We often visited the *Go-Set* offices for interviews. I took Ed's lyrics and wrote the melody and music to fit his words for 'Red-Headed Wild Flower'. It turned out to be a very powerful song on the *Sleeper Catcher* album and a very fitting tribute to the lovely Glenys.

I also remember that Ernie Rose, Graeham and I did the mixing for *Sleeper Catcher*. To me, it was the most perfect album we had recorded to date.

Graeham told me he had written 'Reminiscing' on April 9, 1977. I'm not surprised that our two biggest-selling singles in the US, 'Reminiscing' and 'Lady', were on this album. 'Reminiscing' reached our highest chart position in *Billboard* at number three and has been played more than five million times on American radio.

I recall being in the studio when Bobby Venier blew his flugelhorn solo at the end of 'Reminiscing'. He said, "Play the track for me and I'll just warm up before you record it." Ernie Rose opened a track for him and hit the record button. What you hear on the record is what Bob blew on his very first take.

We pressed the talkback button and said, "Thanks Bobby, that was great."

"Oh come on, guys, I was just warming up. Give me another shot at it!"

We opened up another track and gave him a couple more tries but what he blew was never as magic as that very first take. Bob is a phenomenal musician.

'Lady' was a song that Graeham presented for our very first album and every album after that until it was finally recorded for *Sleeper Catcher*. I'm a big believer in songs finding their own time. It reached number six on the *Billboard* charts and outsold 'Reminiscing' as a single. So far, 'Lady' has received more than four million airplays in the US.

George McArdle:

You can spend months rehearsing and fine-tuning a song. Changing it, pulling it apart, being told by the other guys we hate what you're doing. You get the opportunity to rework it over and over again and that's the beauty of being in a band. When you're with hired guns you don't have that luxury. And 'Lady' was one of those songs that I think benefited a lot from the fact it was a band song.

After recording the album, the band was struck by tragedy. Derek Pellicci,

Ernie Rose, the DJ Barry Bissell and some of our road crew got together for a barbecue. It was really just an excuse to play Beatles music all day. Derek left the gathering around 4 p.m. to visit his father who was in the Alfred Hospital, and when he returned to the barbecue he was hungry and wanted something to eat.

The coals in the barbecue were already dying but Ernie went over with a bottle of methylated spirits and proceeded to pour it onto the coals. He must have held it too close because the flames shot up into the bottle and exploded away from him, across the yard and squarely onto Derek's chest. Derek caught on fire, panicked and started running. The worst thing he could have done.

Jomo (John Money), our stage manager at the time, rugby tackled Derek to the ground and Barry Bissell grabbed a blanket and wrapped Derek in it to extinguish the flames. But by then it was too late and Derek had third-degree burns all over his body. He was admitted to the Alfred Hospital Burns Unit, not far from where his father was.

The first time I went to visit he was tragic to see. His face had blown up and was as round as the moon from his body reacting to the burns. But Derek put on a brave face and was his usual chirpy self.

Obviously, he couldn't join us for the *Sleeper Catcher* tour. We enlisted the services of Geoff Cox on drums to fill Derek's shoes. We all knew Geoff when he was the drummer in the Bootleg Family Band and later a band called Avalanche. When Derek was well enough to join us on the road he played percussion while Geoff played drums. Geoff wasn't the drummer Derek was and I couldn't wait for Derek to be back on the road with us permanently. It was a traumatic thing for him to go through and he still bears the scars of his burns today.

Once again we toured extensively to promote the album around the world. During these months, we supported Jimmy Buffet at The Queen Elizabeth Theatre in Vancouver, Canada. He was very cool and gracious and had a huge following. He personally walked out on stage before our set and said something like, "You guys are in for a real treat tonight. This is a new band from Australia and they are going to blow your socks off." The crowd went nuts and made us feel right at home.

Along the way, we played shows with the likes of Little Feat, The Doobie Brothers, Heart, John Mayall, Bob Seger, Firefall, Dickey Betts, Supertramp, Dave Mason, Poco, America and Foreigner. At the Arrowhead Stadium in Kansas City, at one of those all day and night rock festivals, we supported Ted Nugent, REO Speedwagon and Edgar Winter.

We flew to England to perform at the Reading Festival where we supported Thin Lizzy and Aerosmith. Then more shows in the States with Dan Fogelberg, Derringer and Jean-Luc Ponty. The gruelling touring schedule was getting to George McArdle, who was becoming more and more disillusioned with life on the road. He was searching for something deeper in his life that fame and fortune couldn't give him.

George's birthday is two days after mine and I always treated him like the younger brother I never had. For his birthday that year, Graeham and I gave him a Bible. It was probably the worst thing we could have done because at the end of all the touring for *Sleeper Catcher* George announced he was leaving the group.

In George's book, *The Man From Little River*, he says it was a conflict for him to continue playing in a secular band, quoting the words from 'Witchery'.

I've heard of your good deeds
and I know about your needs, little demon
Excite me with your charms you long to put your arms around me
You cast your spell on me and it's plain to see
It's witchery, it's got me, witchery, it's got you

To me, the lyrics in the song were just playful words about a love affair. And let's face it, there wasn't much I could do about the title considering the original use of the song was as a jingle for a nationwide chain of stores named Witchery. Yes, Graeham and I had given George a Bible for his birthday but we also wrote that song! I think at this stage of his life George was very confused.

George McArdle:
They asked me why I wanted to leave, so I began to explain everything that

had happened to me since my encounter with God at home. I said I wanted to study the Bible and that I believed there was some particular job that God wanted me to do. Nobody stormed out in anger but there was a tangible aloofness which settled over the room.

After the story was finished, one by one the band members stood up and walked out. Eventually, nobody was left except me and the accountant, who actually asked me to tell him more about my experiences.

I believe that George had an incredible God-given talent to play bass but he decided not to continue using that talent as part of Little River Band. He had also recently bought his first house in Parkville and the band was starting to earn some serious money and he chose to give it all away. He gave away his house and all his money and enrolled in a Bible College in Katoomba in the Blue Mountains. George remains a very strong Christian believer to this day.

This is where I have a problem with Christians and certain churches. Why is it they want to keep you within the four walls of Christianity as if it's us against the world? I don't believe that's what Christ taught. How can you be an example to the world if you stay within those four walls?

I wrote a letter once to CCM (Contemporary Christian Magazine) when Christians were writing in, saying they were spinning vinyl records backwards to listen for hidden satanic messages. I commented on how ridiculous this was. First of all, record players are made to spin clockwise, and secondly, if you go looking for trouble you'll find it. Use your common sense. I'm not the kind of Christian who prays for a parking place when I'm needing one. I think that's taking it a bit far.

THE GURU

Sometime during the first three years of Little River Band, Allison and Glenn Wheatley and Narelle and Graeham Goble found out about a guy from New Zealand who was kind of like the Maharishi Mahesh Yogi. His name was John Wilson and he lived up in the Dandenongs, just outside Melbourne, where they went to see him at weekends, to be 'in his presence', so to speak.

'The Guru' claimed he could read people's spiritual meters. If your spiritual reading was not above a certain level, it would be a waste of his time to see you. I think my girlfriend Megan may have gone to see him once as well because her spiritual reading was above the acceptable level.

Anyway, they were all really into Mr Guru and would do just about anything he told them. My spiritual reading wasn't high enough to be seen by 'the enlightened one' but, then, I was fully locked into my Christian beliefs.

So at weekends they'd go to his spiritual retreat in the Dandenongs and spend hours and hours weeding his veggie patch while waiting for The Guru to decide who he would and would not see that day. They must have thought the sun shone out of his arse to wait all that time for a possible word from the holy one.

I don't know why, but for some reason Graeham kept me in the loop. He told me everything The Guru was telling them. They asked him about anything and everything they wanted to know. When both Glenn and Graeham were looking at buying property in the Victorian countryside, they turned to The Guru for 'spiritual guidance' as to where they should buy. They even paid for him to charter a flight in a small plane to fly over certain areas until The Guru pointed out the properties to be bought.

He advised the Wheatleys to buy land in Diggers Rest and they bought twenty acres. Graeham and Narelle bought fifteen acres in Glenburn, near the town of Yea. Later, Graeham and Narelle bought another fifteen acres adjoining this property. This is where they planned to build their dream home.

On one of Little River Band's tours to Adelaide, I showed Graeham my parents' new house. After selling our family home in Harvey Avenue, they bought a very steep block of land in Eden Hills that had an amazing panoramic view of Adelaide. At night, the lights of Adelaide made the view even more spectacular. Dad built a fabulous new house for himself and my mother.

Graeham was very impressed with my dad's craftsmanship and asked him to build a house on their property in Glenburn. By then, Little River Band was well on its way to success and we were all starting to make money from record sales and songwriting royalties. Dad was getting older and work in Adelaide was starting to dry up so he accepted Graeham's offer.

Every time we were back in Adelaide, Graeham and my dad would pore over the plans for Graeham and Narelle's dream house. Dad estimated it was going to take nine months to build. My parents rented out their Eden Hills house and came to live in Melbourne. As Glenburn is about 70 km from the city, they decided to find accommodation somewhere close to Graeham's property. They ended up living in some kind of shed or outbuilding on a property belonging to one of Graeham's neighbours.

It wasn't going to be an easy job because Graeham wanted a sixty-degree pitch on the roofline. Structurally this was going to be difficult because he wanted a slate roof and that would make it very heavy. Graeham wanted the best material for every part of the house.

Dad called on the best tradesmen he knew in Adelaide and started building. After the foundation was poured, a Dutch bricklayer friend of his came over from Adelaide and started laying bricks. It was going to be an amazing house, but the project became a frustrating task for my father because Graeham constantly kept making changes. It drove my father nuts because it kept extending the time for completing the house!

They didn't end up on good terms, because what should have taken nine months ended up taking a year. My father demanded more money from Graeham for the extra time. Graeham refused, saying he and my father had an agreement, but Dad said if he didn't get another $5000 he would go around and break every window in the house.

I remember the distraught phone call from Graeham but all I could say was, "Hey, this is between you and my dad, nothing to do with me."

When the house was finished, my parents were so burned out they took off to Queensland for a well-deserved holiday.

Glenn Wheatley was the first one to bail on the Guru saying, "I'm up there weeding his fucking veggie patch for hours and hours on end, not knowing whether he will see me while I'm there? I don't think so!" And that was the end of the holy man from New Zealand. Eventually, the

Wheatleys sold their twenty acres in Diggers Rest and bought a property named 'Wynkara' on some acreage in Lower Plenty.

Graeham and Narelle named their property 'Serendipity' and continued to pour thousands of dollars into it. As well as buying the extra fifteen acres, they built a graded swimming pool you could walk into from the shallow end to the deep end. They had professional tennis courts built, complete with lights, and landscaped the area around their big house. They planted established trees and paved the road up to the house.

By the time it was all finished they'd poured more than a million dollars into it. Elisha, their first daughter, had already been born and they lived in the house for maybe a couple of years at most. Then, one day, Narelle put her foot down and said she didn't want to live there anymore because she felt too isolated from her friends in Melbourne. Narelle was a very simple girl at heart. She didn't need much to be happy. She actually preferred living in their small house in Elsternwick that they had as their city home.

They decided to put Serendipity on the market, but who was going to pay that kind of money for a high-priced mansion that far from the city? They ended up virtually giving the house away for a little over $300,000, a mere pittance. A butcher, who owned a slaughterhouse in Seymour, made it his family home.

Life lesson number four — don't take real estate advice from a Kiwi Guru who claims he knows how to read your spiritual meter and gets you to work in his veggie patch for free.

Twelve
DONNA MARIE BRUCKS

Donna Marie Brucks

The first time I laid eyes on Donna Brucks was when Little River Band played at The Performing Arts Theatre at the Aladdin Hotel in Las Vegas on June 18, 1978. She was on the arm of Mark Holden who was living in Los Angeles at the time. He was under contract to the Scotti Brothers label.

I remember exactly what she looked like, even though there was no immediate attraction between us. Mark might have introduced her to me that night, though I don't remember. She was on the arm of another man, so I paid no attention. All I knew was that she worked as John Marx's assistant at Headquarters, Little River Band's booking agency in LA. Mark was also signed to Headquarters and that's how he met Donna.

About five months earlier, Donna had decided to pack up and leave St Louis, where she had been living, and move to Los Angeles. In St Louis she had been in a relationship with a guy for six years who didn't do right by her. One day, she'd had enough and told him she was leaving. Donna's father helped pack her stuff and they drove all the way to Los Angeles together, where she rented an apartment just off Sunset Boulevard on Sweetzer Avenue.

A few years later I wrote a song about Donna moving to LA but I called it 'Lucy', probably because Lucy Martin's name was still fresh in my mind. Lucy is the daughter of Judy and George Martin who I met on Montserrat when George produced Little River Band's *Time Exposure* album.

Donna had more to do with our road crew than the guys in the band. Being from Australia we always needed extra equipment because of the voltage difference between the two countries. She always went out of her way to accommodate our road crew whenever they needed something.

It wasn't until July 23 that I saw her again. Little River Band was performing at the Summer Jam 2 concert at the Cotton Bowl in Dallas. It was a stinking hot Texas day. One hundred thousand people turned up to see Fleetwood Mac, the Steve Miller Band, Little River Band, Bob Welch and Billy Thorpe. Billy had just completed recording his *Children of the Sun* album.

Our road crew asked the band if we would pay for Donna to fly out for the concert. It was a week before her birthday and it was the crew's way of saying thank you for going the extra mile. The band agreed, and we flew her and John Marx from Los Angeles to Dallas.

I was in a particularly good mood that day and was being a bit silly in the green room. Derek Pellicci always called me Beebola and because of my love for cheese, being Dutch and all, he would say things like, "More cheesola for Beebola." Part of our rider at every gig was the standard cheese and crackers platter. I was mimicking Derek's phrase that day when Donna walked in with John Marx. I was being silly, really, showing off.

The concert was spectacular that day and the band was in top form. After the show, a bunch of us ended up going to a club called The Bellringer for a few drinks. Geoff Cox was with us, as he was sitting in for Derek who was still recuperating from his barbecue accident.

We were all hanging around the bar, when this guy kept asking Donna to dance. He said he was a pilot and flew some flights for Qantas, which might have been true because he was wearing a Qantas tie.

He was very persistent and wouldn't take no for an answer, even though he could see there was a group of us. Donna probably egged him on by saying that she'd consider dancing with him if she could have his tie. The guy whipped off his tie and gave it to her and continued to ask her to dance. She kept telling him she didn't dance.

The thought that Donna was very attractive had already entered my mind that day and I butted in and said, "Listen, can't you hear what my wife is saying? She doesn't want to dance with you, pal!" He took the hint and left her alone.

Our very short time together was enough to pique my interest. Donna and John Marx flew back to Los Angeles the next day while Little River Band continued on the road. I wanted to see her again and started calling her every day, no matter where I was.

Every time I called I tried to talk her into flying out to meet me on the road. Her answer was always, "Look, don't play with my heart. You're in a rock and roll band and you probably have girls in various cities across the country and I'm not prepared to fly out for a one night stand."

True, there were girls in various cities, but I kept calling her every day. I loved the sound of her voice and she was so easy to talk to.

A few weeks went by and the band was scheduled to perform in Nashville, Tennessee. We were there for three days but only had one show. Graeham and I didn't want to sit around and do nothing for two days so we asked Glenn Wheatley to book us into a studio to record some demos of new songs we'd written.

He booked us into The Goldmine, a studio in the basement of Chris Christian's house in Brentwood. The same Chris Christian who was a member of Cotton, Lloyd and Christian with Darryl Cotton in the mid-70s. 'I'm Coming Home' was one of the songs we recorded during those two days.

Chris was teaching his friend, Brown Bannister, a church youth leader, how to operate a recording console. Brown was the recording engineer for our demo sessions.

A couple of times during those two days a young girl would stop by after school and she and Brown would disappear behind some sound baffles. I guessed they were kissing and cuddling. I didn't think anything of it but I later found out she was a young contemporary Christian singer named Amy Grant. She was about eighteen at the time. Brown would go on to produce Amy's first 12 albums.

By now I was getting the message that Donna wasn't going to fly to meet me anywhere. The couple of days in the studio stopped my calls to her. I remember Little River Band's performance at the Municipal Auditorium in Nashville was a particularly good one. We continued on the tour and I stopped calling Donna altogether.

We played shows in Memphis, Chattanooga, Miami and Orlando. And then we flew up to Toronto, Canada to perform at the CNE Stadium as support to the Eagles. Something happened and we couldn't get a commercial flight, so we chartered a private jet.

After our performance, the Canadian Capitol Records reps arranged for us to watch the Eagles from behind the glass in a private booth at the far end of the stadium. We stood there and heard them perform songs from their latest album, *Hotel California*. It was also in Toronto that Derek Pellicci flew in and surprised us after recuperating from his barbecue accident. From Toronto we flew back to the US where our next scheduled show was in Boston, Massachusetts. We were back on our tour buses.

Remember this was back in the days of handwritten letters from loved ones back home. Every week, either Glenn Wheatley or Stephen White, our tour manager, met us on the bus and handed us our mail from home. Phoning home was expensive and therefore many letters were written back and forth.

On this particular day in Boston, I was handed a huge oversized envelope wrapped in brown packing paper and I remember thinking that it must have cost a small fortune to send something that size from Australia.

There was no return address and nothing was written on the outside of the envelope except my name. I was truly intrigued. I tore the brown paper off and found a large poster board, and there in big letters was written the words:

CALL ME, YOU FUCKER!

I knew immediately who had sent the poster. All I could do was smile. After checking into my room, I called Donna and we picked up from where we left off. I said, "Look, we're going to be in St Louis in a few days after playing Chicago. I'll pay for you to fly to St Louis if you want to meet me there."

Donna was born in Jefferson City, the capital of Missouri, about two hours from St Louis. She agreed to meet me because, in the back of her mind, she was thinking she'd get to see her family if I paid for her to fly there.

I was really looking forward to seeing her again, so while we were in Chicago I bought a beautiful bottle of L'Air du Temps perfume by Nina Ricci. By the time she arrived at Stouffer's Riverfront Towers in downtown St Louis I was at our sound check but I had strategically left the perfume sitting in the middle of the bed in my hotel room.

You know… Donna never made it to Jefferson City to see her family! She did, however, stay on the road with me for a few days. John Marx had to cover for her with his bosses at International Creative Management (ICM), where they both now worked.

It couldn't have been more than ten days before I asked Donna to marry me. And without any hesitation whatsoever she said yes!

I was in a bit of a predicament at the time because I was engaged to Megan in Australia. I even had a wedding suit made in London for the occasion. I had also asked John Marx to scope out wedding rings for me to look at in LA. All these things now had to be undone once I arrived back home in Australia.

The six years of my relationship with Megan had been up and down because of our periods of arguing and not speaking. More than a few people who knew us had observed that about us. I was also away a lot during the years with Mississippi and early Little River Band and I'm sure neither one of us was faithful to the other during those stretches of time.

I found it so easy and effortless to be around Donna. We fitted like a glove. I hadn't known it was possible to feel so comfortable with someone in the way I felt with Donna. I couldn't help but compare the two relationships and it was obvious what I had to do.

From the time I met Donna, my communication with Megan came to a standstill. I'm sure she suspected that something was wrong but I didn't think it was right to tell her over the phone that I had met someone else. I felt the decent thing to do was to tell her face to face.

The band performed in Bakersfield, California and then we were in Los Angeles for three days before flying up to Vancouver in Canada. Donna flew up to meet me. This time she stayed with me for all of our shows down the west coast. We played Seattle and Spokane in Washington, Medford and Portland in Oregon and then back to Los Angeles. On the way back to Australia we had one performance in Hawaii and another in Auckland, New Zealand.

Donna and I were head over heels in love and I told her to follow me back to Australia in three weeks. She had to give up her apartment and sell some of her belongings before she was free to follow me.

I will never forget driving to LAX the day we left. I was in a rental car with some of the guys in the band and Donna was driving her grey Mercedes sedan. At times she would pull alongside our car; we'd make eye contact and I could see the tears streaming down her face.

Donna wasn't sure if she would ever see me again because of what awaited me in Melbourne. But I stayed true to my word, and three weeks later she arrived in Melbourne.

Oh boy, I knew it was going to be messy when I arrived home, but at the same time I knew I had to go through with it. Megan wasn't at Tullamarine Airport to meet me. I think I caught a cab back to my house in North Balwyn. All I had with me was my suitcase and a couple of electric guitars I had bought on the tour.

On entering the house, Megan greeted me and was excited to show me what she had done to the house while I was away. In our master bedroom she had a wooden platform built for our mattress and an abstract design of some tree branches painted on the walls. It all looked fabulous but it meant nothing to me because my heart was no longer there (remember that phrase, 'My heart was no longer there', for a later chapter).

We walked back down to the living room and I pulled out one of my electric guitars and sat there playing it for about half an hour. It took me that long to muster up the courage to tell Megan that I had met someone else and that I wouldn't be staying at the house, not even for one night. She put up a brave front and accepted what I said, showing no signs of emotion.

As soon as I said what I had to say I didn't stick around. I called a cab and drove around to the Wheatleys' place. They were minding someone's house a couple of streets away.

Everything I owned I left in the house I had bought on Panoramic Road, North Balwyn. All I walked away with was my suitcase and the two electric guitars I had with me. It would take me four years to get my house back.

I didn't realise it at the time but it was like I had dropped a bomb on the Tudor family. Every photo of Megan and me was returned, torn into little pieces. Her mother, Jean, wrote me the nastiest and meanest letter and Donna and I received a not very nice phone call from her father, Ron.

I completely understood what they were going through. This time it was Megan who had her heart broken and her parents were just being protective. I knew exactly how Megan felt because I had gone through the same thing when she broke up with me for those couple of months. My breakup with Megan, however, was permanent. I had met the one and only true love of my life.

Thirteen
LITTLE RIVER BAND — PHASE THREE

LRB lineup minus George McArdle

The band had returned from touring around the world on the success of *Sleeper Catcher*, which produced our two biggest hit singles to date, 'Reminiscing' and 'Lady'. We were starting to become the headliners for most of the shows we played, but we were back in Australia and it was time to think about recording the next studio album.

IT'S A LONG WAY THERE — GREATEST HITS

Between the recording of *Sleeper Catcher* and *First Under The Wire*, EMI Australia released *It's A Long Way There – Greatest Hits*, which bought us a bit of extra time between recording studio albums. The album sold platinum in Australia and double platinum in New Zealand.

FIRST UNDER THE WIRE

It was time for us to record a new studio album, and once again we hired John Boylan to produce the project. This time we recorded the entire album in studio A at AAV with Ernie Rose as our main recording engineer and Jim Barton, Ross Cockle and Ian McKenzie as the assistant engineers.

We enlisted the services of session musician bass players Mike Clarke and Clive Harrison to replace George McArdle. As good as Mike and Clive were, the gap George left was almost impossible to fill because of his unique style of playing. He was sorely missed for the recording of *First Under The Wire*.

The album produced David Briggs' finest composition to date, 'Lonesome Loser'. It became a huge hit for the band, reaching number six on the *Billboard* charts.

Graeham Goble:

A song like 'Lonesome Loser' can be a really difficult song to do but it's one of our biggest hits. It's the only song we received a Grammy nomination for. It was for the vocal performance. David always said he was going to write a big hit song for us and he did it.

I used to always wanna pitch our songs as high as we possibly could because you get more energy and more power in the vocals. I think the difference between the way we approached vocals to say a group like the Eagles is that I think we sing harder, a bit like The Hollies. They sing pretty hard as well.

To get the power in the vocals when you go into the recording studio, we put them in the highest key and sang as high as we could because you can do that in the studio. But then when it comes to live performing, after you've done like seven shows in a row and you have to get out and do it again, it's pretty tough. When we started doing 'Lonesome Loser' live, we used to place it towards the end of our set, but then we realised we had to do it in the first four or five songs, just so our voices could do the song justice.

I remember triple-tracking the choruses in 'Lonesome Loser' so what you're hearing is nine voices together. Back in those days there was no 'flying' the choruses in like they do now. Today's technology allows you to sing a harmony chorus one time if the lyrics are the same and then the chorus is 'flown' in — in other words, copied and pasted — to where the other choruses are repeated. It was really tough for me and Graeham because it stayed constantly at the top of our range.

The second big single was 'Cool Change', written by Glenn Shorrock about his frustrations being in the band. 'Cool Change' reached number ten on the *Billboard* charts and ended up becoming another anthem for the group. People still love that song today.

Glenn Shorrock:

You know I was feeling, hey, you know, I'm just with these guys all the time. If there's one thing in my life that's missing it's the time I spend alone. Bing, the light went on!

I think we sang the outgoing choruses of 'Cool Change' around one microphone and we also triple-tracked them. It was just incredible as it was going down to tape. That's probably my favourite part of the song.

Graeham's 'Mistress of Mine' should have been the third single but unfortunately Capitol chose not to release it. Still, the album went platinum in Australia and the US and double platinum in Canada. We were still riding high on the crest of the wave.

Jo Ford and Ray Wilkinson were again hired to come up with suggestions for an album title. They would come to us with a list of possible titles, from which we chose the one we thought was most appropriate. A photo session was organised and a graphic artist hired to come up with their concept.

The mock-up album cover they came up with was rejected by Capitol Records. If you are familiar with the *First Under The Wire* album cover, you will know that the photo with the five of us on the front was taken at the old Waverley football stadium, then known as VFL Park. The gap we left between Glenn Shorrock and Derek Pellicci was intentional, to signify that George had left the band. That was actually going to be the inside sleeve of the album. The more colourful inside sleeve, with a bunch of people carrying the jogger, and the white ribbon flowing through the crowd, was meant to be the front cover. It reminded me a little of 10cc's album cover for *How Dare You!* We bent to Capitol's wishes and the album cover turned out to be what it is today.

We hired Barry Sullivan to play bass, and added Mal Logan on keyboards for the tour. By now, we were headlining and had a double-tiered stage built. Three of us stood on the upper level and the other four were on the main stage below.

At home I had been listening to Ravel's 'Boléro' and suggested to the band we use it as the opening music for our shows. The guys liked the idea. If you're familiar with this classical piece, it keeps building and building from a very soft beginning and rising to a crescendo over some twenty-two minutes of music.

We timed it so that on the downbeat of the very last cymbal crash of 'Boléro' we started the show with the downbeat of Graeham's song 'Hard Life', the first track on side two of *First Under The Wire*. It was a very dramatic and effective way to start our live shows and our audiences seemed to really enjoy it.

By now, we were leasing tour buses to travel from town to town across the US. Stage Coach VIP Inc. was the name of the company, based out of Nashville, Tennessee, and it was owned by a man named D.K. 'Curly' Jones. We had one bus for our road crew and two other buses for the band members. One bus was designated for the smokers in the band. The other one, jokingly, became known as the God bus. I could see the humour in that.

Derek Pellicci and I were always on the same bus because we weren't smokers. When the Walkman was introduced by Sony, we spent many hours sitting in the back lounge on these buses listening to albums, sharing the latest record releases with each other.

BACKSTAGE PASS AND LIVE IN AMERICA

The band bought itself some time before having to come up with another studio album by releasing *Backstage Pass*, a live album. In Australia it was released as two separate albums. *Backstage Pass* was recorded live at the Adelaide Festival Theatre, with the Adelaide Symphony Orchestra conducted by David Measham, over three days in November in 1978.

The other album, *Live In America*, was recorded during our shows on the west coast of America. It featured some new songs from us: I had written 'Red Shoes' and 'I Don't Worry No More', Graeham had written

'Too Lonely Too Long', and David Briggs wrote 'Let's Dance'.

In the US it was released as *Backstage Pass*, a double live album. That same year, Graeham produced *Uncovered*, John Farnham's comeback album. This was something that would soon have a big impact on the band.

For one of our west coast shows, the opening act was Jim Messina from Poco and Loggins and Messina. He had a bass player named Wayne Nelson. Graeham was greatly impressed by Wayne's playing and singing ability. Barry Sullivan had told us he'd had enough of life on the road and wanted to spend more time with his family at home, so the band asked Wayne to become our permanent bass player. It was a stupid mistake on our part. We didn't ask Barry Sullivan and Mal Logan to join the band full-time so why Wayne Nelson? We would have been far better off employing him as a side musician. What were we thinking? The cost of flying an American down to Australia every time we had to rehearse, record or appear on television got to be quite expensive.

As a band, we made so many stupid mistakes that way. Anyway, Wayne joined the band and Mal Logan remained as our keyboard player. Wayne stayed with Donna and me, and whenever his family wasn't with him in Australia, I would also let him drive my old Mercedes around Melbourne.

BIRTLES & GOBLE

We were all starting to feel that we needed a bit of a break after the tour for *First Under The Wire*. It was almost 1980 and we'd been on the road constantly since 1975.

Glenn wanted to record Bobby Darin's 'Dream Lover' as a solo single. He asked John Boylan to produce it for him, and Graeham sang all of the background harmonies. I wasn't asked to sing on it because it would have sounded too much like Little River Band.

By this time, Graeham and I had written quite a few songs that were rejected by the other guys as not being suitable for the band. So we talked to Glenn Wheatley about recording a duo album and using some of these songs. He approached Capitol Records and they agreed to give us a budget for the recording.

Graeham and I split the songs evenly and we resurrected the demo of 'I'm Coming Home' that we'd recorded at The Goldmine in Brentwood, Tennessee. We co-produced the album with Ernie Rose, who also engineered it, and we used some of the guys from the band on the recording, as well as outside musicians.

The album kicked off with 'Lonely Lives', which became our first single. It was co-written by Graeham and me. We used Mark Kennedy to play drums, Michael Clarke played bass and Peter Jones played piano. David Briggs played electric rhythm guitar and Bill Harrower played the saxophones. The strings were arranged and conducted by Graeme Lyall.

It was very commercial but unfortunately it didn't do that well on the Australian charts. When we released 'I'm Coming Home' as the second single, it immediately became a top ten hit. We kept two American musicians — drummer Jerry Kroon and Steve Nathan who played keyboards — from the original demo, while George McArdle played bass, Derek Pellicci played percussion and David Briggs contributed lead guitar.

I had written a song called 'Last Romance', which was a top ten hit for Mark Holden. Graeham and I recorded our own version and used it as the title for the album, *The Last Romance*. Derek Pellicci played drums, Joe Creighton played bass, Peter Jones played keyboards and David Briggs played lead guitar. Other outside musicians we used on the album were Barry Sullivan on bass; Mal Logan on clavinet, piano, synthesizer and Hammond organ; Allan Zavod on Oberheim and Don Burrows on flute.

The fact that we had a top ten hit with 'I'm Coming Home' concerned Glenn Wheatley, who assumed that Graeham and I were considering leaving the band to become a duo act. This was purely a figment of his imagination as Graeham and I had never even discussed this possibility. But because of Glenn's paranoia, Capitol Records totally squashed the album in the US. They released the album but nothing was done to promote it, so it just died.

It was a shame because Graeham and I thought it had some great songs. Graeham contributed 'I Didn't Stand A Chance' and 'How I Feel Tonight', a song he wrote with Megan and me in mind. He wrote the beautiful, haunting ballad 'Whales', while I wrote 'The Netherlands', 'Last Romance' and 'Into My Life', a Christian song. The rest of the songs were co-written by the two of us. A year or so later, The Imperials, an American contemporary Christian group, covered 'Into My Life' on one of their albums.

We also recorded a Randy Newman song, 'He Gives Us All His Love'. Randy wrote the song as a tongue-in-cheek insult to God but we turned it into a serious version of what the lyrics were saying. Apparently, Randy made some smart-arse remark about Little River Band turning his song Christian during his Melbourne concert at Festival Hall.

Throughout the band's career I was approached by other acts to produce them. In Adelaide I went to see a young band called Stars and was instrumental in bringing them to Melbourne and getting them a deal with Mushroom Records. I produced their first and third singles, 'Quick On The Draw' and 'Mighty Rock'. I also wrote 'The Straight Life', which was the B-side of 'Quick On The Draw'.

As I mentioned, 'Last Romance' was a catchy and commercial song that caught the attention of Richard Lush who was producing Mark Holden in Sydney. I can't remember how they heard about it but somehow it was brought to their attention. They recorded the song and it became a top ten hit.

I also produced 'I Could Have Been A Hero' and the B-side 'Can't Say Yes', which was a single for the actor and director Frank Howson, as well as 'Sure Fire Thing', the first single for a band called The Runners.

Frank Howson:

Mike Brady, who had signed me to his Full Moon Records label, asked me who I'd like to produce my single and, without hesitation, I suggested Beeb. We took two of the songs I'd already recorded, 'I Could Have Been A Hero' and 'Can't Say Yes', and Beeb rearranged them and produced the sessions featuring the top session guys around.

I remember Sam See playing guitar on 'Can't Say Yes', and Peter Jones conducting the orchestra on 'I Could Have Been A Hero'. I loved the results and was pleased with my vocals on both songs and attributed that result to the fact that by then I felt very comfortable with Beeb and loved his calm and up-vibe way of producing and getting the best out of people.

David Briggs produced the very first Australian Crawl album, *The Boys Light Up*, which became a huge success in Australia and kicked off their career. It was a fantastic album. We were all starting to take on outside projects to more or less maintain our sanity and get away from the pressures of rehearsing, recording and touring with Little River Band. The band had become extremely popular in the US and the rest of the world.

MRS RUTH LEWIS

About a month before I met Donna, the band was on a flight from Phoenix, Arizona to play a concert at Red Rocks in Denver, Colorado. I sat between George McArdle and an elderly woman with grey white hair who was in the window seat. I had my Bible open and after some time she asked if I was a Christian. I replied that I was.

She told me she was too and that she lived in Lincoln, Nebraska. She was on her way home from visiting her family in San Diego, California. Before disembarking, she asked if she could write to me. I said she was welcome to and that was the start of our very long and special friendship. From that day on, we wrote letters to each other, all of which I still have in a file called The Lewis Letters.

Ruth Lewis became my Christian mentor for more than fifteen years, until the day she passed away in 1993. Having been a Christian all her life, she became my steady rock. I told her about meeting Donna and that I had asked her to marry me. She was delighted. Donna and I weren't attending church at that time, even though we wanted to be married in one.

One day, we drove around looking at different churches in our area, looking for a small church. Our wedding party consisted of just a handful of people. We drove around aimlessly because we didn't have a clue what these churches looked like on the inside.

A letter arrived from Mrs Lewis, saying how happy she was for us. She said they recently had a guest speaker at their church, an archaeologist from Australia. She talked to him afterwards and he was telling her about a wonderful pastor at his church somewhere on the outskirts of Melbourne, the Reverend Max Kingdom. However, the reverend had left and accepted a position as the minister at the Balwyn Baptist Church on Whitehorse Road.

I took her words as a sign that the Reverend Max Kingdom was the man to marry Donna and me. I looked up his number in the phone book and set up an appointment. Donna and I drove over there and talked to the reverend and his wife over afternoon tea.

He asked us why we wanted to get married and we replied that we were very much in love. Then he told us a bit about the ceremony and the procedure. I told him I didn't think it was coincidental that we were led to him through Mrs Lewis' letter, but he made no comment.

As we got up to leave, the reverend's wife asked if we would like to see the inside of the church. "Of course," we said. When she opened the door, we saw that it was a very small church, exactly the size we were hoping to find.

Things like this happened every now and then through Mrs Lewis' letters. If I had a particular question about something pertaining to my faith, I would ask her. She didn't always reply immediately. I think some of my questions probably baffled her and she would take her time answering me. I'm sure she prayed and waited for the correct answer.

The reason we chose the name Hannah for our first daughter was also directly because of one of her letters. Donna was six or seven months pregnant when we were on tour with Little River Band. We were sitting at the back of the tour bus discussing what names we liked. She said she liked the names Sarah and Hannah.

"I'll read to you who Sarah was in the Bible," I said to her. I started reading the story of Sarah but she fell asleep. I got so engrossed in the story that I just kept reading, I didn't get the chance to read her the story about Hannah because we had reached our destination.

As we were waiting to get off the bus, Stephen White, our tour manager, handed us our mail and there was a letter from Mrs Lewis. She was gushing on about the wonderful news of our first child and recounted the story of when she had Sam, her firstborn.

At the same time she was telling us why she named him Sam, she was also telling us about Hannah. In the Bible Hannah was Samuel's mother. I handed the letter to Donna and said, "You've got to read this because you won't believe it!" After she read the letter she looked at me in amazement and we both knew we had to name our first child Hannah. We chose not to know the sex of the baby and, for some strange reason, we never considered any boys' names. And as it turned out, we had a little girl and we named her Hannah.

After Little River Band's tour of 1980 was over, Donna, Hannah and I flew to Lincoln, Nebraska to spend a few days with Mrs Lewis and her husband, Arsenio. On the morning of December 9 she woke us with the news that John Lennon had been shot and killed.

She almost woke us during the night, when she heard the news, but decided not to because Hannah was still a baby. It affected us the same way as the killing of President Kennedy. We sat glued to the television hearing all about it. I just couldn't believe John Lennon was gone.

We were supposed to catch a flight back to Kansas City from Lincoln but the airlines were grounded because of a severe ice storm. Donna's father was meeting us at Kansas City Airport to take us back to Jefferson City to spend Christmas with the family. Donna and I decided to rent a car and drive back to Kansas City instead.

Just as we were approaching Kansas City Airport, a Missouri highway patrolman pulled me over for speeding. The officer asked what my hurry was, and when I replied, he caught my Australian accent.

"Where are you from, man?"

I told him I was from Australia.

"What are you doing over here?"

When I told him I had just completed a tour with Little River Band, he couldn't believe it. He told me he caught the show in Kansas City and asked for my autograph – luckily, he didn't give me his! He let me off with a warning.

The highway patrolman's name was Barry Logan. Twenty-five years later, he signed the guest book on my web site and we have been in touch ever since.

30 CENTRAL PARK ROAD, EAST MALVERN

When Donna and I started our life together, we owned next to nothing. I had left everything I owned at the North Balwyn house I shared with Megan, and Donna had flown to Australia with just a couple of suitcases of clothes.

It took four years to get my house back because Megan hired a feminist female lawyer who advised her to run a de facto case against me. I got Phil Dwyer, the band's lawyer, to represent me, and he was a staunch Catholic.

Over four years, it became a Mexican standoff between Phil and the feminist lawyer, and, of course, it was costing Megan and me money. In the meantime, she lived free of charge in my house because I continued making the mortgage payments.

Still, this was nothing to stop me from starting my life with Donna. When Donna arrived in Australia in September 1978 we stayed with Glenn and Allison for a couple of weeks until the band went on tour to Queensland, New South Wales and back to Victoria.

When we returned to Melbourne we moved in with Jo Ford and Ray Wilkinson who were renting a house in St Kilda. At the time, Jo and Ray were set designers for Crawford Productions. They were two very creative people who came up with the concepts and designs for our album covers. You may remember seeing a bulldog on the covers of *Diamantina Cocktail*, *Sleeper Catcher* and *First Under The Wire*. That was Skittles, Jo and Ray's bulldog, who became a bit of a mascot for the band. Jo and Ray immediately liked Donna, and we lived with them for about three weeks while we looked for our first house to buy.

Even though we quickly found a very attractive Edwardian house at 30 Central Park Road, East Malvern, I dragged Donna along to see dozens of other houses. The housing market was going through a bit of a slump, so every time we came back to the Central Park Road house, the owners made the price more and more attractive. In the end, we negotiated a pretty good deal. The house sat unoccupied, so we arranged a short settlement and moved in.

The fact we owned next to nothing made it possible to start from scratch. We found out about ABAS, the Australian Buying Advisory Service, an organisation that would direct you to the business that had the cheapest price for whatever you were looking for.

We set our wedding date for sometime during January of 1979, but then the opportunity for an American winter tour for the band came up. Glenn Wheatley asked if we would mind moving our wedding day back a month. It made no difference to us, and Donna was excited about possibly being able to see her family in America. The tour wasn't another three-month affair. Wheatley told us it would be four to five weeks at most.

We left just before the end of 1978 and kicked off what was mostly a college tour. The band was still touring on the success of *Sleeper Catcher*, which produced our two biggest hit singles to date, 'Reminiscing' and 'Lady'. Happily, the very last date on the tour was at The Ice Chalet in Columbia, Missouri, just thirty miles from Jefferson City, Donna's hometown.

Some of her family members came to the show. It was the middle of winter and the roads were slippery and icy. I remember it was also cold inside because the stage was built over the ice skating rink. Little River Band played a fantastic show that night, the final night of the winter tour.

When we returned to Australia, Donna and I started planning our wedding. We set the date for February 17, 1979. Jo Ford and Ray Wilkinson helped us design our wedding invitations, which took on the form of sheet music with a song title. I came up with the idea to name the invitation 'Poolside Proposals' because the reception was going to be at the Wheatleys' Wynkara estate at Lower Plenty and they had a swimming pool. It was worded as if the invitation were lyrics to a song.

Donna's mother, Margie, and her brother, Doug, flew out from America and were staying with us. The night before the wedding, Doug, Donna and I were having dinner at La Bouillabaisse, our favourite restaurant near the corner of Malvern and Tooronga Roads in East Malvern. Donna started crying during dinner and both Doug and I asked her what was wrong.

She was getting cold feet and wasn't sure she was doing the right thing. She might have cancelled the wedding altogether if not for Doug. He told Donna she would never find anybody who loved her the way I did. He kept telling her that I was crazy about her, and I was!

There was not a shadow of doubt in my mind. I knew that she was everything in a woman I could hope for, and I wanted to spend the rest of my life with her. I think her nerves were calmed after Doug talked to her throughout dinner, and the following morning she was fine.

We all drove to the Balwyn Baptist Church. My mother and father, my sister, Elly, and her husband, Stewart, were there from my side of the family. Margie and Doug represented Donna's family, and Darryl Cotton was my best man. Reverend Max Kingdom and his wife performed our wedding ceremony. Donna looked absolutely beautiful in her soft pink dress, carrying a small bouquet of fresh flowers.

I remember my heart was pounding with excitement and happiness because I was marrying the woman of my dreams. As Reverend Kingdom was speaking, all I could think about was how grateful I was for this day and thankful that we were led to each other.

The wedding ring Donna slipped on my finger that day has never left my hand. That's how much marriage means to me. For me, it's a lifelong commitment. I'm glad I didn't marry until I was thirty because by then I was ready to settle down and start a family. After the wedding ceremony, we drove to the Wheatleys' estate for the reception.

It was a very casual affair and everybody who meant something to us was there, including all of the band members and our road crew, Darryl Cotton and his future wife Cheryl, and Barry Smith. Darryl and Barry were the two friends who I'd known the longest. Being a once-in-alifetime celebration, it turned out to be somewhat of a boozy affair. Dad dived into the swimming pool with his clothes on. And we have a photo of my mother singing into an empty wine glass, pretending it was a microphone.

Fourteen
Hannah Michelle Bertelkamp

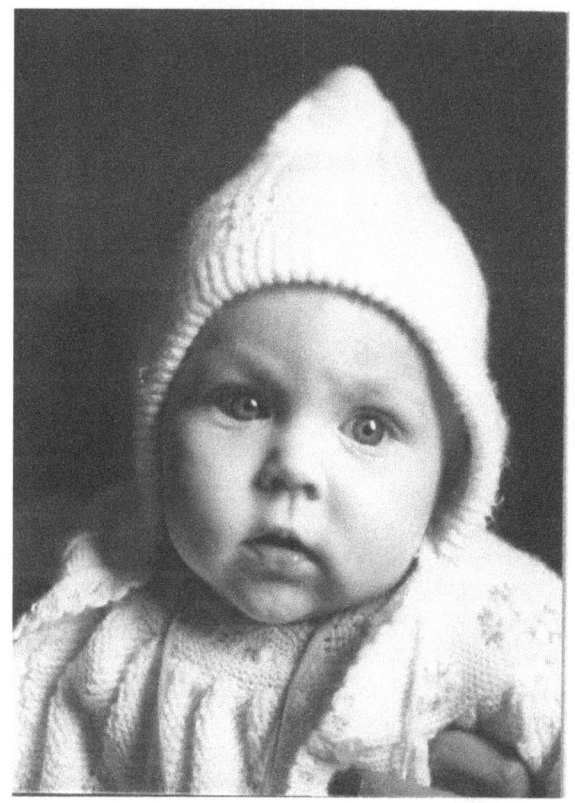

Hannah Michelle bertelkamp

In April 1979 our family doctor confirmed that Donna was pregnant. When we left the practice of Dr Anghie and Dr Rustomjee, I drove down Wattletree Road and turned left into Burke Road. I pulled over and parked the car outside the local chemist shop. I told Donna to wait while I ran inside and came back with a small brown koala that I gave to her. I was so excited about becoming a father. Here was a woman who had had no intentions of getting married, had moved from St Louis to Los Angeles to pursue her career, met me and moved to Australia, got married and was now expecting her first child.

Donna loved being pregnant and we attended Leboyer's natural childbirth classes. It was there we met our good friends Jan and Brian Slattery, who were also expecting their first child. Later that year I was in the studio recording the songs for the Birtles and Goble album, *The Last Romance*. We were all invited to the Wheatleys' house for a New Year's Eve party. Most of the guys in the band were there, as well as our road crew, and some of them were kissing Donna's big pregnant belly. To this day, she's convinced that this threw her into labour.

It was just past midnight when Donna felt her contractions coming on, so we left in a hurry and drove home. It was about a thirty-minute drive and by the time we arrived, the contractions had subsided, so we went to bed.

In the Leboyer birthing classes they told the men not to panic if their wives started getting concerned about their contractions, that there would be plenty of time to get to the hospital.

"Jump in the shower and make yourself a nice cup of tea and Bob's your uncle," they said.

So when Donna woke me very early on New Year's Day that's precisely what I did. I jumped in the shower, made myself a cup of tea and generally just took my sweet time getting ready.

In the meantime, Donna was starting to freak out because her contractions were getting closer and closer together. We packed her bag, got in the car and drove to the city to St Vincent's Hospital.

As you can imagine, there was no traffic on the South Eastern Freeway this early on New Year's Day. I made it from East Malvern to the city in record time, in about 20 minutes.

We checked Donna in and the nurses settled her into the delivery room. We spent many hours breathing and blowing out air as they had taught us in the Leboyer birth classes. After a fourteen-hour labour, Hannah Michelle was born about four o'clock in the afternoon. Donna had delivered her first daughter by natural birth.

There is nothing more miraculous than seeing your own child being born. I wouldn't have missed this for anything in the world. It was truly amazing. After the umbilical cord was cut, the nurses handed Hannah to me. I bathed her before she was handed back to Donna to hold. The nurses moved Donna to her private room and she spent the next week or so bonding with Hannah.

I was still recording the duo album at AAV with Graeham and Ernie Rose and because I knew Donna was in St Vincent's, I would stay at the studio and work late into the night.

The nurses were all fussing over this young American girl who had just given birth to her first baby. I used to leave the studio and sneak in late at night, after the set visiting hours, to see Donna and Hannah.

After a while, the nurses thought they'd put two and two together. They would come into Donna's room, take hold of her hand and say, "Oh, you poor pet, you poor pet." Donna didn't have a clue why they were saying this, let alone what 'pet' meant.

Donna has always looked much younger than her age: she still does as a matter of fact. When we were married, she looked about sixteen. The wisp of grey at the front of my hairline gave me the appearance of a more distinguished looking older man, most definitely quite a few years older than Donna.

I couldn't understand why the nurses started giving me dirty looks every time I showed up to visit Donna and Hannah. They assumed that this older guy who snuck in late every night was probably married and had gotten this poor young 'pet' of an American girl knocked up. She had to explain that we were quite legally married and that I was recording late into the night at the studio.

After about 10 days at the hospital, we got it all worked out, and we brought Hannah home to Central Park Road. We had her nursery decorated with Beatrix Potter wallpaper on the walls and the ceiling.

Hannah's birth ended our sleeping-in days. It didn't matter if the band played a gig at Billboard in the city and I didn't get home until three in the morning, I would still get up at six a.m. when she woke up. We wanted to be there every minute of the day when she was awake. She was our little miracle!

Fifteen
LITTLE RIVER BAND — PHASE FOUR

LRB ON MONTSERRAT: WAYNE NELSON, DAVID BRIGGS,
GEORGE MARTIN, GRAEHAM GOBLE, GLENN SHORROCK,
SEATED DEREK PELLICCI, BEEB BIRTLES

Towards the end of 1980, Glenn Shorrock had had enough of what we'd become as a band. We were already talking about recording our next studio album, which he thought was way too soon. He suggested the band take a year off, for everybody to go and do their own thing, take a break and return refreshed. Glenn's frustrations and suggestions were laid out in a four-page handwritten letter to the band:

> DEAR GUYS.
>
> AS ONE WHO HAS OFTEN AND RIGHTLY SO BEEN ACCUSED OF NON-COMMUNICATION AND INSULARITY, I THOUGHT IT TIME I SHOULD TRY TO COMMUNICATE THE REASONS AND MOTIVES BEHIND MY PRESENT STAND REGARDING MY FUTURE WITH THE BAND.
>
> FIRSTLY, LET ME SAY I AM PROUD AND PLEASED THAT LRB IS WHERE IT IS TODAY, AND THE FACT IS NO ONE CAN TAKE THAT AWAY FROM US BUT AS WE ENTER THIS THIRD PHASE OF THE BANDS CAREER MY RESOLVE & CONFIDENCE IS NOT SO SURE.
>
> THE FIRST PHASE OF LRB WAS ONE OF TEAMANSHIP AND EXPLORATION WITHIN AND WITHOUT THE BAND, AND WE HAD A HUGE COMMON PLATFORM ON WHICH TO BASE IT, THAT IS TO "MAKE IT" AND ALL OTHER CONSIDERATIONS TOOK A DEFINITE SECOND PLACE. OF COURSE DURING THAT PERIOD I BEGAN TO SEE EVIDENCE OF SOME, CAN I SAY, IMMATURITY AND PERSONALITY PARANOIAS THAT ARE WITH US AT THIS STAGE — EVEN MORE SO. THE PRIME EXAMPLE OF THIS WAS OF COURSE THE ROGER McLACHLAN EPISODE.

To sacrifice a great team member and musician and as you know a was to my mind a bad mistake, and although I haven't dwelled on it or carried a grudge of any kind, it has ever since coloured my attitude towards all of you as professional thinking musicians.

Notwithstanding this, Phase One did go according to plan and thanks must be made to David and George for their efforts in this regard.

I include the 1976 American tour as part of Phase One and it wasn't until 1977 that we started to see the fruits of our labours. John Boylan and Help Is On Its Way gaining us our AM credibility and following, along with Grahams hits Lady & Reminiscing etc.... (not forgetting Lonesome Loser Davo!) brought us through to our position today. Of course our live performances have contributed largely to the respect we command around the world today. Our road team deserve a great deal of credit for this and without blowing my own trumpet I feel personally gratified by my own work in this area. Over the last three years we adopted the position of being "just" the singer and spokesman for the band and have largely withdrawn from the politiking and policy making decisions within the band;- just doing my job as it were. This stance of course has led to my insularity which I admit at this time is a problem to myself and I know to all of you, so that now I reluctantly hold the position of Grumpy amongst the Dwarves.

During this time the common ground that swept us through Phase One has slowly been replaced by other considerations and motivations that seem to plague successful bands. So much so ~~is~~ that at this present time it is my opinion that personalities and personal monetary ambition is now the driving force within us and our common ground or platform as professional entertainer/musicians has dwindled to a dangerous low. To me our priority of responsibilities in this area is first to ~~with~~ our audience and ~~secondly~~ to ourselves and families and thirdly to satisfy our ego/paranoias. I feel that at this stage our priorities are clearly reversed. I think it criminal that a group with our ~~experience~~ and ~~a~~ track record exists solely on a repertoire of 17 or 18 songs and anything outside of this flimsy structure sees us floundering embarrassingly, and I find it continually more difficult to maintain the integrity & respect placed in us by our audiences and to a lesser degree by our employers. I simply am no longer able to look my audience in the face! I just feel lately that I'm cheating them. I'm sure most of us ~~feel~~ this way sometimes but we cover it up and compensate for our lack of cohesiveness musically by letting our individual personalities rise to ~~the~~ replace the feelings of inadequacy as a band with a common feeling and soul. Again I must stress I put myself high on this list of offenders but we are all equally to blame. So far we've ~~been able~~ because of financial gain ~~been able~~ to fool ourselves and our public, and so far we haven't lost much ground. But the cracks are getting wider and we musn't underestimate our audiences ability to see it.

How can any musician or performer hope to grow and improve playing the same 18 songs the exact same way night after night for about two years — its ridiculous. And we have to face the fact that individually none of us has improved even 10% but we cover it up in our dillusions of grandeur and egos, and say oh well its just the nature of beast! Well the beast is sick and needs to be made well again!

So that brings us to phase three —
   Its no use patching things up any more not for me anyway. Little River Band is full of so much bullshit it needs an enema if not major surgery!
   Its time for a change and not a cool one if we are going to survive and move on to that elusive "next stage"
   I am not advocating complete replacement of individual members but if surgery is to be avoided then an attitude and role adjustment must be made to happen
   We all have problems musically & emotionally with each other but I think none of us can deny that our most recurring problems lie with Graham, from Glenn Wheatley & the office down through the band and road crew to even hired crew who have no real physical or emotional ties with LRB. It is my opinion that Graham is a square peg in a round hole when it comes to an on the road, live, rock n roll situation, he himself admits to it.
   No one can deny of course the massive contribution he has made as a formative and dominant member of LRB, through the periods referred to before as phase one and

two. In fact it is largely due to his dogmatic approach ~~and~~ ~~attention to detail~~ that we are ~~it~~ where we are today – a successful "pop" group – but I firmly believe that if we are to negotiate phase three successfully this approach must be ~~re~~ replaced by a return to our common ground when we were a peoples band – we must get back the soul and the rock n roll spirit that is lost.

Graham is not this type of character, its just not in him.

And so I reccomend that Graham steps down as a performer in the band and concentrates still ~~with~~ as a member in the areas he excels at, songwriting and helping with the policy making decisions of LRB. Of course his experience in the studio control room should not be lost. The comparison in situation could be made to Brian Wilsons role within the Beach Boys golden times of "Surfs Up" "Carl + the Passions". Of course I advocate that he still be a partner within the corporate + financial structure of the band with an adjustment being made to the live income situation. But thats an area I'd leave to Glenn Wheatley etc.

I also suggest that the performing role of Graham be filled with a percussionist/horn player who can sing, although Wayne is equal to almost all of Grahams parts on stage and more. I think I'm justified in such a drastic suggestion by thinking that with Graham out of the live situation the whole organisation could <u>relax</u> a lot more and get back to ~~a~~ being a band for the people but still having the advantage of Grahams great talents as a songwriter and organiser.

As you know I haven't taken this lightly and I hope I've acted rationally in the best

> INTERESTS OF EVERYONE. BUT ITS SOMETHING I BELIEVE IS AN HONORABLE SOLUTION AND I INTEND TO STAND BY WHAT I SAY AND FEEL. AFTER THE LAST US TOUR I UNOFFICIALLY RESIGNED, NOW I FEEL AFTER GIVING MYSELF TIME TO THINK, THAT UNLESS THE CHANGE IS EFFECTED, AND I MUST SAY AGAIN THAT IT K VITAL TO THE FUTURE OF LRB. THEN THE CHANGE NECCESSARY MUST COME BY ME MAKING MY RESIGNATION AS SINGER FOR LRB OFFICIAL.
> I DON'T WANT THIS TO HAPPEN, IN FACT I WANT TO DO MORE, I WANT TO FIRE ON ALL CYLINDERS AGAIN AND ACHIEVE MY FULL POTENTIAL!
> I'M SURE YOU ALL DO TOO, BUT THE NECCESSARY COURSE ADJUSTMENT HAS TO BE MADE SO THAT WE CAN ALL PUT OUR PERSONALITIES ASIDE AND LET OUR TALENTS, COLLECTIVELY, DO THE JOB.
> DON'T HESITATE TO APPROACH ME ABOUT ANYTHING YOU FEEL YOU WANT TO DISCUSS WITH ME
> Sincerely Glenn.

Glenn's letter didn't surprise me as he kept to himself on the road. He wasn't one to have open discussions with any of us and we were all well aware of the tension between himself and Graeham.

Glenn was right when he stated we had become a successful pop group largely because of Graeham's dogmatic approach. Graeham was the organiser, the conduit between the band and Glenn Wheatley. Graeham was also a master negotiator when he wanted things to go in his favour. He would phone each individual member and persuade convincingly, lobbying to get his way.

I agreed with Glenn stating Graeham was a square peg in a round hole and Graeham admitted he hated being on the road, and our set list was embarrassingly short.

I don't remember discussing Glenn's letter with anyone else in the band. I've often commented in interviews that when a band such as LRB is flying high on success, you kind of become cocooned and lose sight of what's happening on street level. I think that's what Glenn was referring to when he said, "We need to return to our common ground when we were a people's band — we must get back the soul and the rock and roll spirit that is lost."

Even though Glenn felt very strongly about everything he said in his letter the band continued on, business as usual. All of us battled with bouts of unhappiness on the road, we all had our ups and downs at various times. George McArdle couldn't take life on the road anymore, which led to his decision to quit.

We were somewhere on the road in the US before the recording of the *Time Exposure* album when I went through a time of being unhappy in the band. I have always been a pretty moody person and maybe I showed it more than the others.

When Glenn Wheatley joined us for a few dates on the tour he pulled me aside and had a serious talk to me. He suggested that if I was really this unhappy I should quit for my own peace of mind. I gave it some serious thought but felt the time wasn't right yet. What came out of that conversation was my song 'Guiding Light', which was the closing track on side two of *Time Exposure*.

In the lyrics I was crying out to God, asking if I was still doing the right thing by staying with the band. I sang the lead vocal and purposely didn't have the other guys add any harmonies which made the song sound more like it was my own personal plea.

It was also the only song on the album with a string arrangement that George Martin scored. The strings were recorded later in London. He signed his book, All You Need Is Ears, to me with an inscription making a reference to 'Guiding Light'. He told me he played it for Paul McCartney when they were mixing it in London. The thought of Paul McCartney having listened to one of my songs thrilled me.

TIME EXPOSURE

The lineup for Little River Band at this stage of the game was David Briggs, Graeham Goble, Wayne Nelson, Derek Pellicci, Glenn Shorrock and me. We decided not to record our next studio album in Melbourne because of all the distractions of home. And this time we also wanted to work with a different producer to John Boylan. After recording three albums with John we felt it was time to experience working with another producer.

Wheatley talked to a couple of producers, including the engineer/producer Tom Dowd and George Martin of The Beatles fame. Obviously we chose George Martin because of his reputation as the fifth Beatle, and also as producer for the band, America. Recording at Air Studios on Montserrat in the West Indies was an all-inclusive deal, meaning it included accommodation, meals and transportation to and from the studio every day.

Glenn Shorrock lamented that it was too early for the band to record yet another studio album, that we should take a year off and then regroup. Graeham and I disagreed with Glenn as we wanted to keep pushing on. In hindsight, Glenn was right because even though we still had three big hit singles off *Time Exposure* — 'The Night Owls', 'Take It Easy On Me' and 'Man On Your Mind' — the selection of songs was not very strong. It wasn't like *Sleeper Catcher* or *First Under The Wire*.

Glenn wasn't as prolific as Graeham and I in the songwriting department. Whereas Graeham and I were productive on the road and came up with new songs all the time, Glenn preferred to concentrate on just being on the road. He had few new songs to put forward for the recording of *Time Exposure* and that became a problem.

George Martin was a great producer to work with, but I don't think some of us were that thrilled with Geoff Emerick as the recording engineer. Mike Stavrou was the tape operator at Air Studios and the way he was treated by Geoff was appalling. Mike was the mixing engineer on 'Brass In Pocket', the first big hit single for The Pretenders. Though Geoff had won Grammys for engineering *Sgt. Pepper's* and *Abbey Road* and Paul McCartney and Wings' *Band On The Run*, we felt he was out of touch with the recording techniques of the day. He was very old school and his sounds were outdated.

The band split into two factions. We fell into a day and night shift recording schedule, with George and Geoff working during the day, and Ernie Rose recording mostly vocals at night with the singers in the band.

For all of my eight years in Little River Band I always felt I was the meat in the sandwich between Glenn and Graeham. Sometimes I would agree with Glenn's ideas and sometimes I would agree with Graeham. I leaned more towards Graeham's ideas because we both strived for perfection in the studio, whereas Glenn was more into capturing a performance with emotion. He didn't like having to sing a song over and over again. To him, it took the soul out of the performance and he was right, though I think there's a fine balance.

Through working with George Martin, we learned how The Beatles recorded their vocals. The lead singer sang the song maybe three or four times, with each take recorded on a separate track. From those three or four tracks, they chose the best bits and pieces to make up one great track.

The tension between Glenn and Graeham was definitely at its peak during the recording of *Time Exposure*.

Glenn Shorrock:

Graeham and I are two different people, you know? We have great respect for each other professionally, but personally we're different people. I think if we had given ourselves more space than we did before it would have lasted a lot longer.

Over the five years that David Briggs had been in the band, his confidence had escalated to the extent where he became adamant about what needed to be done. I remember a couple of embarrassing moments in the studio where David was quite rude to George Martin, insisting that his way was better and that he didn't need to be told how or what to play. I think David probably sensed that the band was starting to fall apart and he was going to be the guy to take the helm.

David Briggs:

Wheatley had tried to pump us up by saying we needed to deliver a Hotel California *album to elevate us into the big league. For that to happen it required time to write songs. The band needed space and time apart for our personal lives to settle. To write great songs is no easy task.*

I recall Graeham saying he was ready to put his vocals on anything as soon as there was a drum track, so he could get off the island as soon as possible. All of this pressure from Glenn Wheatley to deliver, coupled with the ever-increasing erratic behaviour from Graeham, impacted the Montserrat sessions, taking away the focus on making a quality record.

A very funny memory is that I saw the recording bills/costs written down soon after and Graeham had been flying in Snickers bars from Miami as he felt there wasn't anything there he could eat. The Snickers bars' costs were in the hundreds of dollars per week as I recall.

Graeham was favouring Wayne to sing his songs because Glenn wasn't delivering his best anymore. I think Glenn was well and truly burned out by this stage. He lost his desire to deliver and wasn't singing with the same feeling, more than likely because he didn't believe in the songs we were choosing.

Graeham Goble:

I think what we should have done is close the band down for a while ... Rightly or wrongly, Glenn left because he was really put in a difficult position and I understand that now. But what could I do? I mean, I had to be true to myself. Looking back, I don't see any alternative to what happened. It just happened and that was the way it was.

I had experienced working with John Farnham at that time because I produced his solo album called Uncovered. *I love John's voice and he had a different range, he was a different sort of singer and it was a wonderful experience as a writer to have a different possibility for my songs.*

I don't buy that Graeham was writing specifically for John. Songwriters write for themselves, either from imagination or real life experiences.

I wish it could have been a more pleasant experience for all of us because we were in paradise on the island of Montserrat. It was a spectacular island and the terrain was such a beautiful lush green. I was saddened to hear about the 1995 and 1997 volcano eruptions when two thirds of the island's population had to evacuate. It was so beautiful there.

When George Martin's wife, Judy, and their children flew in from

London to spend Easter together, I went to church with them. Sitting in the pews of a church with glassless windows and with black people making up the majority of the congregation was quite a moving experience. The service was very high Church of England with incense billowing out of thuribles on chains that were swung back and forth by the elders dressed in white robes. It was a highlight of my time there.

Judy and George Martin had two children, Lucy and Giles. Giles was about eleven at the time. We had a lot of fun together. I have a photo of him and me sitting in with the steel drum band we hired one night for some entertainment.

Considering the circumstances, I'm surprised we delivered an album that still managed to have three hit singles. 'The Night Owls', with Wayne Nelson singing the lead vocal, was released as the first single and climbed to number six on the *Billboard* charts.

Graeham Goble:

It was chosen as a single and for the first time we had a top ten hit in America without Glenn being the lead singer. I always look to where things can be as opposed to where they are and I consider that to be as much of an asset as a failing of mine.

'Take It Easy On Me' was also recorded with Wayne singing lead but Glenn objected and said if he was the lead singer of the group he should be doing precisely that. I totally agreed with Glenn on this point. It was released as the second single with Glenn's vocal and Wayne singing the middle eight section that was out of Glenn's range. It reached number ten on the *Billboard* charts. Graeham had written the first two singles.

The third single, 'Man On Your Mind', was co-written by Glenn Shorrock and Kerryn Tolhurst and it reached number fourteen on the *Billboard* charts. It became one of my favourite songs to play live. There's something about the groove of that song that makes it very exciting to play live.

Glenn Shorrock:

Kerryn Tolhurst, who was in The Dingoes, one of my favourite Aussie bands, had 'Man On Your Mind' in a sort of rough form and came to me with it and I helped him finish it, but it was really his song.

Along with Ernie Rose, our sound engineer, we flew Peter Jones over to Montserrat to play piano on the album. Towards the end of our recording we felt some keyboard sweetening was needed in the form of synthesizers. George Martin told us he had recently worked with a keyboard player named Bill Cuomo in LA. So we contacted Bill and flew him out to play synthesizer on some tracks. In rehearsals for the album I had come up with some long sustaining guitar lines played in the form of two closely harmonized notes on 'The Night Owls'. On the actual recording they were played by Bill on his Prophet synthesizer. Montserrat is where Bill and I met for the first time, never remotely thinking we would end up working together in Nashville years down the road. Around the time of *Time Exposure* it was Bill who came up with the arrangement for 'Bette Davis Eyes', a huge worldwide hit for Kim Carnes. It sold thirteen million singles worldwide.

When the recording for *Time Exposure* was completed, we made two big mistakes. One was allowing George Martin and Geoff Emerick to mix the album back in London without a representative of the band being there. Graeham and I, in particular, were very disappointed with some of the mixes when we heard them for the first time.

We decided to remix some of the tracks with Ernie Rose at AAV. Doing this angered George Martin, to the extent that he wrote a letter expressing his disappointment with the band. We stood our ground because some of the instruments we recorded on the album were inaudible. We did what we felt was right for the band's recorded music.

The second mistake was leaving the album cover design up to Capitol Records. The result was extremely disappointing. *Time Exposure*, all right, you couldn't even tell it was our faces from looking at the front or back cover. Yes, we were most definitely one of those faceless '70s bands!

Sixteen
LITTLE RIVER BAND — PHASE FIVE

LRB: Wayne Nelson, Beeb Birtles, Glenn Shorrock, Derek Pellicci, Graeham Goble, Stephen Housden

When we returned home after the recording of *Time Exposure* more changes were around the corner. Graeham was quite vocal about David's conduct in Montserrat during a meeting at Glenn Wheatley's house in South Yarra. He confronted David, and virtually fired him from the band. I don't remember all the details, but David took it like a man and agreed to take his leave.

I have always hated situations like these. Even though I have my own strong opinions, I'm a very non-confrontational person. My heart goes out to the person being ousted. I know it's unavoidable to hurt people's feelings as you go through life, but I try to avoid it at all possible costs. Many times through Mississippi and Little River Band I was persuaded to replace band members. And so when Graeham says, *"I always look to where things can be as opposed to where they are and I consider that to be as much of an asset as a failing of mine"*, I think on more than a few occasions it has come back to bite him in the arse. I think this was also the last straw for Glenn as he and David often hung out on the road.

As a guitar player, my role lay somewhere between a rhythm guitarist and a lead guitarist. David and I worked extremely well together for the years he was with the band. I respected him as a musician and learned a lot from him. His departure had nothing to do with his musicianship, it had more to do with his personality at the time. I'm happy to say that David and I have remained friends over the years, though I know how disappointed he remains regarding his sacking from the band.

For some of our shows in New South Wales, a Sydney band called The Imports supported us. The lead guitarist in the group was an English migrant named Stephen Housden. He was a good-looking guy, flashy and he played great guitar. As usual, Graeham was the one who was the most impressed and he probably had Stephen in the back of his mind all along as a possible replacement for David Briggs.

We approached Stephen and, once again, being the dummies we were, made him an equal member instead of putting him on a wage. We worked him into the band just prior to hitting the road to promote *Time Exposure*. The album was released in August 1981 and we went back on tour the same month. We performed all around the world, again starting in the US.

When we performed in Houston, Texas in October that year, we filmed the concert for a video release. It was called *Live Exposure*. Capitol Records released it in the VHS format on videocassette.

From the US, we went on to England, West Germany, Holland, The Philippines and South Korea before we came home to play another round of shows in Australia. We were all tired from touring and retreated to the comfort zones of our own homes.

Sometime after the recording of *Time Exposure*, Glenn Wheatley negotiated a deal with Warner Chappell Music to buy his music publishing company, Wheatley Music. Warner Chappell was very interested in buying the complete Little River Band catalogue. That meant Graeham Goble, Glenn Shorrock and me as the principal songwriters. He couldn't close the deal without the three of us agreeing to it.

He explained to Donna and me that this deal would not pay me as much money as the other guys because they had written the songs that became Little River Band's biggest hit singles overseas. The deal would net me about $60,000 for thirty of my original songs.

We accepted that this was a fair deal for us. Particularly because at the time we were looking to buy a new house in Manning Road, East Malvern and $60,000 would come in handy. On reflection, I think that Donna and I were a little too trusting and naïve.

Seventeen
LITTLE RIVER BAND — PHASE SIX

LRB: Derek Pellicci, Wayne Nelson, Stephen Housden,
Beeb Birtles, John Farnham, Graeham Goble

After the recording of *Time Exposure* I felt Glenn needed some moral support, so I wrote a letter to him and his wife, Jo, saying that I would stand by him no matter what.

I was about to eat those words.

The working relationship between Glenn, Graeham and me had become very strained and uncomfortable. We had reached that stage where we weren't willing to contribute to each other's songs anymore. It was quite obvious that something had to change. I remember being at Deluxe Audio in South Melbourne one day, rehearsing some new songs. We were working on something Glenn had written but I couldn't get excited about it. It wasn't a very good song.

On the last US tour I had a bit of an altercation with Glenn when we were rehearsing one of his new songs. I was giving what I felt was my absolute best but I just couldn't please him. He turned around and took his frustration out on me without really explaining what it was he was after musically. I took the high road and told him I was doing my best. I might add that rehearsing anything new on the road was never a good idea. We needed to just concentrate on that night's performance.

Around this time I felt I was at my peak regarding song arrangements. It didn't matter whose song it was. Many of the ideas I put forward during rehearsals were accepted and stayed as part of the song arrangement. It was an extremely satisfying time in my life as a musician. Sometimes I would go overboard trying to please Glenn but rarely got anything back from him in return. I found him hard to read at times as he's a man of few words.

I'd had enough and wasn't going to take any more during the rehearsal at Deluxe Audio. I turned to Glenn and said, "You know what? I just can't work with you anymore." I spoke my mind and told him in no uncertain terms how I felt. That led to a meeting between Glenn, Graeham and me at Wheatley's office in Richardson Street, Albert Park.

This time I did the talking. I said it had gotten to the point where I couldn't work with Glenn anymore. Wheatley started freaking out, saying he thought it was a big mistake to replace Glenn as the lead singer. What was Capitol Records going to say? In the other corner, I got major backup from Graeham, who had always been at opposite poles to Glenn. Graeham said he agreed, that he had reached the point where he couldn't work with Glenn anymore.

Wheatley was absolutely on the money during this particular meeting. He definitely wasn't sitting on the fence. This would be the mistake that cut Little River Band's throat!

What we should have done was what Glenn suggested before we recorded *Time Exposure*. We should have taken a year off and had a complete break. But we didn't do that because Graeham and I wanted to keep pushing on. Glenn Shorrock was fired from the band, though he had already been thinking about leaving, according to what he had stated in his letter to the band.

For the rest of my life I will never forget receiving the phone call from Jo Shorrock shortly afterwards. I was in my music room at Central Park Road. She was crying and saying, "How could you, Beeb, how could you after writing that letter to us?" I felt like the biggest piece of shit on earth and just wanted to crawl in a hole and die. I couldn't find the words to reply. I felt I had betrayed both of them.

Eighteen
EMILIA BROOK BERTELKAMP

EMILIA BROOK BERTELKAMP

Sometime during 1981 some of my Dutch relatives flew to Australia to visit my parents. My mother's oldest brother, Simon, his Indonesian wife, Riek, and my mother's older sister, Marie, and her husband, Cees, as well as my parents, drove to Melbourne to stay with us at Central Park Road.

It was not the best time to come calling as Donna wasn't feeling well. Hannah was now 18 months old and we had hired Lulu Cockram to be her nanny. Lulu was fantastic with keeping Hannah occupied with various projects. By then, Donna and Hannah had well and truly bonded.

My Tante (Aunt) Riek predicted Donna was pregnant again. The thought hadn't even occurred to Donna but, to be sure, she made a doctor's appointment. Her pregnancy test was confirmed as positive. We were expecting our second child.

Once again, I loved seeing Donna pregnant, with her belly growing. This all happened during the time when the band was changing lead singers from Glenn Shorrock to John Farnham.

As with Hannah, Donna was registered at St Vincent's Hospital for the birth. Donna wanted to deliver her second baby naturally again. Only this time there was a big difference in her delivery time. I guess because she'd been through this once before, she just assumed it would be another fourteen-hour delivery.

But little Emilia had a mind of her own and on March 23, 1982 she was delivered in a matter of only three hours! The speed of it all left Donna's head spinning as she didn't get much time to prepare. We named our second little girl Emilia after Donna's grandmother on her father's side. Mary Emilia Brucks had passed away the previous year.

So here she was, Emilia Brook Bertelkamp, our second little miracle. As I had done the first time, after cutting the umbilical cord, I gave

Emilia her very first bath. She took more after my side of the family in appearance with dark hair whereas Hannah was blonde and looked more like Donna's side.

Emilia quickly became known as Emmie and during her younger years she was a real chubby bubby. She had rolls of skin on her arms and legs that were so adorable and she had these big brown eyes and little tulip-shaped lips. She was too cute for words and we loved her so much — and still do!

Donna was hopeless with putting the girls down for their naps. She couldn't bear to hear them crying. So when they showed signs of getting grumpy and tired, I'd lift them up in my arms and put their heads on my shoulder and walk into my music room at the front of the house.

I'd place a record on the turntable and dance around with them for a couple of songs until they fell asleep. I could feel their little bodies sag and go limp when sleep overtook them. Then I carefully laid them down in their bassinet. I absolutely loved doing that with both of them when they were little.

10 MANNING ROAD, EAST MALVERN

After four years of going back and forth between Phil Dwyer and Megan's lawyer, the case between us was finally settled out of court. During that time I was able to get some of my belongings back but none of the sentimental items I really cared about and had collected over the years. I had lost a lot of memorabilia and photos from my days with Zoot and Mississippi.

We agreed on a settlement and finally, I got my North Balwyn house back. By then, Donna and I had been married more than three years and we had two daughters. The whole ordeal had become a dark cloud that had followed us around and we were glad to see it finally disappear.

David Briggs' father worked in real estate and he alerted David and me to a block of ten flats in the seaside suburb of Beaumaris. David and I bought them. The flats were managed by a real estate agency but it seemed there was always something that needed to be repaired. We were constantly getting phone calls from the managing company about the plumbing or the electrical side of things.

After a while, Donna and I got fed up. One day, she happened to bump into Dennis Madden, from whom we'd bought our Central Park Road house. Dennis and his wife, Robyn, bought and sold a number of homes in the Malvern and East Malvern areas. They'd buy rundown houses in need of repair, renovate them and then sell for a profit.

Their swan song was a majestic old house at 10 Manning Road, East Malvern that had been a hospital and a dilapidated boarding house. This was going to be their permanent family home. They had been renovating it for more than a year already. In the meantime, Dennis continued to buy more houses to renovate but then they ran into financial difficulty.

Donna and I had been considering buying a bigger house and we came across a stunning one-level Victorian mansion in Hawthorn that sat on about two acres. Unfortunately, the house was out of our price range. When we went to look at it, we took Graeham and Narelle with us. They also thought it was spectacular and fell in love with it.

When Donna unexpectedly bumped into Dennis, she asked if he would give her a tour of the Manning Road house. It was very obvious they had spent a lot of money renovating it. It had a brand new kitchen and all the bathrooms had travertine marble flooring and vanities. It had new electrical wiring, new plumbing, and a central heating system. They had spent about $20,000 alone on new plastering.

All of the stained glass windows were matched to one windowpane, which still had the original stained glass in it. Robyn had chosen gorgeous paint colours and Laura Ashley wallpaper in the upstairs children's bedrooms. Donna fell in love with the house. I put my North Balwyn house up for sale. At the same time, Donna negotiated a deal with Dennis to buy the Manning Road house, with Dennis taking our five Beaumaris flats as a down payment.

It all came together beautifully. In one fell swoop, we sold the North Balwyn house, our Central Park Road house and we were able to rid ourselves of the five investment flats.

As soon as Graeham and Narelle found out we were going to buy Manning Road, they asked our permission to buy the Hawthorn house.

"Permission?" we said. "Go ahead and buy that gorgeous house so we can come and visit it when you guys are living there!"

And that's how the musical houses went 'round and 'round.

In the 1989 edition of *Classic Decorating*, our house was featured in The Australian Design Series. The article was titled 'All Ship Shape', and started:

'Built for an English sea captain, this grand old house was wrecked on the sands of time for much of this century. But a bit of tender loving care has restored it to a home fit for a rock star.'

The writer, Alison Stahle, stated: 'When you're in the public eye and spend months at a time on the road as a member of one of Australia's most famous and celebrated rock bands, home really is where the heart is. And this home, situated in one of Melbourne's older established suburbs, some distance back from the tree-lined street, provides just the peaceful environment that's required.'

And with all the drama surrounding Little River Band at this time, a peaceful sanctuary was just what I needed.

Beeb, Hannah and Donna with mentor & friends, Mrs Ruth Lewis and Arsenio Lewis

David Briggs & Beeb

LRB - on the road

Graeham, Beeb & Glenn playing to a sea of people

Robin Gibb, Glenn Shorrock, Hannah Birtles & Barry Gibb

What the *First Under The Wire* album cover should have looked like

THE NATIONAL ACADEMY OF RECORDING ARTS AND SCIENCES

presents this certificate to

LITTLE RIVER BAND

in recognition of

NOMINATION

for the

BEST POP VOCAL PERFORMANCE
BY A DUO, GROUP OR CHORUS

"LONESOME LOSER"
Single

for the awards period

1979

JAY S. LOWY
NATIONAL PRESIDENT

LRB - Grammy nomination

LRB - Jo, Donna & Glenn at the beach on Montserrat

Glenn and Jo Shorrock at Las Vegas airport, August 16, 1977
Note the newspaper headline!

Whitney Houston & Hannah at
Honolulu Airport, Hawaii

Beeb
Photo by Mitch Karam

In Susan Maxwell Skinner's book, "Diana - Memory of a Rose", Princess Diana was quoted as saying: "I can never resist a good-looking man in Armani", after a long aprés-concert chat with Beeb Birtles. Melbourne 1983

Donna and Beeb

Emmie, my look-alike & me

Our two gorgeous grandsons, Brody & Ashton

Beeb & Stephen Housden

John Farnham & Beeb
Photo by Mitch Karam

LRB left to right: Glenn Wheatley, Derek, John, Stephen, Derek Nimmo, Wayne, Dionne Warwick, Beeb & Graeham backstage at the Universal Amphitheatre in Los Angeles

Two of my loves, Donna and Emmie in sailor suits

One of Donna's favourite photos of Beeb

Beeb's girls: Hannah, Donna & Emmie

My parents, Elisabeth and Gerard Bertelkamp

Lifelong friends, Barry Smith & Beeb, August 2005

LRB - Glenn's acceptance speech at the
ARIA Hall of Fame Awards (2004)

Zoot reunion with Hannah & Emmie
Left to right: Darryl Cotton, Hannah, Rick Springfield, Beeb,
Emmie and Rick Brewer

Songskill logo - created in 1985

Beeb in typical relaxed pose
Photo by Glen Rose

Beeb having the last laugh
Photo by Glen Rose

Nineteen
LITTLE RIVER BAND — PHASE SEVEN

Graeham had produced *Uncovered*, the comeback album for John Farnham and was very impressed with John's singing ability and his endless energy for getting the vocals perfect. He told me John would stand behind the microphone and sing the song over and over until he got it right.

When the time came for us to search for a new lead singer, my thoughts were, *Why confine ourselves to looking just in Australia?* We already had one token American in the band, so I started thinking about a voice that would really complement our vocal harmonies. Our distinctive harmony sound was what set us apart from other rock and roll groups.

The guy who came to mind was Mickey Thomas who had sung that great Elvin Bishop song 'Fooled Around And Fell In Love'. He later became the lead singer for Jefferson Starship alongside Grace Slick. Together they had some big hit songs like 'We Built This City' and 'Sara'. I thought he would be a perfect fit with Little River Band.

Unfortunately that wasn't to be, because the other guys in the band who had worked on *Uncovered* were all enamoured with John Farnham. It's no secret that I wasn't keen on John joining us, but the democratic choice said I was outvoted. It crossed my mind to leave the band then and there, but I decided to hang in and see where it would go. However, I started feeling like I was on the outside.

In the book *Whispering Jack — The John Farnham Story*, published in 1989, the author Clark Forbes writes:

Beeb said he was willing to try with John, but admits their relationship was flawed from the start because he was never convinced the singer was the right person to front LRB. The harmonies were still great, he said, but Beeb became tired and frustrated with John's concert manner. He hated what he described as John's 'clubby routine'.

Here was the difference for me between Glenn Shorrock and John Farnham: John had been a solo artist for most of his career whereas Glenn was always a band singer. I think there's a distinct difference between solo artists and guys who are lead singers in bands. It's a different mentality.

Technically, John can do things nobody else can with his voice, but to me he uses his voice like an instrument. He may be singing from his heart but I don't feel that when I listen to him. Glenn has soul. Everything that comes out of Glenn's mouth is sung with such feeling and that's what was missing for me. You may disagree, I guess it comes down to personal opinion and taste.

The structure of our harmonies with Glenn in the band was such that I sang in full voice above his melody lines. Graeham sang in a very strong falsetto voice a third above me. That was our vocal sound. That sound changed when John joined because he sang in a higher range than Glenn. I had to revert to singing the low harmony underneath John in a range where my voice didn't have anywhere near the same power.

I don't know whether people can hear that in our recordings but for me it took away the edge in our vocal sound.

GREATEST HITS / GREATEST HITS — VOLUME 2

In 1982, EMI Australia released *Greatest Hits – Volume 2*, which included 'Down On The Border', the first single with John Farnham as our lead singer, plus a cover of 'St Louis', originally recorded by The Easybeats, as well as 'The Other Guy' and 'Long Jumping Jeweller'. 'Down On The Border' and 'The Other Guy' were both written by Graeham Goble, and Glenn Shorrock wrote 'Long Jumping Jeweller'. It was a platinum album in Australia and went double platinum in New Zealand.

That same year, Capitol Records in the US released our first *Greatest*

Hits album, which included 'The Other Guy', our last top twenty hit single in the US, and 'Down On The Border'. The album sold gold initially but went on to sell triple platinum in the US.

THE NET

After Glenn Shorrock's departure, Wheatley smoothed things over with Capitol Records and we continued on as usual. We entered AAV to record what would be my last album with LRB. Right from the start I was disappointed with the quality of songs presented for *The Net*, the band's seventh studio album. I couldn't stand the title track that Graeham had written. I hated the recording of it and detested having to play the song live.

Graeham took over the reins to steer the band's musical direction into a harder-edged sound that I thought was totally wrong for us. I felt my songs were more in keeping with the band's known sound. Graeham and I co-wrote 'You're Driving Me Out Of My Mind', which was the opening track on the album. It was released as a single in the US but reached only number thirty-five on the *Billboard* charts.

'Down On The Border', written by Graeham, was the first single in Australia. It became a top ten hit for us. I wrote 'No More Tears', a song of forgiveness about my relationship with Megan. I also co-wrote 'The Danger Sign' with Frank Howson.

Frank Howson:

Chris Gough, who was in partnership with Tim Stobart (who co-owned Richmond Recorders), approached me for a meeting, saying that Little River Band was about to record a new album. He was intending to see Beeb Birtles, so it might be a good idea if I came up with a lyric that he could pitch to Beeb to write some music for.

He was hoping that if it came out well perhaps it'd stand a chance of being on the album. If he succeeded in achieving that, he and Tim would take a cut of the publishing. I took up this challenge and I wrote the lyrics to a song called 'The Danger Sign', a song about divorce, which I had recently gone through.

I remember spending a lot of time, more than usual, crafting the lyrics to be succinct but powerful as I knew the standard of songs recorded by Little River Band was extremely high and it was for an internationally successful act. Every day I'd go back to the lyrics and rework them until I was happy.

I thought 'The Danger Sign' turned out to be an excellent track. It was very driving and a heartfelt song from Frank's perspective.

I wasn't proud of *The Net*, like I had been of previous Little River Band albums. It sounded contrived. When we went on the road to promote it, things just got worse. We lost the support of Capitol Records because they weren't keen on John Farnham's voice. They preferred Glenn Shorrock. Our audiences found it difficult to understand what John was saying because he spoke too fast for them in his strong Australian accent.

Another disappointment for me was that John Marx, our booking agent, was starting to book us into theatre-in-the-round venues where I felt we were watched like monkeys in a zoo. I hated playing those venues and it brought home the realisation that Little River Band was starting to become a cabaret act. I was on board a sinking ship.

On a non-musical level, the other guys all embraced New Age thinking. Stephen Housden was into transcendental meditation. Graeham had always been open to believing in astrology, numerology, palm reading and clairvoyants. I always thought he was a Jack of all trades, master of none. David Hirschfelder, who was our keyboard player on *The Net* tour, was also into all this New Age philosophy. I was definitely the odd one out with my very traditional Christian beliefs.

As the tour progressed, I withdrew more and more from the guys. I kept to myself, sitting at the back of the bus minding my own business. I will say that right up until the very last performance at the Universal Amphitheatre in Los Angeles I never once let the band down on stage. I stayed a professional to the very end.

Wheatley was sick and tired of dealing with the band's petty demands and requests, so he was concentrating more on his other ventures. I could see it was definitely time for a change in the management department.

Because I'm better at putting my thoughts down on paper, I decided to write the guys a long letter outlining the areas where I thought change was needed for our continued success, including my frustrations with John Farnham and Glenn Wheatley. As Glenn Shorrock had experienced before me, every one of the suggestions I wrote in that letter fell on deaf ears.

Previously, my ideas and input into the band had been valued; now I felt I was hitting my head against a brick wall. The band and me simply didn't see eye to eye anymore. I stopped communicating with them altogether.

Graeham phoned Donna in Jefferson City every two or three days asking what was going on with me. All Donna could say was that I had written my letter of explanation to them and they had chosen to ignore it, so she couldn't shed any further light on the situation.

This all took place over about nine months, a period when I agonised over what my future should be. Never before in my life did I pray more intensely for an answer. I was beating myself up pretty good because I was questioning my judgment. I was miserable. And true to my style, I tried to place the decision-making in the band's hands rather than me having to do it.

There was a break in the middle of the tour where most of the guys went back to Australia. I stayed in the States and flew back to Jefferson City to join up with Donna and our girls at her mother's place. The next leg of the tour was starting in Japan, so Donna and I planned a little getaway, without the girls, in Hong Kong.

Afterwards, we rejoined the band in Japan. From there we flew to Anchorage, Alaska for a show and then on to Kansas City for a concert at the Starlight Theatre. We played dates in Canada and the US and completed the tour with four sold-out nights at The Universal Amphitheatre in Los Angeles.

After the final gig, a band meeting was called because the guys and our manager wanted to know what I planned to do. Donna pumped me up before the meeting, telling me to hang in and fight for my beliefs and my ideas, so it was with that attitude that I entered the backstage green room.

Very little was said by any of them until John Farnham took the floor as if he had taken it upon himself to become the band's spokesperson. He was the very last person I wanted to hear from. I didn't give a shit about what the newbies thought. I was bitterly disappointed that the two people with whom I had worked the longest and given my heart and soul to for eleven years through Mississippi and Little River Band, Graeham Goble and Derek Pellicci, didn't have anything to say. Even Glenn Wheatley, with whom I had shared eight years of incredible success, didn't say a word, though by this stage he'd had it with the group.

Throughout the meeting it still wasn't clear to me what my decision would be until John said, "Look, Beeb, don't be a lamb led to the slaughter. None of us want you to leave the band, we want you to stay, but we want your heart to be into it."

The words had barely left his lips when the light bulb went on inside my head. It hit me like a ton of bricks and in that instant I knew I had to stay true to myself. I wasn't going to lie to them. I said, "Well, there's no way I can do that because my heart isn't here anymore." And with that, I quit Little River Band and walked out of the meeting.

That incredible feeling of having an enormous weight lifted from my shoulders confirmed that I had made the right decision and that this was God's will for me. As hard as life has been at times since then, I will never regret making the decision to quit Little River Band when I did.

And here's confirmation that I knew I was right. Within five years of me leaving Little River Band they executed all the things I addressed in my letter to them.

1. John Farnham was no longer the lead singer, in fact, Glenn Shorrock was back in the band.
2. Glenn Wheatley was no longer their manager.
3. The music reverted to the band's more melodic sound.
4. They even went back to John Boylan as producer for the *Monsoon* album.

They were scrambling to recapture the successful years, but by then it was too late. Something was still missing. Am I being egotistical here to suggest it might have been me? I suspect I wasn't asked back into the lineup because of my strong Christian beliefs. I wouldn't have returned to the band then anyway because it would have been too soon.

It was now October 1983. Nineteen years would go by before I would share the stage with Graeham Goble and Glenn Shorrock again.

Twenty
FOR THE RECORD

Shortly after quitting Little River Band, when we were all back in Melbourne, Wheatley asked to meet me to see what I wanted in the way of compensation. It never crossed my mind to put a dollar value on what Little River Band was worth at that time.

We met for lunch in South Melbourne and I told him all I wanted was my two amplifiers in their road cases and my pedal board. That was it. He said he would have his lawyer send me a release form signing all my rights to the Little River Band name and trademark over to the remaining guys. I had no intention of signing any kind of release form. I still have that release form today without my signature on it.

Capitol Records paid us advances of one million dollars for every album we recorded. We used to spend about half of that on recording expenses. These advances were recouped as long as the album was successful and sold more than a certain amount of units.

The albums recorded after I quit the band hardly sold at all, so they didn't recoup the advances that were paid by Capitol Records. Consequently, the royalties from the lineups who had recorded the successful albums were paying for the advances to the lineup that recorded the non-successful albums.

It shouldn't have been the responsibility of the band members who had been part of the successful lineups to pay back the advances of the new lineup. Yet, here we were, losing out on royalties that were rightfully ours because all the royalties got lumped into the same pot. A business manager should have had no problem keeping the royalties in separate bank accounts.

Our Capitol Records' contract stated that we had the right to audit the company's books once every three years. Wheatley totally dropped the ball. On June 13, 1985, band members and their wives had a very heated meeting with him about all of this stuff. It pissed Wheatley off that Donna and I placed a tape recorder down on the table so we could record the meeting. Our trust in him had long disappeared.

In the late '90s, Wheatley released a book called *Paper Paradise* (the title made me think of some fancy brand of toilet paper!). I thought it lacked attention to detail.

Wheatley commissioned Ed Nimmervoll, a friend of mine, to write the book for him. In the book, Wheatley states that Donna hated him, which was far from the truth. Wheatley's first wife, Allison, and Donna were very good friends and remain so to this day. When Allison left Wheatley, who did he turn to and cry on her shoulder? Donna. She held his hand throughout that whole ordeal. I remember all his phone calls to our house on Central Park Road.

As much as Little River Band couldn't have made it without Wheatley initially, we made it possible for him to build his management and music publishing business.

Graeham Goble, Glenn Shorrock and I were all signed to Wheatley's first music publishing company, Tumbleweed Productions, before he later changed the name to Wheatley Music. We were on a 75/25 split with him on our songwriting copyrights. The songwriters earned 75 per cent and 25 per cent went to Glenn Wheatley. It was a very fair deal at the time.

In the US, to be both a manager and music publisher is considered a conflict of interest and is against the law. In Australia, because of our much smaller population, the law allows it.

As Little River Band gained success overseas, other Australian artists approached Wheatley about management. He managed Australian Crawl, Stylus, Ross Wilson, Real Life — who had an international smash hit with 'Send Me An Angel' — and Pseudo Echo. He also managed Darryl Cotton for a short period of time.

Wheatley and I saw things differently. Maybe I couldn't get past the fact that he was just a musician himself trying to be a businessman. I'd been accused of sitting and reading newspapers at band meetings but when discussions start going 'round and 'round, about the same bloody thing, without a firm decision being made, I tend to lose interest very quickly. Shit or get off the pot! Once I make a decision, I stick with it, come what may. Some of those band meetings dragged on and on for hours because of Wheatley and Derek.

Wheatley made decisions he thought were fantastic at the time but came back to bite us in the butt years later. When Capitol Records offered Little River Band an $8 million deal to record eight albums over a certain number of years, Wheatley asked Stephen Shrimpton, who was then head of EMI Australia, if he would release us from our contract with them. It was just prior to Stephen leaving for England to head up Paul McCartney Limited. Stephen agreed to let us out of our recording contract.

The deal with Capitol was set up in such a way that EMI Australia would continue to earn an overriding royalty from the first two albums we recorded for them. Over the years, it became an accounting debacle because no one kept an eye on what should rightly be paid to EMI and the band. Capitol paid an overriding royalty on not just the first two albums but on all of our albums. Well, that was money the band was losing out on!

Little River Band audited Capitol Records' books just once, early on in our career, and turned up $100,000 in unpaid record royalties. We settled out of court for half that amount. It clearly stated in the Capitol recording contract that Little River Band had the right to audit Capitol's books every three years.

The final straw for me was when Wheatley hired my ex-fiancée to work for him. He didn't ask Donna and me about it, didn't consider our feelings whatsoever. This became the final wedge between us.

EON FM

In 1979, radio in Australia was still only broadcast in the AM format. I guess the success of Little River Band being the first Australian group to crack the US while still residing at home brought us admiration and respect from the media.

When a consortium of investors, headed by Bill Armstrong, came together to invest in Australia's first FM radio station, Wheatley was offered a position on the board. Each member of Little River Band was given the opportunity to invest by buying 20,000 shares for $1 each. As a board director, Wheatley was allowed to buy more shares than we were. The offer was too good to pass up, so we all invested $20,000 each. The band's shares had to be kept to a minimum because the other investors didn't want Glenn Wheatley and Little River Band having a monopoly in EON FM Pty Ltd.

Having toured the US for a number of years and done interviews at radio stations where one side of the building housed the AM station and the other side the FM station, we knew that FM radio would definitely take off in Australia.

It couldn't have been more than a year or so later when, for whatever reason, both Graeham and Derek decided they were going to sell all of their EON shares. They were asking $1.25 a share.

Donna and I, and Jo and Glenn Shorrock, jumped at the opportunity and each bought 10,000 of Graeham and Derek's shares.

Five years later, EON FM was sold to another consortium of investors who were buying up every one of the FM radio stations in the capital cities around Australia.

Twenty-one
RIVER OF NO RETURN

Shortly after I quit Little River Band, Derek Pellicci also left the group. Graeham rang me at home and asked if I could recommend a drummer. Having read that Cold Chisel had recently broken up, I suggested they get Steven Prestwich, which they did.

Glenn Wheatley stepped down as Little River Band's manager and focused on managing John Farnham. They were already planning John's return to being a solo artist. Apparently, Wheatley mortgaged his house to finance the recording of *Whispering Jack*.

In 1987, the guys decided to re-form Little River Band with Graeham Goble, Stephen Housden, Wayne Nelson, Derek Pellicci, and Glenn Shorrock back as lead singer. I had heard something about them re-forming but I wasn't asked to be a part of it. In my mind, re-joining the band at this stage would have been too early. With Geoffrey Schuhkraft now managing the band, they scored a record deal with MCA Records. This was a brand new deal, not to be confused with the flow of royalties coming from Capitol Records.

They had to set up a new company for the MCA royalties, so they formed We Two Pty Ltd, with the five members all being equal shareholders. Another big mistake! In doing so, the lawyer who drew up the legal paperwork transferred the rights to the Little River Band name and the platypus trademark symbol from Little River Band Pty Ltd to We Two Pty Ltd.

The new lineup recorded two albums for MCA, *Monsoon* and *Get Lucky*. I didn't listen to *Monsoon* or *Get Lucky* until a few years later when I picked up the CDs in a bargain bin at a used vinyl and CD store.

After mild success with both albums and, of course, the ongoing touring schedule, one by one the original members of Little River Band left the group. I've never asked Graeham why he left in 1991 but I suspect it probably had something to do with the tension between him and Shorrock.

On September 28, 1992, Wayne Nelson's 13-year-old daughter, Aubree, was killed in a freak car accident, resulting in him quitting the band. Next it was Glenn Shorrock, who left for the second time, selling his share in the company for $83,500. Derek Pellicci was the last to leave, also selling his interest in the company for something like $80,000. Stephen Housden, the last man standing, continued to tour as Little River Band, hiring side musicians to complete various lineups of the band.

I saw the band play just once, in Nashville when they performed at a small club called Café Milano. The lineup included Stephen Housden plus a bunch of new guys and just one original member of the band, Roger McLachlan, who had agreed to do the tour. Before the show I picked Roger and Stephen up at their hotel and drove them to my house in Brentwood where they requested I make them tea and vegemite on toast. Everything was still friendly between us. I had recently completed recording *Driven By Dreams*, my solo CD, so I invited them up to my music room and played it for them. They were very complimentary, to the extent that Stephen said this was exactly the kind of music he would like to be writing and recording. Then I drove them back to the city for their performance that night.

When they performed 'Happy Anniversary' that night, Stephen mentioned I was in the audience and had me stand up and take a bow. It made me feel awkward. It never feels right for me to be seated in the audience, no matter who I go see. I always think I belong up there, on stage. After all, it's been my life since I was 16 or 17.

This from Donna:

It was great to hear all of the old tunes but something was desperately missing. It was Beeb's harmonies in each and every song. Because I'd toured with Beeb and the band in the heyday, I knew the songs inside out. So as I watched this lineup perform, I just started to hear Beeb's part in my head to complete the sound.

After the show, one of the guys rushed up to me and said he was so happy to meet me and that he was 'the new Beeb Birtles'. Say what? I am not known for my tact ... more so for having no filter, so I said something like, "Whoa, don't flatter yourself. You are no Beeb Birtles. You did not deliver, nor would I expect you to be able to." Needless to say, that conversation wrapped up quickly and he sauntered off with his tail between his legs.

In the late '90s, in a phone conversation with Bill Cuomo, my business partner in Nashville, Stephen claimed to have every right to the name. He said he had 'kept the name alive' for seventeen years whereas my time with the band had been just eight years. Bill promptly pointed out to Stephen that my years with the band were the most important of the band's entire career. They were the eight years that set him up to be able to continue to reap the financial benefits.

At the time of writing, Stephen Housden doesn't even perform with Little River Band anymore, even though he still owns the rights to the band's name. Wayne Nelson, who returned to the band after playing bass in the John Farnham Band for a few years, has appointed himself as Little River Band's lead singer and I suspect he is leasing the name from Stephen Housden.

This band is nothing like the band that I co-founded. To me, it's no longer the Little River Band, it's the Little River *Brand*, and I am disappointed for the fans, but heartened by their comments and support. I recently saw one comment on YouTube that stated: 'Calling this band LRB is like calling the Ringo All-Starr Band the Beatles.'

Looking back, I think we should have handled David Briggs and Roger McLachlan's dismissals more delicately. I didn't even know that Roger was dismissed the way he was until I read his contribution to this memoir. I remember David's sacking because I was there and I won't ever forget the way Graeham got in David's face. Considering the contribution David and Roger made to the band's music, I don't think they deserved what they got.

You can't change the course of history, and whereas Ric Formosa, George McArdle and I left of our own accord, I can't help but wonder how things could have turned out had the classic lineup of the band stayed together. After I quit the band I wrote a song called 'Hired Hand' and one of the verses reads like this:

I get accused of being The Lone Ranger
Don't see my face around yet I'm no stranger
You underestimate my contribution
In the midst of confusion
It's a world of confusion

Every now and then LRB fans will send me links to interviews Wayne Nelson has done with various magazines and newspapers. He continually refers to the 'ever revolving' door of past members that have come and gone through Little River Band's lineup. I got so fed up with reading these articles, I sat down and wrote the song 'Revolving Door' as a direct response to Stephen Housden and Wayne Nelson.

You know when the well runs dry
Your view of the open sky
You can kiss it all goodbye to the wind
You've milked it for all these years
With no one to interfere
And you claim you'll be the last man here till the end
My friend

I got news for you
Don't let that revolving door
Spit you out across the floor
And leave you scrambling for more clout
There's always room for reasonable doubt
So don't let that revolving door
Hit your arse on your way out

Your gift of inheritance
Has cost you the price of friends
And you know that it all depends on the song
Court action is guaranteed
When driven by fear and greed

And you've had so many mouths to feed for so long
But it's wrong

I got news for you
Don't let that revolving door
Spit you out across the floor
And leave you scrambling for more clout
There's always room for reasonable doubt
So don't let that revolving door
Hit your arse on your way out

You say you keep the name alive
Pulling the wool down over their eyes
You speak of toiling sweat and blood
Dragging the name down through the mud

Lately, I take great delight in telling people that it's very satisfying to know there is a tribute band out there performing the hits we recorded as Little River Band all those years ago. Stephen Housden may own the name but it will never ever be his band.

Twenty-two
MIDLIFE

twenty-two

MIDLIFE

After quitting the band in October 1983 I had no idea what I wanted to do. I was thirty-five years old and when I sat back and analysed what I had become, it dawned on me that for the last two years with the band I had just been going through the motions. I wasn't singing with any feeling anymore, I had lost my soul.

What else could I accomplish in Australia? I had climbed to the top of the ladder and there wasn't another rung to go higher. I suggested to Donna that we should think about moving to the States but she wasn't keen because she absolutely loved her life in Melbourne.

Hannah was nearly three and Emmie was 18 months and I was happy to spend time at home watching them grow up. Hannah was about to start school at Korowa Anglican Girls School as the youngest student ever enrolled.

As a songwriter I was quite prolific for the next two years, but I wrote a lot of bitter songs about my time with the band, songs not worth recording. I guess I had to get them out of my system to clear my brain.

I bumped into Zoot's old manager Wayne de Gruchy not long before he died and he asked me what I was going to do next. I told him I didn't know. Always the visionary, he said I should form a stripped-down band of four members, two guitars, bass and drums. Back to the kind of lineup Zoot was. I didn't take his advice.

I also received a phone call from someone in the business asking if I would be interested in joining Wendy Saddington's band. I said no. That wasn't for me. I think it was just too early for me to jump straight back into something. Or was it? I really needed some time off after all the years on the road. I had been constantly touring since 1968 and was well and truly burned out and needed some time to recharge my batteries.

I think my mind got the better of me because I kept going 'round and 'round thinking about what I should do. Should I just write and produce? Should I form another band and start all over by going back into the pubs? I didn't really want to do that! Should I approach a music publishing company as a songwriter? Should I write jingles? I was confused and had definitely hit a brick wall.

Around the same time I left Little River Band, Sherbet broke up, leaving Daryl Braithwaite out on his own. I conceived the idea of forming another successful Australian duo. This was more than a decade before Savage Garden came along. Except for Air Supply, Australia had not seen a successful pop duo since Bobby and Laurie, who had some fantastic hits in the late '60s and early '70s. I also kept Hall and Oates in mind as a more current example of a very successful recording duo.

Daryl and I knew of each other although we had never met. I contacted Daryl and his wife, Sarah, and invited them over to our house, where I explained the concept. They both thought the idea was terrific and we made arrangements to start writing some songs together. Some film people contacted me and asked me to submit songs for their upcoming productions.

Daryl and I actually got a little ahead of ourselves by having some publicity photos taken and appearing on *Hey Hey It's Saturday*. We were mostly working in the music room at my house, recording some pretty bad sounding demos on my Revox tape recorder.

One day we were recording some vocals with a friend of Daryl's, a guy called Brett Goldsmith, and I could hear one of them mimicking my voice from another room. I got the feeling there and then that Daryl didn't really respect me and I knew that the duo wasn't going to work. I thought my initial idea for wanting to form the duo was a good one, and it all started with good intentions but after a while the novelty wore off. I could tell Daryl was losing interest. When he was at our house shortly after that I had to virtually drag it out of him by saying, "Look, I'm getting the feeling that you really don't want to pursue the duo thing." He sheepishly admitted that he didn't think it was right for him, so we parted company. Ironic, isn't it, me dragging something out of someone else?

During my last year with the band I had written what I thought was a really great song, 'Dreams'. I wrote it to a set of lyrics Frank Howson had given me. It was going to be the theme song for a movie on the life of Les Darcy, the famous Australian boxer. Frank gave me the script to read and it blew me away. I thought it was fantastic.

I wrote the music with a very driving drumbeat as if I was watching the footwork of two boxers sparring in the ring. I remember playing it for David Hirschfelder out on the road somewhere when I was tuning up just before a show.

The movie on Les Darcy never eventuated, which was a crying shame. Frank Howson used the song in another one of his movies, *Boulevard of Broken Dreams*. I felt they really missed the mark on that one because the Les Darcy script was quite phenomenal.

Frank Howson:

I realised that 'Dreams', although written about Les Darcy, also suited the subject matter of Boulevard Of Broken Dreams. *So I asked Beeb to sing it for the soundtrack with Lisa Edwards doing backing vocals. The soundtrack album was nominated for an ARIA Award for Best Soundtrack Album.*

I believe after Beeb left LRB, Wayne Nelson asked if 'Dreams' could be on the next LRB album, but Beeb refused permission. So it finally found its home on the Boulevard Of Broken Dreams *soundtrack. It may very well, arguably, be the best song we ever collaborated on.*

In 1985 I decided to form my own music publishing company, which I named 'Songskill'. I was introduced to a young graphic artist by the name of Mykl Pratt. I explained what I was looking for and he came up with an absolute killer logo. The bonus was that his design won the prestigious 1985 Melbourne Art Directors Club Award for 'best corporate image'. To this day, I still use Mykl's logo for my music publishing company.

I may have heard about the organisation Youth With A Mission through Word Records, a Christian record label in Melbourne. It was through YWAM that I met Steve Grace, an Australian contemporary Christian artist. Steve asked me to produce his début album. It was 1988 and I hadn't spent much time in the studio since leaving Little River Band.

We recorded his album at Sing Sing in Richmond. Phil Butson, who was a partner in the studio, recorded the project with us. Everything I had learned from being in the studio with Little River Band came flooding back to me. Steve's album was called *Children of the Western World* and it turned out to be a very good record.

It was so good that we talked Word Records into creating a new label, Triune, for the release. When it was released it earned the distinction of being the biggest-selling contemporary Christian album Australia had seen to date. Only Amy Grant sold more albums than Steve Grace and she was an established American contemporary Christian artist.

Recording Steve's album restored any confidence I might have lost. I loved being back in the studio creating new music, whether it was inspirational music or not.

Twenty-three
THE MOVE TO AMERICA

I'd been pestering Donna to move to America ever since I quit Little River Band in late 1983. I was floundering, not doing much of anything and getting bored. She told me to go over to the States by myself to see what I could get going, but that she was going to stay in Australia, to give the girls the stability they needed.

I understood what she was saying but I just didn't have it in me to leave Donna and our girls. At the time I think I wanted to run away from it all, not really knowing specifically what I would do in America. I did, however, want a new start for myself.

Sometime during 1991 I received a phone call from Donna's sister, Debbie, in America. Debbie told me their father had been tragically killed in a car accident on the way to their cabin at The Lake of the Ozarks, which is about a 45-minute drive south from Jefferson City in Missouri. I had to tell Donna the devastating news. She was in that state of not really knowing whether it was real. It all seemed like a bad dream.

This was on a Friday and I knew I had to get Donna and the girls on a plane to the US because it was important they had closure. With such short notice, I had to stay in Melbourne and keep everything going at home. I phoned our travel agent and she was able to get Donna and the girls on a flight to the States that weekend.

When they returned, we sat down and talked about everything. The funeral made it clear to Donna that she didn't want to be so far away if something should happen to her mother. Donna and her mother have always been very close, and I love Margie like she's my own mother. I completely understood how Donna felt.

She came home with a cassette of a sermon that was preached during a service at her sister's church. The sermon was called 'A Place Called

There' and it was based on the story in 1 Kings 17.1. The brook dried up and Elijah was told to go to a place called 'there' where he would receive many blessings. The pastor said, "There comes a time when the brook dries up and the blessings cease to flow. Some people hang on when they should be moving on." Donna took it as a sign that the time had come for us to move to America.

For all of the eight years after quitting Little River Band I felt I wasn't getting anywhere by staying in Australia, so I was elated with Donna's decision. I was forty-two and I remember Derek Pellicci coming over when he found out we were leaving. He said something along the lines of, "Mate, I really admire you for packing up, selling everything and moving to the States."

But just like when my Adelaide musician friends had talked about the possibility of becoming famous all over Australia, I didn't think anything of it. The move wasn't a big deal to me. I felt I was following in the footsteps of my father. I felt I had the same pioneering spirit. And it wasn't like we were moving to some foreign country we didn't know. As a family we had made countless trips to the States, and all of Donna's family was there.

Donna and I were fortunate that our house was completely paid off due to the sale of EON FM. We paid a little more than $500,000 for the Manning Road house and in the nine years we lived there, we put a very minimal amount of money into it.

We had to vacate the house by January 3, and we decided to spend our last week in a hotel on Queens Road, seeing friends at various times, to say our last goodbyes. Then, on January 11, 1992, we left Australia for good.

FROM JEFFERSON CITY, MO TO NASHVILLE

We decided to settle in Jefferson City, Missouri because Donna had family there and we were familiar with the surroundings. For as long as I have known Donna, Jefferson City was my home in the US. If I was on the road, Donna and the girls stayed at her mother's house. Margie Brucks has lived her whole life in Jefferson City, and Donna's next oldest sister, Debbie, and her family, also lived there.

It was an adjustment for our girls, who were eleven and nine at the time.

First of all, they had attended Korowa, a girls school in Melbourne, but now they had to go to school with boys as well. Their classmates couldn't get enough of their Australian accents, which they promptly lost over about three weeks. They also came home in tears a couple of times because they said the boys were teasing them. The boys weren't teasing them, they were merely flirting with them, but my girls didn't know the difference.

People talked to me about Branson, the touristy town about three hours from Jefferson City. I decided to check out the music scene there because quite a few people told me that Branson was going to be the new Nashville. Rodney Dillard, from The Dillards, had recently bought the best recording studio in town. I met Rodney and he showed me around the studio. He was a very cool and down-to-earth guy.

However, I didn't think Branson had much to offer me, other than playing live music in the huge entertainment theatres some prominent country artists had set up. And it wasn't just country artists. People like Wayne Newton, Andy Williams, Boxcar Willie and some well-known gospel artists had their own theatres there. I wanted to pursue writing music rather than performing. I returned to Jefferson City knowing that I didn't want to move to Branson.

Within three months of getting settled in Jefferson City, I started commuting to Nashville, which is about a seven-and-a-half hour drive. I did that for more than a year until I couldn't stand it anymore. I told Donna we had to move. There really wasn't much to do with music in Jefferson City. Some friends of Donna's were moving back to Jefferson City at the time and bought our house, which freed us up to look for one in Nashville.

After looking at numerous houses, with not one of them really standing out as 'the one', we bought an attractive brick house in the subdivision of Brent Meade. We left Jefferson City in August 1993 and moved into our house the day before school started on August 17. Once again, Donna and I set up home while the girls went to school during the day.

Dropping the Little River Band name opened every door for me with music publishing companies on Music Row. I came armed with cassettes of my pop and rock demos. Basically it came down to this: they didn't know what to do with me. Nevertheless, I spent the next five years writing with other songwriters who had publishing deals on Music Row. Looking back on that period in my life, I don't know whether I learned much or not. I had Songskill, my own music publishing company, already in place and financially I didn't need what they called 'a draw', a weekly wage on which to live.

I was astounded that some writers would sign to music publishing companies just for the draw and forsake ownership in their copyrights. Not in a million years would I ever give away my creativity for free. That's how desperate some of these writers were to score a hit song.

It got to the stage where I grew tired of writing really dumb songs and I cut my ties with most of these songwriters. I was never short of a musical idea to bring to the table but when one of my co-writers started telling me not to play what she called the 'fancy stuff', I lost the desire to co-write. I needed to keep challenging myself when it came to song writing. I'm always chasing something different, whether it's an interesting chord progression or an outrageous groove. To me, country music doesn't groove.

Twenty-four
SONIC SORBET RECORDS

Sonic Sorbet Records logo

In 1998, about five years into our life in Nashville, I gravitated towards working with ex Los Angeles musicians with whom I immediately clicked. Bill Cuomo was one of them. Bill and I first met on the island of Montserrat when Little River Band recorded *Time Exposure*. Little did I know that our paths would cross again nearly two decades later in a rather chance encounter.

Scott Whitson, our insurance agent, also happened to be Bill's insurance agent. When Scott was at Bill's house one day, knowing Bill worked in the music business, he asked him if he knew any of the guys in Little River Band. Bill said, "As a matter of fact I worked with the band when they were recording their *Time Exposure* album with George Martin."

Scott replied, "Well, Beeb Birtles lives just ten minutes up the road from you in Brentwood."

Scott relayed the story to me and I searched for Bill's name in the phone book. I called the number for the only Cuomo listed and it turned out to be Bill's mother who had also moved to Nashville. She gave me Bill's studio number and I contacted him. We set up a meeting and I drove down to see him and check out the studio.

That led to me recording some demos of songs I had written. During the recording, I was telling Bill about my recently launched website and how many hits it was getting. I was bowled over by the amount of fans out there still interested, not only in Little River Band, but me as well.

Bill Cuomo:

Beeb and I talked about the kind of pop/rock music we liked and he told me of his desire to record a solo CD. Since there were eighty million plus baby boomers in the US alone that would likely be a great audience, we discussed how we might be able to deliver that music to them. I suggested that we form an independent record label since we both had a long history in pop music.

With a web presence, we figured we could use that experience to help draw traffic to our record company website. We were both very excited — despite knowing the risks of running a label — as we could target and reach our desired audience as well as write and record the kind of music we loved. Our aim was to sell our recorded product via online and direct mailing.

For a long time, we couldn't settle on a name for our company. It wasn't until we were recording electric guitars with Jerry McPherson for my solo CD, *Driven By Dreams*, that we stumbled across it. Jerry was fishing for a certain sound from his pedal board when he said, "I'm trying to find the right tone but it's like a sonic sorbet of sounds down here." The light bulb went on and I turned to Bill and said, "That's it, that's our name!" And so thanks to Jerry McPherson, Sonic Sorbet Records took on life.

We liked the name because it encompassed the word for sound, 'sonic', and 'sorbet', as in many flavours. It was apparent to both of us, considering our combined experiences in the recording business, that we could produce and write just about anything. Country music was already starting to lean more towards pop and rock, so we had that covered. Bluegrass, country, alternative rock, hard rock, comedy, you name it, we could do it all under the umbrella of Sonic Sorbet Records.

We completed the recording for *Driven By Dreams* sometime in late 1998. To this day, Bill and I are still so proud of that CD. The music and the chosen songs were perfectly suited to my voice. All of the band tracks were recorded with me playing acoustic guitar. Drums, bass guitar, keyboards and my acoustic guitar made up the basic tracks and from there we did the overdubbing and vocals. Bill always remarks about my Maton acoustic having the 'sonic balls' to be able to drive the band. It's his all-time favourite acoustic to record. We laughingly refer to *Driven By Dreams* as the CD that refuses to die as from time to time we receive emails from people telling us how great it is.

Bill:

Our confidence in the CD got ahead of us. We spent a lot of money paying promotional people who promised us the moon as we slipped further and further into debt. We spent thousands of dollars trying to get Driven By Dreams *off the ground with airplay. Peanuts for a major label, but we were a small, inexperienced and low-budget label, basically a two-man operation.*

Our aim was to sell product online but we were just a bit ahead of the curve. In the early 2000 years, people still didn't feel comfortable giving out their credit card information to buy product online. If we wanted to sell in retail stores, we had to contend with a string of distributors who would all take a financial slice of our CD, leaving us with less than 30 per cent of the original price. We also needed radio to secure retail.

So we decided to pursue radio and enhance our musical presence. We achieved some milestones too, which was quite encouraging. In the Pacific Northwest and the Southeast we received medium to heavy airplay in what they call secondary radio markets. We got to speak with program directors and DJs who were all very enthusiastic about Driven By Dreams. *We managed to get 'Someday' into the top 5 in the Pacific Northwest and 'Relentless' into the top 10 in the Southeast, in particular Georgia and Florida. But that did not come without costs.*

We put up advertisements at local colleges seeking two interns to help us with our efforts at having our own 'promotion department'. We realised that we didn't have the financial resources or personnel to attack the entire radio nation, so we set out to focus on one region only.

Having decided to take on promotions ourselves, in order to save money and perhaps do a better job, we found that we were able to get through to program directors and disc jockeys with a fair amount of ease. This was largely due to our combined music/record history. It turned out that many country jocks were former pop/rock DJs familiar with the records that Beeb and I had done. Soon we had promotion guys calling us asking how we managed to get through to the people they failed to reach. We always told them, "Just talking about music!"

Twenty-five
BIRTLES SHORROCK GOBLE

BIRTLES SHORROCK GOBLE

Sometime in late 2001 I received a phone call from Graeham Goble. He told me that quite a number of opportunities for Little River Band to get back together and perform again had come up. He asked me if I was open to a reunion of what fans were calling the classic lineup, including David Briggs, George McArdle, Derek Pellicci and Glenn Shorrock. We were going to call ourselves the Original Little River Band.

By then, it had been eighteen years since I quit the band. I told him that I would be interested in a reunion because, in my mind, time had healed many things. I was also keen to hear our three voices together again after all these years. I sent Graeham my solo CD, *Driven By Dreams*. After listening to it, he informed both Glenn Shorrock and Glenn Wheatley that I was still singing really well. They particularly liked one of my songs, 'Photogenic'. Glenn Wheatley was again going to be involved on the management side, something I wasn't exactly jumping up and down about.

I didn't know it at the time, but the reunion idea didn't actually come from Graeham or Wheatley. It was Paul Rodger's idea. Paul was in partnership with Michael Costa in a company called Stream AV. I knew Michael was a recording engineer. He had reached out to me via email a couple of times during the '90s.

In Paul Rodger's own words:

In 2001, Stream AV started providing DVD authoring services to Warner Vision, which was, at the time, the largest producer and distributor of concert DVDs in the world. I was travelling to Sydney every other week to see them and on one of those visits I was talking with Warner Vision's production team about how successful the Eagles' Hell Freezes Over *DVD was. I said that we should do a similar thing in Australia.*

Darryl O'Connor, the managing director of Warner Vision, laughed and asked me who would be big enough and have the appeal to that market to make it worthwhile. I said I thought LRB would be a great choice and the room fell silent. Darryl said that LRB would be the right fit for them but how could we get it to happen? I said that Michael Costa was in contact with Graeham Goble and that we could ask the question. Warner Vision said if we could pull it together they would fund the production.

On my return to Melbourne I asked Michael what he thought and he said, "It will never happen!" I asked him to put me in touch with Graeham Goble, which he reluctantly did. I spoke with Graeham and then Derek Pellicci to see if there was even a possibility, but both of them were hesitant.

Over several weeks I continued to speak with Graeham and Derek and gave them copies of various concert DVDs so they could see the possibilities. At some point Graeham started to come around to the idea and he contacted Beeb and Glenn Shorrock.

Glenn wasn't happy with Derek following Little River Band's first re-formation at the end of the '80s. An ultimatum had been delivered to Glenn, to get him to commit to touring with the band for a certain amount of time every year. Glenn sought legal advice but was told it was two (Stephen Housden and Derek) against one, and he was forced to sell his share in We Two Pty Ltd. Glenn had the company valued and was informed it was worth $250,000. So Glenn sold his share to Housden and Pellicci for one third of that amount. It left a bad taste in Glenn's mouth to the extent that he didn't want anything more to do with Derek.

Paul Rodger adds:

At some point, someone asked if we had spoken to Glenn Wheatley. Big mistake! I made an appointment to see Wheatley, who I knew from the productions we had worked on for John Farnham. I walked into his office in the tradition of the Blues Brothers and said, "We're putting the band back together." Wheatley's jaw hit the floor! He was amazed that I had got it to the stage we had, but in true form, he thanked me and told me he would take it from here. I wasn't happy about being dismissed from the process, but at that point I was more interested in producing the DVD than the management of the whole project.

We informed Stephen Housden that we intended to perform under the name 'The Original Little River Band'. Stephen's lawyer, Thomas Stevens, claimed we didn't have any rights to the Little River Band trademark anymore and he sent us a 'cease and desist' order. He claimed Stephen Housden now legally owned the LRB name and trademark. What was about to unravel would cost us — Graeham Goble, Glenn Shorrock and me — more than $300,000 in legal expenses.

As reported by Nui Te Koha in the Herald Sun on December 14, 2001:
A musician trading as the Little River Band has vowed to block plans by the group's original members to tour the US under the name.
Stephen Housden, a member of the Little River Band since 1982 and who bought the worldwide rights to the famous band name four years ago, says he will not allow a re-formed version of the group to use the LRB name in any shape or form.
'I can tell you now, there's no hope of them coming to America because I own the trademark in America and I own it for the world,' Housden told the Herald Sun *from his home in Ireland yesterday. 'I've been working in America for the last 20 years in the Little River Band and this new group just cannot happen.'*

We were forced to hire Dr John Bleechmore QC as our legal representation as we were dragged into the Australian Federal Court over who legally owned the rights to the Little River Band name. It also ended any chance of re-forming the classic lineup of the band. Seeing as we were the three main songwriters and singers of most of the hits, we decided to go out under our own last names, Birtles Shorrock Goble, and put together a backing band with younger musicians.

In the US that was going to be a hard sell because being one of those faceless '70s bands, all Americans knew was Little River Band. Some people may remember that Glenn Shorrock was the lead singer but the rest of us were basically unknown. Nobody in America knows who Birtles, Shorrock and Goble are unless we advertised that we were the 'original founding members' or 'the original voices' of Little River Band. And that led to another fight with Stephen Housden, this time in a district court in Florida.

In the settlement, reached in the Australian Federal Court in June 2002, we agreed we would only use the LRB name to describe ourselves as former members of the band. We assumed this settlement would be worldwide, so we didn't respond to the action being taken in Florida. The Florida court had no knowledge whatsoever about the Australian settlement. So we reached a second settlement with Housden in July 2005.

In a nutshell, as Birtles Shorrock Goble, we were allowed to say we were the founding members or the original voices of Little River Band but in advertising, the Little River Band name could not appear in typeface larger than two-thirds the typeface size used for Birtles Shorrock Goble.

Our side of the story is as follows:

In 1975, Little River Band formed a trading company called Little River Band Pty Ltd. This company became the legal owner of the Little River Band and the LRB trademarks. It was this company that signed a recording contract with EMI/Capitol records. The original members who were shareholders in Little River Band Pty Ltd and who signed the deal with Capitol Records were Glenn Shorrock, Graeham Goble, Beeb Birtles, Derek Pellicci, David Briggs, George McArdle, and Glenn Wheatley as the band's manager.

By 1986, LRB had completed its eight albums deal with EMI/Capitol and the band ceased working. The trademark remained in the ownership of Little River Band Pty Ltd that was owned and controlled by the original lineup and Glenn Wheatley.

In 1988, a new company was set up for the re-formation of LRB to take advantage of a new recording contract that was offered by MCA Records. Without consultation, the lawyer who documented the new company, legally transferred (not licensed) ownership of the Little River Band trademark from the original trading company, Little River Band Pty Ltd, to a new company, We Two Pty Ltd. This new company did not include all the original members but it did include Glenn Shorrock,

Graeham Goble, Derek Pellicci, Wayne Nelson and Stephen Housden.

At that time, no one was aware that a legal transfer of the trademark had occurred in the large amount of documentation that formed the new trading entity. Subsequently, Graeham Goble and Wayne Nelson left We Two Pty Ltd, returning their $1 company shares to the other three.

In about 1994, Derek Pellicci and Stephen Housden approached Glenn Shorrock and demanded that he commit to seven months a year touring the US. As this arrangement was unsuitable to Glenn, Pellicci and Housden, using their two-thirds majority, put an ultimatum to Glenn: He could buy them out or they would continue without him. The company, We Two Pty Ltd, was valued.

Glenn Shorrock sought legal advice to see if an injunction could prevent Housden and Pellicci from continuing. The advice was that he could not. So Glenn took a settlement of his then one-third share, and Housden and Pellicci continued as a partnership. Shortly after, Pellicci sold his half share to Stephen Housden, and Housden then owned 100 per cent, which included the trademark.

All of the original members of LRB were not paid for the loss of the name. Glenn Wheatley, Graeham Goble, Beeb Birtles, David Briggs, George McArdle, Roger McLachlan and Ric Formosa received nothing and consequently lost all rights to the LRB trademark.

As far as the Original Classic lineup is concerned, Little River Band's name and goodwill was never for sale. They thought it would be theirs forever. LRB continued to perform in the US with Stephen Housden and hired side musicians. At some point, Wayne Nelson returned to LRB and took on the role of lead singer. Stephen Housden retired from touring around 2007 and was replaced by a hired guitar player. Stephen Housden currently lives in Ireland off the profits he makes from the touring income from Little River Band. The original members who wrote and recorded all the hit records receive nothing from the touring activities of Little River Band.

In 2002, discussions were held to reunite the 'Classic Lineup' and call it 'The Original Little River Band'. Immediately, Stephen Housden, along with his wife, June Housden, launched legal action to protect their 'money-tree'. A Federal Court case was held in Melbourne. On the third day the original members' case collapsed when Stephen Housden's legal team produced a document showing the legal transfer of the trademark.

The document was a copy because the original could not be found, and was signed by Glenn Wheatley and Graeham Goble. Both Glenn Wheatley and Graeham Goble have no memory of signing the document and there were no witnesses to the agreement. Why would we have signed away the ownership of LRB for no consideration?

Beeb Birtles, Glenn Shorrock and Graeham Goble decided to re-form, using the name BIRTLES SHORROCK GOBLE (BSG). Stephen and his wife, June, spent a staggering amount of money in legal action to prevent BSG from working, particularly in the US. Their legal action has been successful in making it impossible for a promoter to adequately advertise BSG in the US. BSG have tried to mount a tour of the US but could not find a promoter willing to tour the act because of the legal restrictions surrounding the trademark.

On October 17, 2004, 'The Classic Lineup' was inducted into the ARIA Hall of Fame. Stephen Housden almost prevented this from happening. Eventually, Housden agreed to issue a 24-hour license to the original members, allowing them to perform one song at the awards and use the name Little River Band.

In 2005, the historical story of the Little River Band, a DVD titled It's A Long Way There, was manufactured, pressed and scheduled for release by EMI/Capitol, but Stephen Housden and Wayne Nelson threatened to sue EMI Records and the product was withdrawn. It was never released.

Graeham actually wrote an excellent song about the whole situation. It's called 'Someone's Taken Our History'. Both Glenn and I sang harmonies on it.

Where once Wheatley smelled money in the re-formation of the Original Little River Band, the whole wrangle now ended his involvement with us. He was already showing signs of frustration and virtually washed his hands of us. The four of us had been on the nightly television news and all over the newspapers concerning our Federal Court case but I guess as soon as he couldn't get his name in the news anymore he decided that was as far as he was going to go. I lost all respect for Wheatley when he refused to chip in one-fourth of our outstanding Queen's Counsel bill to Dr Bleechmore for $64,000, claiming his name didn't appear on the piece of paper.

Stephen White, who was Little River Band's tour manager for many years, took over the management for Birtles Shorrock Goble in 2002. Some of the shows we played that stand out in my mind are the Grand Prix Ball for the Formula One racing event in Melbourne; A Blue Night, a fund raiser for Motor Neurone Disease at the Crown Palladium in Melbourne on May 24, 2002; and the Farmhand Concert for Drought Relief on October 26, 2002. After a couple of tours around Australia, we parted ways with Stephen White and Paul Rodger took over as manager.

Paul Rodger:

I was still talking to Graeham Goble and Warner Vision about the DVD, but I knew that Glenn Wheatley and Stephen White were trying to get me out of that too. Warner Vision then had a change in management and the offer to finance the DVD evaporated. When a tour was announced, I noticed that there was one date at The Enmore Theatre in Sydney.

I organised to get the bosses from all the big labels to the show, including George Ash and Rod Cameron from Universal. At the end of the show, Rod said, "We'll talk." I also received favourable input from all the other label executives. The following week I was asked to put in a budget to Universal for what I thought it might cost and a week after that George Ash and Rod Cameron flew down to Melbourne to have dinner with Graeham and me, where they offered us the deal.

I think it was just after the Enmore gig that Stephen White sent the guys a very aggressive email about me and that he could do the Full Circle *DVD for you. With the finance from Universal in place, Birtles, Shorrock and Goble appointed me as manager and as the producer of* Full Circle.

FULL CIRCLE

On July 17, 18 and 19, 2003 we recorded and filmed three nights at The

Forum Theatre in the heart of Melbourne. *Full Circle* was released as a CD and DVD and featured our hits as well as some new songs. Paul Rodger negotiated a deal with Universal Australia for the release.

The CD and DVD went gold and Universal tried very hard to have it released in the US and were in negotiation with Capitol Records, our old record label. However, because of the loss of the Little River Band name and the injunction against us in the Florida Court of Law, Capitol got cold feet and passed on it.

Full Circle has become a very sought after DVD because it's scarce and unavailable in the US NTSC television format. I have LRB fans contacting me all the time asking where they can find a copy.

The last time that Birtles Shorrock Goble appeared together was for the Countdown Spectacular 2 concerts around Australia from August 18 until September 5, 2007. Graeham and I worked on a medley of our hits. It flowed seamlessly and left the crowds yearning for more. We appeared as the second last act on the bill, with Rick Springfield closing the show. Kind of ironic, isn't it?

Twenty-six
ZOOT REUNION

ZOOT: RICK SPRINGFIELD, RICK BREWER, DARRYL COTTON,
MATT BISSONETTE, BEEB BIRTLES
PHOTO BY KRISTINE S. FLUCK

Sometime during 2011 I received a phone call from Darryl Cotton. He said, "Now, before you immediately say no to this, I want you to hear me out, okay? Would you be interested in a Zoot reunion for the Rick Springfield and Friends Cruise in the Caribbean in November 2011?" For some reason, Darryl thought I wouldn't even consider it, but I was actually more excited about this than a Little River Band or a Birtles Shorrock Goble reunion. Hell, at least Zoot still owned their name!

So here we were, forty years to the month since Zoot broke up and all of the band members agreed to do the reunion. It was very exciting to me. Darryl and I discussed the possibility of this going further than just the cruise. We were planning to take the group back to Australia for some concerts. After all, Zoot was still very well known and respected in Australia.

Leading up to the cruise, Darryl and I Skyped a couple of times and talked about song choices and actually rehearsed certain vocal harmonies. Over a few months we pulled together a set that we ran by Rick Springfield. Rick, being as busy as he always is, was happy to let Darryl and me handle this part of the reunion. Between the three of us, we compiled a set of songs that would please Zoot fans.

Not having been on a Rick Springfield and Friends Cruise, Darryl, Rick Brewer and I really didn't know what to expect but we went with open minds. My main concern was getting enough rehearsal time to put a decent set together. I had to really stay on top of Springfield's people to make it happen. We rehearsed one afternoon at Markee, a rehearsal and recording studio in Deerfield Beach, Florida, and that put our minds somewhat at ease. The other full rehearsal was on the actual day of the concert on board the Carnival Destiny.

Rose Tours did an excellent job of organising the cruise. We were very impressed. To me, it was a big enough deal to bring my whole family, including Darin, my son-in-law. Not a day went by without Darryl telling me he was kicking himself for not bringing his wife, Cheryl. I really felt for him because it ended up being so much fun. Five days through the Caribbean, departing from Miami and sailing to Ocho Rios in Jamaica and on to Grand Cayman Island before returning to Miami.

Every night on the cruise was a music night. The other guests included Jack Wagner, a soap opera star who is also a singer; Mark Goodman, one of the original MTV VJs and Doug Davidson, Rick Springfield's best friend, who is also a soap opera star. In Ocho Rios, everyone disembarked for a beach party, which was a blast.

For two nights running, all of Rick's ardent female fans — about 700 in total — filed past the entertainers on the cruise to receive an autograph and have their photos taken with us. They also ran a competition for the best door prize. Just about every cabin door was decorated with photos of Rick from all phases of his career.

The detail was quite amazing. Some doors had twinkle lights on them, while some had rose petals, because if you've ever been to a Rick Springfield concert you'll know he smashes a bunch of roses against his guitar strings and sends the petals flying in all directions. It looks spectacular! And, of course, the Zoot naked bum shot featured heavily on some doors and these women were desperate for us to autograph our own bottoms. Quite hilarious!

Not one of us knew what awaited us a few months down the road, with Darryl's announcement that he was dying from liver cancer. We had our hopes pinned on Zoot performing a forty-year reunion tour around Australia and New Zealand.

The five-day cruise flew by and then it was time for everyone to retreat to their corner of the earth. We all left on a high because the Zoot concert, after just one-and-a-half rehearsals, was received so well that we thought we would definitely get together again for a repeat performance.

Rick's people recorded and filmed the concert, which was released as the *Zoot Live – The Reunion* CD/DVD on the Ambition label in Australia and the US. Zoot claimed many more fans from Rick's ardent following and most of them bought the CD/DVD, which has now gone into its second pressing.

Twenty-Seven
IN MEMORIAM JOHN D'ARCY & DARRYL COTTON

Darryl Cotton

In July 2006 I was very saddened to hear that John D'Arcy had died. John had been such a major influence in my early years in music. He lost his life to stomach cancer and I posted this tribute on my personal website:

WE WERE LADS

A popular greeting amongst friends in the early '60s was, 'Hello, lad' or 'G'day, lad.' John D'Arcy and I were 'lads' who met at Plympton High School the year his family migrated to Australia from England.

Music was the common thread that drew us together. John was from Manchester, hometown of The Hollies, and brought with him the latest musical influences. He wasn't particularly the hippest-looking cat in school because he wore glasses and kind of resembled Buddy Holly, but with his IQ he could have been a member of The Zombies, reputed to be the band with the highest IQ out of any of the English pop bands.

He was a stickler for getting the vocals absolutely perfect. My ear training began because of John D'Arcy. He was the guy who piqued my interest in popular music, in particular with singing harmonies that he himself so loved. And if it wasn't for him, I wouldn't be the guitar player, the singer and the songwriter I am today. John kicked all of that off for me.

We worked together through several formations of the same band. Times Unlimited became Down The Line when Darryl Cotton joined, and shortly after we changed our name to Zoot.

As I write this, I have nothing but the fondest memories for this guy who was there for a season in my life, certainly a very integral season. I remember that I could always make him laugh, but the most precious memories are those of making music together in our very first bands.

Years later, he came to visit me in Melbourne after I had experienced success with Zoot, Mississippi and Little River Band and he told me that he should have followed his heart with music instead of his head with studying. But I don't think he made a mistake. John was too intelligent to risk his career on music alone. He continued his studies as Darryl Cotton and I took off for Melbourne with Zoot in search of fame and fortune.

It makes me think about the seasons of life. You never know how you're going to touch somebody's life, even if you only connect for the shortest time. And as far as John D'Arcy is concerned, at the time we didn't give it much thought. We were young, we just went along with everything, and we pursued the things that brought us happiness — and along the way we became lads.

DARRYL GRANT COTTON
FRIDAY, JUNE 1 2012

It is 11:30 at night when my mobile phone rings and wakes us.

"Who would be calling me at this hour?" I say to Donna. "Probably someone in Australia who has their times mixed up again," I add, "I'm not getting up to get it." But then we hear the little musical chime, letting me know that someone has left a message. Something inside me tells me to get up and listen to it.

My thoughts immediately race toward my aging mother, Elisabeth, who is now eighty-eight and declining in health. I listen to the message as Donna asks from the bedroom, "Is it bad?"

"It's really bad," I say. "It's Darryl." I'm dumbfounded by Darryl's message. He was so apologetic for calling us late at night but said he had been diagnosed with liver cancer and the doctors have given him weeks to live.

"Beeb, I just want you to know that I have no regrets. I've lived a really good life, I've never fucked anybody over and I just want to tell you that I love you, mate." Whenever Darryl is nervous he reverts to using the word 'fuck'. Before he hung up he began to cry. It is heartbreaking to hear.

I call him back immediately and we talk for some time about his diagnosis. Needless to say, Donna and I don't sleep very well that night, and the next day we discuss my need to fly back to Australia. I phone Jeff Joseph, Zoot's manager, to hear what he has to say about Darryl's diagnosis and he suggests I fly home to say goodbye to my best friend sooner rather than later. I book a flight that weekend.

THURSDAY, JUNE 7 2012

I arrive in Melbourne at 9:20 in the morning. Jeff Joseph picks me up at Tullamarine Airport and we drive straight to John Fawkner Hospital where Darryl is checked in.

"You're unbelievable, mate," he says to me, as Jeff and I walk into his hospital room. We hug each other.

His skin colour is yellowy but not ghastly awful and he is having a pretty good day. His stomach is very bloated from the condition of his liver, something the doctors are addressing with some kind of diuretic medicine. Normally, fluid in the stomach is drained via a needle, but Darryl's stomach isn't bad enough yet.

It is a day-by-day situation, with Jeff and me waiting for a call from Darryl to tell us whether he is up for visitors. He tires quickly and isn't sleeping well at night but I am able to visit him on my first two days in Melbourne.

SUNDAY, JUNE 10 2012

I speak to Darryl and he decides to pass on seeing anyone today. Just his immediate family are with him. He is having another round of chemo tomorrow and then the doctors are sending him home for a couple of days. I think the change in scenery will do him good.

WEDNESDAY, JUNE 13 2012

Jeff Joseph and I drive out to Darryl's home to visit. His skin colour is ashen and his eyes are sunken, but he is in pretty good spirits. He wants to go over the funeral arrangements with Jeff and talk about the benefit concert to be held at The Comedy Theatre in the city.

"That's so ironic," he says, "that's where I performed Joseph and the Amazing Technicolor Dreamcoat."

Donna and I attended one of those performances and Darryl was fantastic.

Darryl sends Jeff out of the room so we can talk privately for a while. He says, "I've never given much thought to where I go after this life but lately I've been thinking about it." He says various religious groups have come to his door to tell him about this, that and the other.

I cut him short and say, "Forget about all that. Who cares what those fanatical organisations tell you, this is between you and God." I tell him I believe we are made up of mind, body and spirit. We exercise the body and look after it the best we can, we use our mind to think and act, but we spend little time developing our spiritual side. He tells me that what I have said makes a lot of sense.

I understand now the reason I'm here is to make Darryl right with God. I hope I'll get the opportunity to pray with him before I leave to fly back to the States. He's my best friend and I need to know that he is going to Heaven. Tomorrow is going to be an extremely tough day for him because his children, Amy and Tim, are flying back to the US and Canada, where they live. I can't imagine having to say goodbye to my children, knowing I may never see them again. My heart goes out to Darryl, Cheryl, Amy and Tim.

TUESDAY, JUNE 19 2012

I see Darryl one more time the day before I fly back to the US. He is back in hospital. We don't get a chance to sit alone because other people are coming in and out of his room. I say goodbye and kiss him and say that I hope we can still talk on the phone once I get home.

Both Donna and I talked to him one more time from America, and towards the end of our conversation, I said to him, "Daz, you know I'm a believer, right? If I was to ask you to accept Jesus as your Lord and Saviour into your heart would you say yes?"

Darryl said, "Yes, mate." And those were the last words Darryl spoke to me.

Darryl hung on until July, all the while getting weaker and withering away. Right to the end, he was dictating to Jeff the things he wanted read at his funeral service. Darryl passed away in his sleep at seven in the morning on Friday, July 27.

The memorial service was held at The Comedy Theatre in Melbourne on August 1. It was a packed house with everybody paying their respects to Darryl. Just two months, from the time I received his phone call to his memorial service, and he was gone.

With Donna's help, I composed this piece to be read at Darryl's funeral service:

I wish I could be here in person today to pay tribute to my amazing friend, Darryl. First of all, I want to give my condolences to Cheryl, Amy and Tim for their loss. Darryl was a great husband and father and an incredible friend to me.

We started playing music as kids in high school in Adelaide and worked our way up to become one of the most popular bands in Australia. And even though the band parted ways in 1971, our friendship remained. Forty-five years later, our friendship stayed intact to the extent that we talked about performing together again. We spoke on the phone every few weeks.

I will forever cherish the memories of the Zoot reunion as part of the Rick Springfield and Friends Cruise last November and the time I spent with him when I flew back to Australia to see him recently. Words cannot express how much I will miss him but I will endeavour to do so in the best way I know how — in a song.

Goodbye my friend . . . until we meet again.

Twenty-Eight
WATCHING THE SUNSET

BEEB BIRTLES
PHOTO COURTESY OF JOSH OGLE

In 2015 an attempt was made to celebrate the 40th anniversary of the formation of Little River Band. There was talk of Universal Music Group (UMG) releasing a 40th anniversary CD with some previously unreleased live recordings, but it all fizzled when UMG was advised by their legal department they would have to get clearance from Stephen Housden for use of the name. I think this was the final nail in the coffin for the founding members.

Lately, I find myself telling people I don't even want the name back anymore. What's it really worth now because of what it has become? There are not enough years left to re-establish the great band that Little River Band once was. We're all much older now, so let's just move on with our lives.

We carved out our place in world music history and we were the first Australian band to have a gold album in the US, quite an achievement. We opened the floodgates for others to follow. And the legacy we leave behind can be heard on the recordings we made.

My preference these days is to work as a songwriter and a producer in the studio. The thought of playing the same songs over and over, year after year, doesn't excite me, so I took the other route. Perhaps at times, it hasn't been as successful as I had hoped but it has definitely been very satisfying and rewarding. Over the years I've sometimes thought perhaps I should have mingled more, been more outgoing and let people know that I was still around – but that's not who I am. I don't have a need to be in the limelight whereas some artists are desperate to remain in the public eye. I'm more the kind of person who, when I have something to say, will come out and say it and that's it. I'm more a family man.

I've never given much thought to retirement. I know I will always want to do something, especially if it's connected to music. There will always be another idea for a song or someone wanting to record some songs.

Through the years I've been called an enigma, a loner, and a dark horse by some people, yet I will strike up friendships with strangers, no matter where I am. I like people and I'm interested in their lives, where they come from, where they live and what they do. I view myself as a creative soul, an ideas person. I see possibilities not just in songs and music but in everything around me. For the most part, I'm a pretty positive-thinking guy.

I know I have the insecurities that many creative artists have. At times I do a pretty good job of beating myself up because of those insecurities but I'm very fortunate that I have a wife who balances me. In fact, we balance each other. Donna is my rock! After all these years of being together, I'm still in awe of her. She is the most nurturing, loving mother to our girls and I know that she is the reason why our family is as close as it is. She will always put family first. Donna is strong, but at the same time she is very compassionate. She will do anything for you.

From the day we met, we loved being together. I can't tell you how many women have said to her over the years, "How can you stand having your husband around all the time? That would drive me nuts!" And then we've had other women tell us, "I want what you guys have." People pick up on what we have as a married couple.

We became grandparents in 2014. Hannah delivered her first baby, Ashton Brooks Yeomans, on June 15, 2014. He is the most gorgeous little boy we could have hoped for and we can't express the thrill of having our first grandchild.

My mother passed away on December 2, 2015. I flew home to attend her funeral, which turned out to be a beautiful and very moving service. On the day before, I went to see her one last time with Elly and her family. She was lying in her coffin, looking totally at peace and holding a crucifix between her hands. I touched her hands and said in Dutch, "Ik hou van jou, Mum (I love you, Mum)." And so as one generation passes, new life springs forth.

On May 27, 2016 Hannah delivered her second son, Brody Bennett Yeomans, who, from what we can tell, looks very much like his older brother, Ashton. What a thrill it will be to see these two grow up together.

Every Day Of My Life

Life seems to move so much faster the older we get.

I think the words of my song, 'Driven By Dreams', that I co-wrote with Bill Cuomo and Billy Henderson say it well:

DRIVEN BY DREAMS

When I was young, had my whole life in front of me
No need to think about my future being the key
To open unlocked doors, everything just seemed to flow
I never thought about money to be made
As long as I could play the music of my day
And travel round the world, giving it my heart and soul

I was driven by dreams and not by my fear
On the crest of the wave year after year
And though my life came crashing down or so it seems
I'm still standing here driven by dreams

Now I'm a man with responsibility
I think too much about what lies ahead of me
The more the doors stay closed, the more I wanna find a way
It's just the desperation of a restless mind
And lack of confidence I've lost somewhere in time
But to a dying world I have so much more to say

I am driven by dreams and not by my fear
On the crest of the wave year after year
And though my life came crashing down or so it seems
I'm still standing here driven by dreams

I was, still am, and always will be, driven by dreams.

ACKNOWLEDGEMENTS

My heartfelt gratitude to Jan Nimmervoll for granting me permission to use Ed's words in his biography of me. Jan was also responsible for introducing me to Jeff Jenkins who edited my memoir. Many, many thanks to you, Jeff.

Over a period of seven years writing this memoir I could never think of an appropriate title. After Darryl Cotton's death in 2012, I developed a friendship with Bruce Hutchins, who was also a good friend of Darryl. When I mentioned to Bruce that for the life of me I couldn't think of the perfect title, right off the top of his head he said, "I know what you need to call your memoir: *Every Day Of My Life*." I couldn't believe my ears. It was perfect! My gratitude to you, Bruce.

My decision to start writing a memoir in early 2008 was not so much for myself as it was for the preservation of a slice of Australian rock and roll history. My intention was also to give the reader insight into what European migrants endured by packing up and leaving their homeland and families to make a new start in the Great Southern Land. My gratitude to my parents is immeasurable.

My thanks also to my sister, Elly, for scanning some of our old family photos and sending them to me. Love you, El.

My deepest gratitude to Julie and Mark Zocchi and Elly Cridland at Brolga Publishing for their enthusiasm and belief in my manuscript.

I'd like to also acknowledge all the road crews, stage managers, guitar technicians, lighting technicians, spotlight operators, sound engineers, tour managers and bus drivers. The show must go on and without all of you this would have been impossible. Thank you. Also to the many band members and musicians with whom I had the pleasure of working over the years, I thank you for sharing your God-given talent in creating this wonderful gift of music.

AWARDS AND ACCOLADES

1969 – Best Group – Go-Set Pop Poll Awards – ZOOT – Australia
1971 – Best Group – Go-Set Pop Poll Awards – ZOOT – Australia
1971 – Best Bass Guitarist – Go-Set Pop Poll Awards – BEEB BIRTLES – Australia
1971 – Best Single for 'Eleanor Rigby' – Go-Set Pop Poll Awards – ZOOT – Australia
1971 – Gold and eventually Platinum single for 'Eleanor Rigby' – Australian Recording Industry Association (ARIA) – ZOOT – Australia
1976 – Gold album sales for *LITTLE RIVER BAND* – Australian Recording Industry Association (ARIA) – LITTLE RIVER BAND – Australia
1977 – Australian Record of the Year for 'Help Is On Its Way' – King of Pop Awards – LITTLE RIVER BAND – Australia
1977 – Best Australian International Performers – LITTLE RIVER BAND – King of Pop Awards – Australia
1977 – Platinum album sales for *LITTLE RIVER BAND* – Australian Recording Industry Association (ARIA) – LITTLE RIVER BAND – Australia
1977 – Gold album sales for *LITTLE RIVER BAND* – Recording Industry Association of New Zealand (RIANZ) – LITTLE RIVER BAND – New Zealand
1977 – Platinum album sales for *AFTER HOURS* – Australian Recording Industry Association (ARIA) – LITTLE RIVER BAND – Australia
1977 – Gold album sales for *DIAMANTINA COCKTAIL* – Australian Recording Industry Association (ARIA) – LITTLE RIVER BAND – Australia
1977 – Platinum album sales for *DIAMANTINA COCKTAIL* –

Australian Recording Industry Association (ARIA) – LITTLE RIVER BAND – Australia

1977 – Double Platinum album sales for *DIAMANTINA COCKTAIL* – Australian Recording Industry Association (ARIA) – LITTLE RIVER BAND – Australia

1977 – Recognition from EMI Records Australasia for more than 1 Million International Album Sales – LITTLE RIVER BAND – Australia

1977 – Keys to the City of Melbourne for outstanding achievements and success overseas – LITTLE RIVER BAND – Australia

1978 – Platinum album sales for *DIAMANTINA COCKTAIL* – Canadian Recording Industry Association (CRIA) – LITTLE RIVER BAND – Canada

1978 – Gold album sales for *DIAMANTINA COCKTAIL* – Recording Industry Association of New Zealand (RIANZ) – LITTLE RIVER BAND – New Zealand

1978 – Gold album sales for *DIAMANTINA COCKTAIL* – Recording Industry Association of America (RIAA) – LITTLE RIVER BAND – U.S.A.

1978 – Best Group Performance – Australian Recording Industry Association (ARIA) Awards – LITTLE RIVER BAND – Australia

1978 – Album of the Year for *DIAMANTINA COCKTAIL* – King of Pop Awards – LITTLE RIVER BAND – Australia

1978 – Record of the Year for 'Reminiscing' – LITTLE RIVER BAND – King of Pop Awards – Australia

1978 – Best Australian TV Performer for 'Help Is On Its Way' – LITTLE RIVER BAND – Paul Hogan Show – Australia

1978 – Gold album sales for *SLEEPER CATCHER* – Canadian Recording Industry Association (CRIA) – LITTLE RIVER BAND – Canada

1978 – Gold album sales for *SLEEPER CATCHER* – Recording Industry Association of America (RIAA) – LITTLE RIVER BAND – U.S.A.

1978 – Platinum album sales for *SLEEPER CATCHER* – Recording Industry Association of America (RIAA) – LITTLE RIVER BAND – U.S.A.

1978 – Platinum album sales for *IT'S A LONG WAY THERE (GREATEST HITS)* – Australian Recording Industry Association (ARIA) – LITTLE RIVER BAND – Australia

1978 – Double Platinum album sales for *IT'S A LONG WAY THERE (GREATEST HITS)* – Recording Industry Association of New Zealand (RIANZ) – LITTLE RIVER BAND – New Zealand

1978 – Most Popular Australian Album for *SLEEPER CATCHER* – LITTLE RIVER BAND – King of Pop Awards – Australia

1979 – Platinum album sales for *SLEEPER CATCHER* – Australian Recording Industry Association (ARIA) – LITTLE RIVER BAND – Australia

1979 – Platinum album sales for *FIRST UNDER THE WIRE* – Australian Recording Industry Association (ARIA) – LITTLE RIVER BAND – Australia

1979 – Double Platinum album sales for *FIRST UNDER THE WIRE* – Canadian Recording Industry Association (CRIA) – LITTLE RIVER BAND – Canada

1979 – Gold album sales for *FIRST UNDER THE WIRE* – Recording Industry Association of America (RIAA) – LITTLE RIVER BAND – U.S.A.

1979 – Platinum album sales for *FIRST UNDER THE WIRE* – Recording Industry Association of America (RIAA) – LITTLE RIVER BAND – U.S.A.

1979 – Grammy Nomination for Best Pop Vocal Performance by a Duo, Group or Chorus for 'Lonesome Loser' – The National Academy of Recording Arts and Sciences (NARAS) – LITTLE RIVER BAND – U.S.A.

1979 – Best Australian Album for *FIRST UNDER THE WIRE* – LITTLE RIVER BAND – TV Week/Countdown Music Awards – Australia

1979 – Platinum sales for the single 'I'm Coming Home' – Philippine

Association of the Record Industry (PARI) – BIRTLES & GOBLE – The Philippines

1979 – Most Outstanding Achievement – LITTLE RIVER BAND – TV Week/Countdown Music Awards – Australia

1979 – Most Popular Group – LITTLE RIVER BAND – TV Week/Countdown Music Awards – Australia

1980 – Platinum album sales for *BACKSTAGE PASS* – Australian Recording Industry Association (ARIA) – LITTLE RIVER BAND – Australia

1980 – Advance Australia Award – LITTLE RIVER BAND – Australia

1981 – Gold album sales for *TIME EXPOSURE* – Canadian Recording Industry Association (CRIA) – LITTLE RIVER BAND – Canada

1981 – Gold album sales for *TIME EXPOSURE* – Recording Industry Association of America (RIAA) – LITTLE RIVER BAND – U.S.A.

1981 – Gold album sales for *TIME EXPOSURE* – Australian Recording Industry Association (ARIA) – LITTLE RIVER BAND – Australia

1982 – The Mo Awards Rock Group of the Year – LITTLE RIVER BAND – Australia

1983 – Platinum album sales for *GREATEST HITS (VOLUME TWO)* – Australian Recording Industry Association (ARIA) – LITTLE RIVER BAND – Australia

1983 – Double Platinum album sales for *GREATEST HITS (VOLUME TWO)* – Recording Industry Association of New Zealand (RIANZ) – LITTLE RIVER BAND – New Zealand

1983 – Gold album sales for *GREATEST HITS* – Recording Industry Association of America (RIAA) – LITTLE RIVER BAND – U.S.A.

1983 – Gold album sales for *GREATEST HITS* – Canadian Recording Industry Association (CRIA) – LITTLE RIVER BAND – Canada

1983 – Gold album sales for *THE NET* – Australian Recording Industry Association (ARIA) – LITTLE RIVER BAND – Australia

1986 – Triple Platinum album sales for *GREATEST HITS* – Recording Industry Association of America (RIAA) – LITTLE RIVER BAND – U.S.A.

1995 – Platinum album sales for *THE CLASSIC COLLECTION* – Australian Recording Industry Association (ARIA) – LITTLE RIVER BAND – Australia

1995 – Double Platinum album sales for *THE CLASSIC COLLECTION* – Recording Industry Association of New Zealand (RIANZ) – LITTLE RIVER BAND – New Zealand

2003 – Gold sales for *FULL CIRCLE* DVD – Australian Recording Industry Association (ARIA) – BIRTLES SHORROCK GOBLE – Australia

2004 – The Mo Awards Classical Rock Performers of the Year – BIRTLES SHORROCK GOBLE – Australia

2004 – Australian Recording Industry Association (ARIA) Hall of Fame – LITTLE RIVER BAND – Australia

2006 – Australian Songwriters Association (ASA) Hall of Fame – BEEB BIRTLES – Australia

2007 – 'Lady' – over 4 Million airplays on commercial radio – LITTLE RIVER BAND – U.S.A.

2007 – 'Reminiscing' – over 5 Million airplays on commercial radio – LITTLE RIVER BAND – U.S.A.

2007 – 'Take It Easy On Me' – over 1 Million airplays on commercial radio – LITTLE RIVER BAND – U.S.A.

2007 – 'The Other Guy' – over 1 Million airplays on commercial radio – LITTLE RIVER BAND – U.S.A.

CHART POSITIONS
IN THE U.S.A.

LITTLE RIVER BAND

'It's A Long Way There' – November 1976 – number 28

'Help is On Its Way' – September 1977 – number 14

'Happy Anniversary' – January 1978 – number 16

'Reminiscing' – August 1978 – number 3

'Lady' – January 1979 – number 10

'Lonesome Loser' – August 1979 – number 6

'Cool Change' – November 1979 – number 10

'The Night Owls' – September 1981 – number 6

'Take It Easy On Me' – December 1981 – number 10

'Man On Your Mind' – April 1982 – number 14

'The Other Guy' – December 1982 – number 11

'We Two' – May 1983 – number 22

'You're Driving Me Out Of My Mind' – August 1983 – number 35

IN AUSTRALIA

ZOOT

'You Better Get Goin' – 1968
> Kent Music Report – number 87

'One Times, Two Times, Three Times, Four' – 1968
> Go-Set chart – number 32
> Kent Music Report – number 25

'Monty And Me' – 1969
> Go-Set chart – number 33
> Kent Music Report – number 36

'It's About Time' – 1969
> Kent Music Report – number 73

'Hey Pinky' – 1970
> Kent Music Report – number 61

'Eleanor Rigby' – 1970
> Go-Set chart – number 4
>
> Kent Music Report – number 4

'The Freak' – 1971
> Go-Set chart – number 27
>
> Kent Music Report – number 27

MISSISSIPPI

'Early Morning' – 1973
> Adelaide – number 23

'Will I' – 1973
> Adelaide – number 8
>
> Melbourne – number 7

LITTLE RIVER BAND

'Curiosity (Killed the Cat)' – October 1975
> Adelaide – number 17
>
> Brisbane – number 4
>
> Melbourne – number 15
>
> Perth – number 21
>
> Sydney – number 21

'Emma' – January 1975
> Adelaide – number 5
>
> Brisbane – number 6
>
> Melbourne – number 20

Perth – number 35

Sydney – number 35

'Everyday Of My Life' – May 1976

Adelaide – number 29

Brisbane – number 14

Melbourne – number 24

Perth – number 24

Sydney – number 24

'It's A Long Way There' – November 1976

Adelaide – number 15

Perth – number 32

Sydney – number 32

'Help Is On Its Way' – April 1977

Adelaide – number 7

Brisbane – number 1

Melbourne – number 1

Perth – number 3

Sydney – number 3

'Witchery' – August 1977

Adelaide – number 25

Brisbane – number 19

Melbourne – number 26

'Home On Monday' – October 1977

Adelaide – number 34

'Shut Down Turn Off' – April 1978

Adelaide – number 15

Brisbane – number 10

Melbourne – number 15

Perth – number 17

Sydney – number 17

'Reminiscing' – July 1978

Brisbane – number 23

Melbourne – number 31

'Lady' – October 1978

Adelaide – number 33

Brisbane – number 13

'Lonesome Loser' – August 1979

Adelaide – number 27

Brisbane – number 19

Melbourne – number 22

Perth – number 25

Sydney – number 25

'Long Jumping Jeweller' – January 1981

Brisbane – number 14

Perth – number 40

Sydney – number 40

'The Night Owls' – September 1981

Adelaide – number 26

Brisbane – number 15

Melbourne – number 12

Perth – number 19

Sydney – number 19

'Down On The Border' – August 1982

Adelaide – number 7

Brisbane – number 6

Melbourne – number 7

Perth – number 8

Sydney – number 8

'St. Louis' – December 1982
 Adelaide – number 34
 Melbourne – number 32
 Perth – number 39
 Sydney – number 39

'The Other Guy' – February 1983
 Adelaide – number 32
 Brisbane – number 34
 Melbourne – number 10
 Perth – number 18
 Sydney – number 18

'We Two' – June 1983
 Adelaide – number 38
 Melbourne – number 21
 Perth – number 53
 Sydney – number 53

BIRTLES & GOBLE

'Lonely Lives' – April 1978
 Brisbane – number 40
 Sydney – number 29

'I'm Coming Home' – March 1979
 Adelaide – number 6
 Brisbane – number 4
 Melbourne – number 6
 Perth – number 11
 Sydney – number 8

ORDER

Every Day of My Life
BEEB BIRTLES

ISBN: 9781925367973   Qty

RRP   AU $34.99   .....

Postage within Australia AU$5.00   .....

TOTAL* $_____

* All prices include GST

Name: ....

Address: ....

....

Phone: ....

Email: ....

Payment: [ ] Money Order   [ ] Cheque   [ ] MasterCard   [ ] Visa

Cardholder's Name: ....

Credit Card Number: ....

Signature: ....

Expiry Date: ....

Allow 7 days for delivery.

Payment to: Marzocco Consultancy (ABN 14 067 257 390)
                PO Box 12544
                A'Beckett Street, Melbourne, 8006
                Victoria, Australia
                admin@brolgapublishing.com.au

Be Published

Publish through a successful publisher.
Brolga Publishing is represented through:
• National book trade distribution, including sales, marketing & distribution through Dennis Jones and Associates Australia.
• International book trade distribution to
    • The United Kingdom
    • North America
    • Sales representation in South East Asia
• Worldwide e-Book distribution

For details and enquiries, contact:
Brolga Publishing Pty Ltd
markzocchi@brolgapublishing.com.au
PO Box 12544
A'Beckett St VIC 8006

ABN: 46 063 962 443
(Email for a catalogue request)

www.ingramcontent.com/pod-product-compliance
Lightning Source LLC
Chambersburg PA
CBHW070628160426
43194CB00009B/1393